WILLIAM
WALLACE

CHRIS BROWN is completing his PhD at St Andrews University. His other books include *The Second Scottish Wars of Independence, Robert the Bruce: A Life Chronicled* and *The Battle for Aberdeen 1644*, all published by Tempus. He is currently writing *Scottish Battlefields: 300 Battlefields that Shaped Scottish History*, forthcoming from Tempus. He lives in Fife in Scotland.

Praise for *The Second Scottish Wars of Independence*

'Fills a yawning void in the Scottish popular historical market... lucid and highly readable'
History Scotland

'Awesomely well-illustrated... a lucidly written account of another troubled period in Scottish history which is bound to appeal to the general reader'
The Scots Magazine

Praise for *Robert the Bruce: A Life Chronicled*

'An excellent anthology' *The Scotsman*

'Indispensable' *The Daily Mail*

'A masterpiece of research... truly a book to treasure' *The Scots Magazine*

Praise for *The Battle for Aberdeen 1644*

'Readable and balanced' *The Scots Magazine*

WILLIAM WALLACE

The True Story of Braveheart

CHRIS BROWN

TEMPUS

First published 2005

Tempus Publishing Limited
The Mill, Brimscombe Port,
Stroud, Gloucestershire, GL5 2QG
www.tempus-publishing.com

British Library Cataloguing in Publication Data.
A catalogue record for this book is available from the British Library.

ISBN 0 7524 3432 2

Typesetting and origination by Tempus Publishing Limited
Printed in Great Britain

Contents

Acknowledgements

As ever, pride of place goes to my wife Pat, who has suffered the life and times of William Wallace with a stoical grace, and to my children – Charis, Christopher, Colin and Robert – and my parents Peter and Margaret, who have also been subjected to more 'Wallace' than is fair to ask of anyone. Yet again, Robert has rescued me from self-inflicted computer disasters. Jonathan Reeve at Tempus has proved to be a patient man indeed; he has waited longer for this manuscript than is at all reasonable. Friends at St Andrews University Scottish History Department have, over the past four years, given me a great deal of their time: Dr William Knox, Mr Alex Woolf, Dr Hamish Scott and others too numerous to mention. I am grateful to them all, and to the staff of Easy PCs of Kennoway for their help in making the manuscript file printable, and to the late Kay Urqhart, good friend, good company and the mainstay of my babysitting in the days when I was a single parent. I am particularly indebted to Professor G.W.S. Barrow, who very kindly read the unedited manuscript of this book and made many valuable corrections and suggestions. This is my fourth book. I had expected that by now I would have found an effective and reliable means of blaming others for my mistakes… it is a tragedy that I have not yet been able to do so.

Chris Brown, Kennoway, 2005.

CHAPTER ONE

William Wallace, Knight of Scotland

P erhaps the ultimate Scottish hero, Wallace has been dear to the hearts of Scots and others, of all ages, classes, political and religious persuasions, for seven centuries. His determination has been used to inspire soldiers, athletes and political movements. His life has inspired novelists, poets, songwriters and film-makers. A brief survey of the World Wide Web indicates a vast interest in the man, with more than one million entries for Sir William Wallace. By the same measure, it could be argued that the public interest in *Braveheart* is rather stronger, since there are more than twice as many websites dedicated to the Mel Gibson portrayal of the Guardian's political career.

Wallace has been the subject of a great many Victorian statues of questionable artistic value, several novels, at least one stage play, a film, a strip cartoon book and a number of popular, if somewhat fanciful, 'biographies'. All of these have been the work of people who have been enthused and inspired (understandably) by the life of one of the greatest, if not *the* greatest, of Scotland's heroes. Novels, films, plays and cartoons share a common factor: nobody expects them to be strictly realistic portrayals of personalities, events or conditions – they are fantasies devised for entertainment. It could be argued, with some justice, that the latter statement also applies to the bulk of the 'biographies' of William Wallace that have appeared in recent years. For several writers the starting point, mainstay and – in at least one example – the entirety of their primary research has been the study of Blind Harry's *Wallace* epic. Whether the poem is a great work of fifteenth-century literature or nothing more than sheer hagiography in doggerel verse is open to debate; whether it is a generally useful record of the life and work of William Wallace is not. Harry's claim to have used an existing

biography of Wallace written by his chaplain, Blair, may be true, but that
does not mean that the Blair manuscript, assuming that it ever existed,
bore any great resemblance either to Blind Harry's eulogy or the life of
Wallace. The shortcomings of *The Wallace* as a historical record have been
demonstrated many times and need no rehearsal here; what is more of an
issue is the manner in which Wallace's life has been approached. Since few,
if any, of the Wallace biographers have made any serious examination of
the social, cultural, economic, political or military conditions of the lesser
nobility in either Scotland or England in the late medieval period, they
have been prone to assumptions – and perhaps a spot of wishful thinking
– about the nature of the society in which William Wallace grew up and
in which he made his career.

It has, for example, become an article of faith among Scots that Wallace
was a man of the common people, separated from a privileged, foreign
and oppressive noble class by language and social ethos. Nothing could be
further from the truth. William Wallace was a product of the Scottish noble
class, not an enemy of it, and not distanced from it in any cultural or political
sense.[1] Like the other members of his class he grew up in Scottish communities, among Scottish people, speaking Scots,[2] but that does not have the
same romantic appeal as the struggle of a man to overcome the prejudice
and ineffectiveness of a class of aristocratic 'chancers', which is, broadly, the
view offered in several recent biographies. The origin of the recent spate of
Wallace books is, to a considerable extent, a product of the success of the
Braveheart film: it is, as they say, 'an ill wind…'. However, there has been a
steady rise in interest in medieval Scotland among historians over the last
forty years and much of the credit for that must go to Professors Geoffrey
Barrow, Ranald Nicholson and Archibald Duncan, very much the architects
of current thinking relating to Scotland in the later Middle Ages.

In 1965 Professor Barrow published the first scholarly examination of
the life and reign of Robert I. Entitled *Robert the Bruce and the Community
of the Realm of Scotland*, it was revolutionary in that it was a formal political biography of a Scottish king, not a collection of tales and traditions.
In the same year, Professor Nicholson published *Edward III and the Scots,
the Formative Years of a Military Career*, a detailed study of the final attempt
of Plantagenet kings to bring Scotland directly under their sway. Both
Barrow and Nicholson discovered that a great deal of light could be cast
on affairs in Scotland through the study of English state records. In a sense
this had been long recognised. In the late nineteenth century the Reverend
Stevenson and Joseph Bain published collections of material connected
with Scottish affairs. These volumes, *Documents Illustrative of the History*

of Scotland and *Calendar of Documents Relating to Scotland*, have provided
medievalists with a wonderful resource for over 100 years. Neither Bain nor
Stevenson was an analytical historian so much as an antiquary, and Bain's
lengthy introductions to each of the four volumes he compiled have not
lasted the test of time so well as the body of the work. There is no such
thing as a perfect work of history and both Bain and Stevenson misdated
or misinterpreted the significance, or sometimes the origin, of the odd
document here and there, but their scholarship and industry has been a
boon to anybody and everybody with an interest in medieval Scotland.

There have, then, been two significant strands of inspiration driving the
growth in medieval studies: the romantic – *Braveheart* and many attractive
and romantic volumes – from one direction and scholarship – Barrow,
Nicholson, A.A.M. Duncan, Norman Macdougall, Bruce Webster, Stephen
Boardman and many more – from the other. There has been a good deal of
academic research into a very wide range of social, economic and political
activity in thirteenth- and fourteenth-century Scotland in recent years
and a great deal of fine work has been published; unfortunately, as any
academic will be only too ready to tell, new work does not necessarily
make much impact on the perceptions of the public. It is forty years since
Barrow's *Robert the Bruce* was published; it is only in very recent times that
his findings have started to make any impression on the kind of material
that is easily available to the public.

Any book in print is, of course, easily available to the public, but generally
the public will not be aware of its existence. If moved to take an interest
in history, they are inclined, naturally enough, to look for information at
the point of easiest access. In the past this has generally been a matter of
consulting the encyclopaedias or the sort of general histories of Britain that
are familiar to most English and Scottish people from schooldays. 'British'
histories are very frequently 'English' histories with, sometimes, a nod in
the direction of Scotland, very often at Scottish heroes, including William
Wallace: what we might reasonably, if a trifle uncharitably, call the 'Myth
and Legend' school of learning. This has led to a historical problem in
itself. In the main, English/British histories have indicated that Scotland has
been essentially the same as England at any point in history, just a slightly
poorer and more primitive version. This is simply not the case. There was a
great deal of similarity in certain aspects of social and commercial practice
in both countries, but an English traveller was just as much 'abroad' in
Scotland as they would have been in France or the Netherlands. The difficulty is that a great many Scottish people have had to 'unlearn' that sort
of accidental conditioning before they can make any real headway in the

study of their past. This is not an area in which there has been any great improvement in recent time. Scotland is the only country in Europe where there is absolutely no legal requirement for schoolchildren to be taught the history of their country. The fact that there is no adequate history textbook for Scottish schools compounds the problem, but in any case the teachers, mostly the product of Scottish education themselves, have little or no grasp of their country's history: the problem is circular. Sadly, neither the Scottish government nor Scottish education authorities seem to have any interest in doing anything very practical toward improving the situation, so Scottish schoolchildren will continue to be denied proper access to the history of their country.

The popular view of Scottish society in the Middle Ages has been strongly coloured by the *Braveheart* image and bolstered by many recent writers. A picture of a community that lived in mud and stone shanties, wore animal skins and conducted such trivial business as they had either by barter or by violence, under the heel of an uninterested, greedy and largely foreign aristocracy which imposed its authority with the noose. None of this is supported by evidence, but is widely accepted nonetheless. How such a crude and primitive society as twelfth-, thirteenth- and four-teenth-century Scotland managed to maintain commercial, cultural and political ties with every other country in northern Europe, build wonderful cathedrals, monasteries and castles, produce writers, scholars and soldiers of outstanding quality and survive a sixty-year series of wars of acquisi-tion launched by a massively more powerful neighbour without effective and sophisticated administrative, judicial and above all fiscal systems does not seem to have inspired popular histories to the same degree as tales of gallantry and treachery.[3]

Fortunately, the 'Braveheart Scotland' tendency has been offset to some degree by the remarkable wave of high-quality research that has been pub-lished over the last three decades. The first two volumes of the *Edinburgh History of Scotland*, though a little dated due to archaeological and his-torical developments in the 1980s and 1990s, between them provide a first-class introduction to the institutions and practices of medieval Scotland. Professor Duncan's *Scotland. The Making of the Nation* explores the develop-ment of Scottish society from what we misleadingly call the 'Dark Ages' to the close of the reign of Alexander III; Professor Nicholson's *Scotland. The Later Middle Ages* takes the reader from the demise of Alexander to the death of James IV at Flodden in 1513, though it is arguable whether or not Scotland was still truly a 'medieval' society by that point. Duncan, Nicholson and Barrow were instrumental in providing a framework from which other historians could develop the various strands and themes of Scottish society. Several of these are important contributions to the theme of this book, William Wallace, not so much because they examine his life and actions, but because they examine the structures of the society in which he lived. Dr Fiona Watson's *Under the Hammer*, a study of the invasion and occupation of Edward I, is an invaluable guide to the practices of the Edwardian administration, its effectiveness, its procedures, its effect on Scottish society, and the challenges that it faced.

Any consideration of the career of William Wallace would be redundant without giving some thought to the great men figures of his time, most obviously his chief adversary and eventual nemesis, Edward I. There are many biographies of Edward available, but few, if any, that compare to *Edward I* by Michael Prestwich. There is, at present, no modern scholarly biography of Alexander III which could give the reader an introduction to the society of Scotland during the youth and early manhood of William Wallace; however, there is a collection of essays ranging across economic, ecclesiastical, political and military issues in later-thirteenth-century Scotland edited by Norman Reid entitled *Scotland in the Reign of Alexander III*, which cannot be too highly recommended to anyone with an interest in the life and times of William Wallace.

The political leadership of lords is an important factor in medieval history, whether in France, England, Scotland or Spain. Lordship was a rather more sophisticated relationship than we might expect and will be examined elsewhere in this book, but the interests and actions of the great magnates call for detailed study if the reader is to understand the values, benefits and problems of lord-tenant relationships. Alan Young's *The Comyns, Robert the Bruce's Rivals* and Michael Brown's *The Black Douglases* each provide an illuminating view of Scottish noble families at work. *The Comyns* shows the growth in status of a relatively minor family, who, through consistent service to the Crown and careful management of their interests, came to be one of the foremost interest groups in the country in the course of little more than 100 years. *The Black Douglases* looks at the spectacular growth of the Douglas family in the fourteenth century, in particular the meteoric rise to prominence of the 'Good Sir James', also known as 'The Black Douglas', and the means by which his personal advancement became a vehicle for the elevation of the tenuously-linked Douglas families in Lanarkshire and Lothian from minor barons and lairds to membership of a vast and powerful affinity. Like the Comyns, James Douglas made his career in Crown service. Although a close associate of the king, Douglas did not join the ranks of the great magnates until the death of Edward Bruce in

Ireland made a gap in the Bruce party leadership that needed to be filled by a man with martial talents.

The social and economic history issues of medieval Scotland have not yet been so carefully examined by historians as the political arena, but there are useful volumes to be found, in particular Elizabeth Ewan's *Town Life in Fourteenth Century Scotland*, David Ditchburn's *Scotland and Europe* and Geoffrey Barrow's *Scotland and Its Neighbours in the Middle Ages*. Although the history of later medieval Scotland is dominated by war, there has been surprisingly little in the way of military history; though there have been a great many political histories which, for obvious reasons, can hardly avoid the topic of warfare, there has as yet been no adequate work published on the nature and practice of military service in medieval Scotland. It is not clear why this should be the case; the material is reasonably plentiful, much of it from English state records that have been available in print for 100 years and more. The absence of such a volume has led to a general perception of medieval Scottish war that almost completely fails to coincide with any of the evidence. In general terms, there was no great distinction in military dress or normal military practice between Scotland and England, or for that matter France or the Low Countries. Fortunately there have been several good studies of particular events of a military nature. There are no modern scholarly examinations of the battles of Stirling Bridge or Falkirk, but C.J. MacNamee has made an excellent survey of William Wallace's 1297 campaign in Cumbria, Westmorland and Northumberland, published in vol. 26 (1990) of *Northern History*.

Not unnaturally, Scottish historians have expended a great deal of ink on the subject of Sir William Wallace, but can hardly be expected to provide an objective view of, arguably, Scotland's greatest hero. For English historians, Wallace is a mixed bag. Many English historians, from Charles Oman (if not before) to David Starkey, have taken the view that the success of the house of Wessex in achieving dominance in southern Britain was both inevitable and desirable, and that the extension of the rule of that house, or at least its successors, to a place of superiority throughout the whole of Britain was therefore, to use a technical term from Sellar and Yeatman's masterly survey of 'memorable' English history, *1066 and All That*, a 'good thing'. From that perspective, Wallace, like Robert I, Prince Llewellyn or Owen Glendower, inevitably represented an obstacle to their preferred optimum outcome: the British Isles united in one (English) kingdom under one (English) king. The chief problem with achieving a unitary English state in medieval Britain before Edward I's reign was that no one felt particularly strongly about it; the problem after 1296 was that interest

among the English generally was not so well developed or so consistent
as it was among English kings.

At various junctures, generally under threat of military force, Scottish
kings had accepted the suzerainty of English ones, though the exact extent
of that suzerainty was never clearly defined – an indication, perhaps, that
the *realpolitik* relationship between Scottish and English kings was that both
parties were involved in face-saving exercises. The Scottish kings may have
resented the implications of homage to English kings, but the demands
made, when they were made at all, seem to have been gestural rather
than practical, indicating that English kings were unsure of their capacity
to conquer Scottish kings, but that Scottish kings doubted their capacity
to successfully confront their English counterparts. Although the obligations of Scottish kings may have been nominal, they felt strongly enough
about it to fork out 10,000 merks to Richard I in 1189[4] in exchange for
a full discharge from all and any obligations due from Scottish to English
kingship. There would seem to have been no resistance to this measure
in the political community of England: no sense that Richard was selling
off the assets of English kingship, no sense of national pride injured. The
inevitability and desirability of a unitary English kingdom stretching from
the Channel to the North Sea does not seem to have strongly motivated
English political society at the close of the twelfth century. By the close
of the thirteenth century the unification of Britain had become, arguably,
the most significant political issue in both England and Scotland. This
matter was driven chiefly, if not entirely, by Edward I's personal ambition.
If it were at all possible, he intended to make Britain one kingdom under
his kingship. If we assume that his goal was laudable, then William Wallace
must surely be seen as little more than a political vandal.

Remarkably, Wallace has not, to any great extent, been the target for
opprobrium from Unionist or English nationalist historians, perhaps on
account of his outstanding heroic reputation. Like Robert E. Lee or Erwin
Rommel, for some historians his reputation has stood higher than his cause.
This was not the case in his own lifetime. The popularity of Mel Gibson's
character from *Braveheart* among the cinema-going English of the late
twentieth century was not a reflection of the popularity of the prototype
among their counterparts at the close of the thirteenth century. Wallace
was, to medieval English observers, a barrier to the 'settlement' of the
'Scottish problem'. As such, it is hardly surprising that English chronicles
and state records describe him as a ruthless revolutionary. Of course, one
person's terrorist or gangster is another person's freedom fighter or partisan;
the distinction is very much in the eye of the beholder.

It is only fair to bear in mind that there was not exactly a 'Scottish problem' in the first place. If one great barrier to British unification through English expansionism in the twelfth and thirteenth centuries was disinterest in the project among the English, the great barrier to unification after 1296 was the determination of enough Scots, enough of the time, that there should be no unification at all. In the late-thirteenth and fourteenth centuries, the chief obstruction to that unification was the attitude of the Scots to what they saw as subjugation by a larger, wealthier, more populous neighbour. The importance of William Wallace to that cause cannot be questioned. His significance lies not only in his military and political successes of 1297–98, but in his commitment to his chosen cause over the next seven years. Although he never recovered the power and influence he lost after the battle of Falkirk, his adherence to the Balliol party and the political independence of his nation never wavered. Unlike several more prominent figures, Robert the Bruce among others, Wallace was absolutely steadfast in his allegiance and, like his colleague Andrew Murray, he has enjoyed a certain reputation for constancy that is shared by only a very small segment of the Scottish noble classes during the Wars of Independence.

CHAPTER TWO

Of Noble Kin:
The Society of William Wallace

Over the centuries, Scots and others have developed a picture of William Wallace as a man of the people: not perhaps quite a farm worker, but certainly one of the 'common people' of thirteenth-century Scotland rather than one of the lords. In fact, Wallace was a member of the nobility; minor and obscure nobility perhaps, but nobility nonetheless. This is a matter of considerable importance in any assessment of Wallace's career and his impact on the political sensibilities of the Scots, both in the medieval period and, to a remarkable degree, thereafter as well.[1]

The society of thirteenth-century Scotland in which Wallace grew up was essentially a feudal one: it was not identical to that of England or France, but it bore many resemblances to both. The word feudal conjures up that familiar, if misleading, schoolbook illustration image of a pyramidal structure of society. The king sits at the top; below him is a small group of major lords, below them lesser lords, then knights, then squires, then farm tenants and finally serfs. Although such a depiction of medieval society makes for a very nice illustration, it does little to actually show the nature of rank and status relationships in medieval societies, and it is worth giving some thought to the realities of feudal society in Scotland to achieve a better understanding of the community in which Wallace lived and made his career. The king was certainly the top bough of the feudal tree, and to a great extent kings did depend on the support of the great lords or magnates, or at least on their acceptance of or acquiescence in his rule. The magnate class included the earls and the bishops, clearly denoted by their titles as superior members of the community, but it also included some great barons and heads of religious houses who did not, in any legal sense, enjoy a greater status than other barons or prelates, but whose wealth, influence or extent of property brought them into the magnate group (or they were the heads of families that enjoyed traditional status in a particular locality). In a sense, each of these men had a personal relationship with the Crown. Most of the temporal magnates held their property from the king in exchange for a variety of judicial and administrative obligations and for military service.[2]

For great lords like the Comyns or the Bruces, military service obligations were not particularly heavy, given the extent of their properties. Even for an earldom the service owed seldom exceeded ten knights, and it is believed that the customary duration of service was generally – perhaps almost universally – a period of forty days. It is not clear that the 'knights' in such arrangements were men bearing that title. In operational terms there was no real difference between knights and men-at-arms, save that a knight might be expected to fulfil a command function and that the title carried an extra shilling a day in wages. Each was obliged to equip himself to the same given standard. A man might make a lengthy career as a man-at-arms and never aspire to becoming a knight, and the fact that a property was held for the service of one knight did not mean that the tenant either was a knight himself or that he would employ a dubbed knight to discharge his obligation. Apart from anything else, there would be an obvious dif-ficulty if the landholder happened to be a woman; the service owed for the property would still have to be provided, though there would be no question of a female landholder ever being knighted.[3]

Self-evidently, no landholder could discharge a burden of ten knights personally. Service of forty days for each 'unit' of knight service owed would come to 400 days a year out of 365. The chief means of providing for knight service was subinfeudation. A person holding land from the king might in turn grant land to a relation or associate in exchange for military service. The need for landholders to provide property or cash settlements for their children led to a degree of fragmentation of both properties and service obligations, to the extent that there are instances of landholding for fractions of knight service, generally a half or a quarter, but sometimes as little as a twentieth of a knight's service.[4] Quite how such fractions of service were discharged is unclear. Major portions of service, such as a half, could have been given on a pro rata basis, the service of twenty days rather than forty, but the service of a twentieth of a knight would only provide a man-at-arms for two days, an enlistment of limited value. There is some evidence to suggest that there was an accepted relationship between the service of men-at-arms and of other troops, specifically archers and the lighter-armed cavalry troopers known in Ireland and England as hobelars, allowing the substitution of lighter troops for men-at-arms. It is clear that there were alternative mechanisms which were acceptable to, or at least accepted by, both superiors and vassals, which allowed the discharge of military service obligations by a greater variety of methods than simply personal service in the field or at the castle.

Military responsibility was not limited to the individual arrangements between superior and vassal. All men were obliged to serve in the army as required in defence of the realm. Tenure for military service was an additional burden, one that depended, at least in theory, on the financial capacity to bear it; only men with a substantial income could afford the necessary investment. An act of Robert I in 1318[5] is the earliest extant state-ment of the extent of military responsibility for Scots, but it should not be assumed that army service was not defined from an earlier date, by custom if not through legislation. The 1318 act was primarily concerned with the arming standards of men whose landed status was not sufficient to draw them into tenure agreements. The burden was not a particularly heavy one. The poorest men in the kingdom were obliged to provide themselves with no more than a spear or a bow and some arrows. The role of such men would largely be limited to responses to invasion. The bulk of the large armies raised by the Scots throughout the Wars of Independence would be drawn from wealthier classes of men. Those with rents worth £10 or goods worth £40 per annum were expected to equip themselves with a spear, an aketon (a padded jacket), a 'good iron' and armoured gloves. A 'good iron' was probably a steel cap. Men equipped to this sort of standard were in fact typical of the infantry element of all European armies. The chief difference between a Scottish soldier and his counterpart from elsewhere lay in his language and cultural background, not in his appearance. Although such men were recruited by the thousand when required, large field armies were something of a rarity. Wallace and Moray raised considerable forces for Stirling Bridge and the force that Wallace led at Falkirk seems to have been a strong one, but as a general rule the Scots tended to avoid major formal confrontations.

As a younger son from a modest estate, William Wallace might conceivably have served in the infantry had he not made a career of military leadership; however, his social status would more likely have led him to serve as a man-at-arms. Although the rank and file of major armies consisted of close combat infantry, the majority of warfare, in Scotland as elsewhere, was conducted by heavy cavalry. The reasons for this are wide-ranging. Partly it was a matter of economics. Although men-at-arms were expensive to train and support, even a modest force of them, particularly one with possession of the local castles, could dominate a relatively large area and provide a reasonably imposing presence in the community.[6] Being mounted, men-at-arms could respond to situations quickly, whether to intervene or to escape a larger force, but the social factors are perhaps the most significant. The men who were wealthy enough to support themselves as men-at-arms were also the men whose lifestyle afforded them the time and opportunity to learn and maintain the relevant skills. Further, since these men provided a focus of political admin- istration and therefore of allegiance in their localities they were, in a sense, representative of the will of the community. No doubt Scotland, like any other country, experienced a degree of class resentment before the Wars of Independence though there is little, if any, evidence to indicate it, but it does not seem to have been a feature of politics *during* the war, which would surely have been an excellent opportunity for the disadvantaged classes to further their position. This may in fact have occurred to some extent, in however a gradual and piecemeal fashion. Before the Wars of Independence most Scots were 'attached' to the land. They might have tenure rights on that land, but they themselves were owned by the landholder.

The terms most commonly used to describe these people – *rustici, nativi, bondi* and *servi* – all indicate a degree of servile status. The terms may have held a distinction that is lost to us, but they were all, in the loosest sense, serfs. By the middle of the fourteenth century serfdom would seem to have disappeared as a condition in Scotland. Throughout Europe servile status was in something of a decline, but not to the degree apparent in Scotland. To what extent the change can be attributed to the war is impossible to say, it would seem unreasonable to think that the war was not a factor. Professor Nicholson has suggested that the rapid recruitment of Wallace's army in 1297 was fuelled by widespread social discontent;[7] however, it is not clear what evidence there is to support that observation. There is little or no trace of class resentment tending toward violence in later-thirteenth- century Scotland, nor were there any events to compare with the Peasants Revolt in England or the Jacquerie disturbances in France in the four- teenth century. This does not mean that medieval Scotland was free from class conflict, or that the Scots of the day all existed in a companionable consensus, but it does suggest that class envies and insecurities were not of sufficient moment to bring about any event of great significance.

To some extent, the war itself was probably a factor in reducing the potential for social unrest within Scottish society, as opposed to unrest between interest groups. From the opening of hostilities in 1296 until the release of David II there was only a very short period, August 1305 to February 1306, when there was no party active in the cause of either King John or Robert I. The demands of the war required co-operation against a common enemy if the Scots were to succeed where the Welsh and Irish had failed in resisting the encroachment of English kings. On a more personal level, the war also made opportunities for advancement. The rate of attrition among the minor nobility was painfully high, but such men needed to be replaced if they were lost or if they were forfeited. Several minor nobles made spectacular careers in the service of Balliol, Plantagenet and Bruce kings; we should not doubt that more obscure men improved their fortunes in the same way. Gilbert Harper,[8] a man of very obscure origins, served Edward Bruce as a man-at-arms in Ireland. Although he was considered to be of too low a station to be made a knight, he could afford the very finest in arms and armour; the men who found his body apparently thought that they had recovered the corpse of Edward himself. It would seem unlikely that Gilbert Harper's adoption of the military and (to a great, though not unlimited, extent) cultural status of a man-at-arms was the product of service in war.

There was almost certainly some degree of resentment of the Plantagenet government, by virtue of its foreign nature, if nothing else. Although there is little evidence to suggest that Edward I's government imposed heavier taxation or demanded service of any kind beyond the customary limits, there must clearly have been some issues at work to persuade thousands of Scots to risk their necks in war against an obviously powerful enemy. It is possible that the Scots thought it likely that the occupation would lead to higher taxes, perhaps even to compulsory military service abroad; possibly the garrisons and administrators Edward put in place were heavy-handed – Edward himself seems to have thought this was a possibility, since he issued a writ declaring that in future his officials would be more accommodating. A motivational factor that is sometimes belittled and often ignored in medieval history is nationalism. A number of twentieth-century historians have seen European nationalism as a product of the wars of Napoleon, arguing that prior to the nineteenth century the bulk of the populace in most countries were not concerned about national identity. In England and Scotland, at least, this is simply untenable. Thirteenth-century Scots were perfectly well aware of their nationality, as were their counterparts in England. The extent to which nationalism formed a vehicle for the careers of William Wallace and Robert Bruce and the extent to which they constituted vehicles for nationalism is a moot point. Scots who accepted the rule of either may have done so not out of a fondness for the Balliol or Bruce cause, but because they believed that those parties represented the most effective opposition to the English.

This does not mean that the non-noble classes of Scotland were united in opposition to Plantagenet government. A group of tenant farmers on royal estates ('King's husbandmen') approached Edward I in the hope of securing the same tenurial rights as their counterparts in England.[9] Apart from demonstrating the willingness of Scots of all classes to accept Edwardian rule when it took their fancy to do so, their action shows that even Scots of a very obscure status could be aware of themselves as a political entity, could compare their conditions with their counterparts in another country, and were prepared to approach the king to seek an improvement in their status. At all levels of society, the extent to which the communities of Scotland accepted Edwardian government varied accord-ing to the prevailing political and military situation. No doubt a very large proportion of the population would have been more than happy to be simply left in peace: a common, and rational, reaction to war on one's doorstep. Even so, on the occasions that Scottish leaders called for widespread military service they do not seem to have toiled for recruits. In the weeks before Bannockburn, when, admittedly, Scotland had been at war for most of the preceding twenty years and had presumably become a rather militarised society, Robert I could afford to turn men away because they were inadequately equipped.[10]

The great formations of spearmen that are considered characteristic of Scottish medieval armies were not the means by which war as a whole was conducted; the normal practice of war was the business of men of some substance – the free tenants, the gentry and nobility. Regardless of the source of landholding privileges, whether from the Crown or from a feudal superior, in theory free tenants enjoyed heritable tenure as long as they fulfilled their contractual obligations. In practice, they naturally had to maintain a good relationship with their superior. The incidence of 'in capite' tenancies (tenancies 'in chief': land held directly from the Crown rather than from another noble) varied considerably across the country; in Lothian the political community largely comprised free tenants of the Crown. In areas dominated by a regional magnate (such as the lords of Badenoch or the earls of Buchan in the north-east or the earls of Carrick in the south-west) a greater proportion of the political community were vassals of magnates. The implications for local political leadership are fairly obvious. Men and women whose place in society stemmed from their relationship with a local potentate would be inclined to be sympathetic to the interests of that person. As feudal dependants of the Stewarts, the Wallace family would have been obliged to give military, judicial and administrative service, and, to a great extent, whatever other support they could offer, politically and socially. In general terms baronial free tenants enjoyed much the same status as royal ones, but the nature of the Wallace family tenure at Elderslie may explain their absence from the Ragman Roll; it is possible that as baronial free tenants their homage was 'taken as read' by virtue of their superior's undertaking, whereas men and women of similar, or lesser, status in society were obliged to make a personal declaration of homage and fealty because they were 'in capite' Crown tenants. If that were the case, Malcolm Wallace (brother of William and the holder of the property) would not have needed to avoid appending his seal to roll; he would not have been asked to do so in the first place. This does not imply that the Wallaces were not a part of the local political community, only that their political status was, in the view of the occupa- tion government at least, defined by their relationship with their feudal superiors. The validity of the assumption of political loyalty on the basis of feudal obligation was, however, open to question. The presence of feudal inferiors in the ranks of Scottish armies opposed to their superiors in the ranks of English ones drew comment from chroniclers, and an English spy reporting to Sir Robert Hastang (Edward I's sheriff of Roxburgh) in 1299 described Malcolm Wallace as a member of the Earl of Carrick's following. The earl was of course Robert Bruce, but Malcolm Wallace was a vassal of the Stewart, so practical operational leadership would seem to have been rather more sophisticated than a simple matter of tenure connections.

Accepting 'feudal' as an appropriate term for Scottish structures of gov- ernment in the late Middle Ages is not the same as assuming that the whole country, or even the entirety of any region within the country, was comprised entirely of feudal landholding units, nor that terms or practices were universal within those land units that were 'feudal'. In England, the conquest of 1066 allowed William the Conqueror to apportion property as he saw fit. Land divisions seem to have remained largely unchanged at the practical level of farms and estates, but William and his successors were able to impose some degree of common practice in relation to property rights and landholder responsibilities. In Scotland the situation was rather more complicated: 'feudal' tenures were introduced piecemeal, each grant made on its own terms. A number of Crown properties were converted to military tenures and no doubt other existing tenures were converted to a 'feudal' arrangement with or without the consent of the landholders in question, but others continued to operate on the basis of property rights that had been established long before the arrival of knight service. The great English medievalist Maurice Powicke was of the opinion that there was 'no articulated system of knight service in Scotland';[11] writing twenty

years later, Professor Barrow was equally sure that there was.[12] Neither
chose to elaborate on exactly what they meant by an 'articulated system',
of service.

In France, England or Scotland, knight service was a personal contract
to provide heavy cavalry service for a specified period of time and with
a specified level of equipment. The quality of horse and arms changed
over the years to reflect husbandry and technology developments, but the
amount of service in terms of numbers was only very rarely altered. That
amount bore no real relationship to the value or acreage of the lands for
which service was due. One landholder might have 2,000 acres for the
service of one tenth of a knight, while their neighbour with an estate of
similar size and value was obliged to provide the service of a whole knight.
In that sense, no European country had an 'articulated' system of knight
service, though in Scotland it was probably an even more ramshackle affair
than in France or England, due to the higher incidence of tenures that
were not 'feudal' in any sense.

Sir Malcolm Wallace's status as a 'vassal' of the Stewart was hardly servile
and certainly not dishonourable. Even kings gave their homage and fealty
to other kings for the sake of retaining property. The obligations attached to
his landholding were of an 'honourable' nature. In peacetime a considerable
portion of the tenants' obligations lay in 'suit of court'. Crown tenants,
and perhaps baronial tenants as well, served as jurors in the sheriff court.[13]
Baronial free tenants also served as jurors in the court of the baron or earl
from who they held land. Although criminal cases undoubtedly formed
a significant part of the workloads of the courts, there was a great deal of
other judicial activity. It is worth examining one particular aspect of juror
activity outside the criminal law in some detail. In the event of a free tenant
dying, the Crown would issue instructions to the sheriffs of those counties where the deceased held land to ascertain the extent of the property,
rights due to the Crown from the property and both the legitimacy and,
to some degree, the suitability of the heir – the latter being largely con-
fined to questions of the sanity of the heir, not his skills as a landholder.
These enquiries are known as Post Mortem Inquisitions; where they have
survived they give some insight to various aspects of landholding, as well
as the work of jurors.

In 1296 the occupation government selected a number of Lothian men
to conduct an inquisition into the estates of the late Robert de Pinkneye,[14]
an Englishman who had inherited Luffness Castle and property around
Balnacref (Balincreiff) in the constabulary of Haddington (a constabulary
was a division of a sheriffdom; the sheriffdom of Edinburgh was divided

into three parts, Edinburgh itself and the two subordinate constabularies of Haddington and Linlithgow). The first point of interest is that the jurors were all Scots. Edward had no intention of making major or immediate sweeping changes to the fabric of Scottish society; the only tier of government that he wanted to alter was the top one, kingship. If he could persuade the Scots that there were no radical alterations proposed for the political community at large, he might be able to bring Scotland under his rule without too much difficulty. In any case, in the short term at least, he could not allow the general conduct of commercial and social life to grind to a halt; that would hardly be a demonstration of 'good lordship'. Without the active participation of the minor nobility in administrative spheres, Edward's government would hardly be able to function at all. If the 'business' of Scotland was not carried on under Edward's kingship, what was the point of conquest? Edward wanted an asset, not a liability. For the nobility there was really very little choice. In those parts of Scotland where Edward could effectively exert his will, the failure of free tenants to discharge their obligations was likely to lead to forfeiture, possibly even execution. The men concerned (and it would invariably have been men) might well be loath to avoid jury service. Refusal might well have implications for their own standing within the community; also, war or no war, life must go on – why should the heir to a property be denied possession of his rightful inheritance merely because there had been a war?

The deliberations of the jury probably did not take very long. They had to establish the extent of the property, its commercial value to the heir, such portions of the property as were held by others and on what basis, and the extent of military and other service due to the Crown. Where necessary, the jurors might have to conduct a survey, called a 'perambulation', to ascertain the exact bounds of the property. This was not the case in the de Pinkneye inquisition, possibly because the jurors, all local men, were sufficiently aware of what those bounds were, or possibly because there were no boundary disputes with the neighbouring landholders. The report of the jury opens with a description of the property, finding that the late Robert de Pinkneye had held the 'tenement of Balincref, and the chief messuage, with garden and pigeon house in the enclosure', worth 34s 4d per annum. What exactly these terms imply is not always precisely clear. Evidently Balincref or 'Balnacref' – medieval spellings tend toward diversity rather than consistency – was a distinct vicinity whose limits were locally understood, and the chief house of the property had a garden, which we should probably take to mean something more along the lines of a market garden, or even allotment (though on a rather grand scale), to supply the household with the vegetables and fruit that we know were consumed in Scotland, though not grown as field crops such as kale, onions or raspberries. The pigeon house remained a feature of Scottish life until relatively recent times. Raised in purpose-built towers known as 'doo cots' (dovecotes), pigeons provided a source of fresh meat in winter for the tables of the gentry, and no doubt for others when the gentry were not looking – a reasonable reaction if you had a colony of rapacious pigeons in the vicinity of your crops. Additionally, Robert had ten carucates (approximately 100 acres each) and fifty acres of arable land held 'in demesne'. This was relatively unusual in a Scottish context, where the tradition of the landholding classes was to rent land out for a fee (*firma*, hence 'farmer') rather than to manage it personally. In this context however, 'in demesne' may mean that the land in question was the proportion of the property he retained to provide his income, as opposed to portions of the property that he had granted to others. Each of these acres was valued at 21d per annum, '*with its meadow and grazing*'. Throughout the medieval period it was quite common to assess only the arable acreage of a property, but it was generally assumed that there would be a quantity of grazing land attached to the arable, not physically, but as a unit of land tenure. The property also had two mills, valued at £8, from which £1 per annum was given to the clerics of the hospital of St Cuthbert in alms from Robert de Pinkneye, in addition to nine bovates and nine acres which they had received from Robert and his predecessors over the years.

A number of cottars had smallholdings on the estate and paid fixed rents amounting to £5 12s 6d, and there were a number of breweries paying fixed rents of £1 9s 4d, from which Alicia de Graham was paid 13s 4d (one merk) as part of her terce from her late husband, Roger de Lelman. The connection between Lelman and Pinkneye is unclear, but evidently Alicia's claim on the estate was not in dispute. Alicia's terce is an example of the wide range of demands that might fall upon a landholder; the sum was not large in terms of the Pinkneye estate, but it might be only one of many such obligations to family connections. Robert's brother, Henry, also had a commercial interest in the estate: six bovates which he held from his brother. Although the land was valued at £4 per annum, Henry actually paid 1d. Obviously that minute rental was a reflection of the relationship between Henry and Robert, not a reflection of the commercial value of the nine bovates. Henry's tenure was probably limited to his own lifetime; he would have to make provision for his children's future himself. If nothing else, the successor to Robert might, in due course, have to make provision for his own younger brother. Henry was not the only major secular tenant on the estate. The castle of Luffness, the demesnes of the castle and three carucates of land were rented out to Roger de Bigerton for the sum of £26 13s 4d.

At first glance this might appear to be a more carefully assessed sum, a figure of some nicety that reflects the commercial value of land in East Lothian in the late thirteenth century; however the sum is deceptive. At two-thirds of a pound to the merk, it is clear that the rental paid was forty merks per annum. This *might* have been based on a commercial valuation but is likely to have been very favourable to the tenant. What appears to us as a favourable rental need not have appeared so at the time. It is quite possible, even likely, that some apparently favourable rentals were in fact the consequence of moneylending, or at least of capitalisation of assets in some form. Many apparently generous donations of land to religious houses were in fact accompanied by a substantial cash payment to the 'donor' from the recipient of the land; it would be unreasonable to assume that activity of that nature was limited to ecclesiastical investors. It might seem curious that Robert should have let out his castle at Luffness; however it should be borne in mind that he was the owner of the estate, not necessarily a resident. Without residents, the castle would either be a pointless financial burden on Robert or it would fall into disrepair. Roger held a further property from Robert de Pinkneye. It consisted of 'twenty merks' of land at Bynyn (Binnin) in the 'county' (constabulary) of Linlithgow. The jurors have not chosen to explain, or perhaps had no need to explain, precisely what they meant by 'twenty merks' of land. The terms 'marcate' was used fairly extensively in both England and Scotland. Obviously there is a link with the word 'merk' (or 'mark' in England) but it is not clear what the relationship was. The most likely possibilities are that, at some point in the past, a 'marcate' had either been worth one merk per annum in produce, or as a rental unit; the latter would suggest that the produce expected from a marcate would be worth much more than one merk, to allow the tenant to generate a profit. Alternatively, the term may have had less 'site-specific' application, but was understood to indicate an order of magnitude rather than a land unit of exactly that value.

Grants that involve the terms 'marcate' or 'librate' often represent an intention to provide land, often in a particular sheriffdom, as opposed to specific named estates. When Edward III granted several properties in the sheriffdom of Edinburgh to Sir John de Strivelin in 1335–36, he did not indicate which properties in the sheriffdom were to be given to Sir John. At that juncture Edward III happened to have a good deal of property in Lothian that he could grant out, due to the fact that he had recently forfeited 100 or so Lothian landholders for supporting the Bruce monarchy. In such circumstances, someone must have conducted a survey to ascertain which properties were available and what combination of them would constitute 100 or 200 marcates. In the absence of any evidence to indicate otherwise, it would seem most likely that administrative work of that nature would have been undertaken by jurors owing suit to the sheriff court. Those jurors would not only have a good knowledge of the local properties, they would have an understanding of the practices involved in effecting a change of lordship; also, since they would have been representatives of the local political community, their verdicts and reports might help to enhance the credibility of the administration that Edward had imposed.

There were two other sitting tenants on the Balnacref estate: Alexander de Lindsay, who held one carucate, valued at £4 per annum, for a rental of 1d, and Thomas de Coleville, tenant of Gosford, an area within the estate. Gosford was estimated by the jurors to extend to three carucates and to be worth £10 per annum. Thomas did not pay a cash rental at all, but instead was obliged to provide one quarter of a knight's service. How that service was expressed is not made clear, but that is probably because there was no need to do so; everyone concerned – the tenant, the landholder, the jurors and the sheriff – were all perfectly well aware of what exactly 'one quarter of the service of a knight' entailed.

For all the lands at Balnacref and Luffness, Robert de Pinkneye had owed the service of one knight – presumed to be a period of forty days – and for his property at Bynyn, Linlithgow, he owed the service of three-quarters of a knight. Self-evidently he could not discharge both obligations at the same time. In part, his problem was solved by subinfeudation. Thomas de Colville was obliged, as we have seen, to give one quarter of a knight's service. We might reasonably look to Robert's brother, Henry, who held £4 worth of property for 1d per annum, to be a likely candidate to discharge the balance, given his favourable rental, but if that was the extent of his wealth he might have been pushed to provide himself with the quality of equipment required for knight service. On the other hand, Thomas de Colville evidently could either provide himself with the necessary arms and horse or could afford to pay someone else to perform the service of one quarter of a knight on his behalf.

It would be unrealistic to consider Balnacref as a 'typical' Scottish property: what, after all, would constitute a 'typical' business today? All the same, the Balnacref inquisition does illustrate a number of the issues that 'typically' might apply to any property in Scotland. Estates, baronies and lordships might look like single entities held by an individual, but in practice were more often than not a patchwork of short-term, long-term, lifetime and heritable leases.

Like many other landholders, Robert's position as a rentier landlord was derived from his personal liability to provide the king with armoured cavalry service. The amount of military service required obviously varied considerably from one property to the next, but in addition to what we might call the 'field service' burden of knight service, the free tenant would also have to make a contribution, known as 'castle guard', to the security of his superior's home. Though no doubt castle guard was originally envisaged as an obligation to serve in person for a given period, it would seem that from the early twelfth century, if not before, it was acceptable – even customary – to commute such service for money payments. There are a number of reasons why commutation should have been attractive to both tenant and superior. In peacetime, the castle guards were likely to be redundant – a drain on the superior, who presumably would have to provide board and lodgings. In wartime, the addition of a couple of men-at-arms to the complement of even a very small castle was unlikely to make any real difference to its security. For the tenants commutation was bound to be more convenient than standing guard over someone else's property. At the time at which the original grants had been made, mostly in the early twelfth century, castle guard payments probably represented a worthwhile contribution to the security of those royal and baronial castles that attracted it, but since the payments were fixed in perpetuity, the process of inflation gradually eroded their value; by the close of the fifteenth century castle guard payments had dwindled into an almost insignificant source of income for feudal superiors, hardly enough to make a dent in the costs of maintaining even the most insignificant of castles, let alone a garrison.

The military obligations of the nobility and the more prominent burgesses and tenants were not strictly limited to knight service; indeed, so few of the men who owed that service were actually knights that we might more realistically refer to it 'man-at-arms' service. There is a slight possibility, however, that the distinction between knights and men-at-arms was one of the methods by which fractional knight service was assessed. It was a generally established rule of thumb in France and England, and therefore very likely elsewhere as well, that a knight was entitled to double the pay of a man-at-arms. There was no real difference in the nature of their service, so far as we can tell; it was the superior social status of the knight over his undubbed companion that brought him two shillings a day instead of one. If that relationship was carried into other areas of military responsibility, it may have been the case that the service of a man-at-arms for forty days was acceptable as the equivalent of half a knight's service for twenty days, or that the quarter of a knight's service owed by Thomas de Colville on behalf of Roger de Pinkneye might actually take the form of ten days' service from a man-at-arms. Professor Duncan has suggested that there was an accepted rate for the substitution of archers for knight service; however, while there are several extant charters that specify archer service, there are none at all that specify the service of a man-at-arms as opposed to that of a knight, though there are references to 'armed men' – *armati* – to serve alongside archers, presumably in a junior leader role.[15] This is curious, given that the bulk of the day-on-day warfare that lasted intermittently from 1296 to the middle of the fourteenth century was conducted by men-at-arms; English and Scottish chronicles and records are largely devoted to the activities of the noble class at war, because the majority of the action was conducted by men-at-arms and most men-at-arms were of the nobility.

Military service obligation for land was additional to the service owed by all the adult males of Scotland. Known as 'Scottish' or 'Common Army' service, this was an obligation on all men over the age of sixteen and under the age of sixty.[16] The fact of the obligation to bear arms is well understood; what is less clear is the extent of the burden. In 1318 Robert I laid down a scale of arms according to income. After the nature of medieval legislation generally, the 1318 rules are probably more in the nature of codifying exist-ing obligations and/or restating existing legislation than evidence of a new system. All 'fencible' men (those liable for military service) were obliged to have arms and to bring them to community training days. It would be most unlikely that those men in the community who had the obligation – or had made the choice – to acquire more sophisticated arms would have abandoned their man-at-arms status to take part in these events. They may not have taken part at all; there is a sense in which medieval armies con-sisted of two distinct armies in co-operation, one of men-at-arms and one of infantry. However, it would be more likely, given that such men would be relatively well known and of some status in the community, that they would be encouraged to adopt junior leadership roles in training for the day when they might have to take the field as part of a large conventional army, such as those at Falkirk, Bannockburn or Myton.[17]

These training days were held only a few times a year, and it should not be assumed that they were all either well attended or well conducted, so the level of expertise acquired was probably not very sophisticated; however, the evolutions required of a body of spearmen are not terribly sophisticated either, and a certain amount of familiarity with those evolutions must surely have developed in most communities over the years. The essential requirements, if a formation of spearmen were to function adequately, can be seen in the foot drill manuals of any army since the invention of manuals, but with the complication that 'cadenced marching' – that is to say, marching in step – had yet to be introduced. This might seem like a trivial consideration, but is in fact quite a major advantage in moving formed bodies of men; they move more quickly and at a more consistent rate and are less likely to trip over one another if they march in step. In particular, a formation moving in line rather than column loses its 'dressing' – its regularity – very easily even when the troops are marching in step. A formation of spearmen would need to keep very good dressing to avoid becoming disrupted and vulnerable to attack. Since these training days were local affairs, such training as did take place was limited to the local men; when called to the ranks of a large army they would have to act in co-operation with the men of other localities. To achieve any degree of cohesion, there would need to have been a good deal of authority wielded at junior leader levels if the resulting army was to consist of practical formations for the battlefield, rather than a large number of independent followings.

Common army service was not the mainstay of the Scottish military effort in the fourteenth century, but it was an integral part of the military system as a whole, and the numbers involved were considerable. In the late sixteenth century, when the population of Scotland was, if anything, smaller than it had been in 1298, the 'common army' of the sheriffdom of Carrick amounted to well over 1,000 men.[18] An indicator of the extent to which the Plantagenet administration failed to win over the population as a whole is the fact that none of the Edwards made any attempt to raise the 'common army' of any of the Scottish counties under their control, nor, so far as we know, did Edward Balliol during his attempt to procure Scottish kingship. It was certainly under consideration by Edward I; a draft for a writ to call out the men of Stirlingshire has survived, though there is no evidence that such a writ was ever issued or promulgated. Since Edward had been able to call upon service from even the most newly conquered areas of Wales with some degree of success, it seems reasonable to assume that he had, at some point, expected that he would be able to do the same in Scotland; apparently he did not feel that he could do so with any prospect of gaining men. Were he to demand service and not achieve a credible force, his authority would be undermined. Better by far not to put it to the test – a policy apparently adopted by his son and his grandson.

As well as judicial and military duties and a general obligation to be supportive of the superior, free tenants frequently had an obligation to join their superior in the hunting field. As well as contributing to the table, hunting provided an opportunity for social intercourse and, to some extent, for the practice of field and leadership skills for the battlefield. If nothing else, there was the opportunity for the lord's dependants to sharpen or develop their equestrian abilities and to become accustomed to acting collectively on horseback over a variety of terrain. As a younger son, William Wallace would not have been expected to inherit the family property, but we should not assume he grew up excluded from noble traditions of military or hunting service. Had he married an heiress – the ambition of younger sons generally – he would have had to discharge the obligations attached to her property. Extinction in the male line was not uncommon, so marriage to an heiress was not so unlikely a proposition as it sounds and younger sons therefore needed to have the various social, judicial, equestrian and military skills necessary for life as a free tenant.

Advantageous marriage was not the only career path for younger sons, though in an economy more than 90 per cent dependent on agriculture it was surely the most popular. The only real alternatives were the Church and commerce. The latter might still be founded on matrimony. Marriages between minor nobility and burgess families were not uncommon as a means of enhancing the prestige of the burgess family and improving the finances of the noble one. Younger sons from minor noble families could be married off to burghal families and thus introduced to commerce, in exchange for a good dowry from the bride's family.[19] Towns were reckoned, with some justification, to be unwholesome places, but they were the focus of marketing. The more significant towns, the burghs, had a formal, incorporated status, generally defined in a charter stating the rights and responsibilities of the town to its superior. Baronial and ecclesiastical burghs were no a great rarity in medieval Scotland, but almost all of the most important burghs held charters from the Crown. The responsibilities included the supply of men for the king's army and money for his treasury. The site rent of the burgh was not generally a great sum, but the burgh authorities would also have collected the customs dues and such taxes and aids as the king might be able to extract from Parliament. The most important of these revenues was unquestionably the export duty on wool. Other goods were exported, particularly fur, hides and leather, fish, woollen and linen cloth and horses; however, since they were not subject to duty the extent of the trade cannot be gauged.[20] In exchange for these responsibilities the burghs were entitled to a monopoly of trade within stated bounds, sometimes called the 'liberties' of the burghs, and the right to self-administration. Largely, if not universally, the merchant guild of the burgh came be the dominant force in internal politics and administration. Only a very small proportion of the inhabitants of a burgh were actually burgesses.[21] Admission to the guild was dependent on a certain level of economic status and attachment to persons already admitted. In effect, the merchant guild in most towns formed an oligarchy, interested chiefly in furthering the interests of the members of the guild rather than those of the town, though to a considerable extent these did tend to be sympathetic considerations: that which was good for the merchants tended to be good for the community as a whole. Traditionally, it has been assumed that the merchants co-operated to marginalise the suppliers of produce and goods; however, recent research indicates a more consensual relationship between producers and sellers. Without some degree of consensus, it is difficult to imagine how medieval towns could have survived economically, let alone managed to thrive.

That they did thrive is beyond question. In 1153 there were, to the best of our knowledge, sixteen burghs in Scotland; at the close of the reign of William I (William the Lion) there were nearly forty, and more than fifty by 1300.[22] This may be more a matter of the survival of evidence than the foundation of burghs. Many Scottish towns date their foundation from charters. The granting of a charter is not, however, very good evidence for dating the origin of the burgh; it is only evidence of the burgh being granted certain privileges. The community might have existed for centuries without acquiring the status of a burgh. There are exceptions; it seems very likely that a number of burghs in Moray were founded as planned, enclosed settlements belonging to the king, constructed to help him bring the area more securely under royal control after revolts in the twelfth century, but most burghs would appear to have developed naturally as commercial centres due to their location on navigable rivers, natural harbours or in the vicinity of secure centres of government like Stirling Castle.

A burgh did not need to be a royal foundation, though increasingly from the twelfth century (if not before) the elevation from town to burgh required royal sanction; if the status of a royal burgh was to be worthwhile it had to have privileges reserved to the burgesses and not easily acquired by newcomers to the commercial world. Several burghs were either baronial or ecclesiastical. In both cases, the intention was to give the lord or the prelate an opportunity to take advantage of a privileged position in the market.[23] Not only would they enjoy the commercial privileges of the burgesses – the merchant guild oligarchy that ran the town, not the craftsmen and servants that lived there – but they could regulate certain aspects of it, in particular letting shop and stall space and administering the sort of minor commercial justice issues that arise in any marketplace. Such issues would generally be resolved by the payment of a fine (Latin *finis*, 'an end'), which would, naturally enough, be retained by the superior.

Unlike its baronial and ecclesiastical counterparts, the royal burgh was, theoretically, free from the influence of great nobles, since it was the property of the king leased to the burgesses. In practice, burghs could not afford to offend neighbouring magnates. Apart from their general influence in the vicinity and the possibility that they might exert armed force on the burgh if pushed, the local magnatial house would often have constituted an important source of revenue; magnates might be rich (compared to those around them, at any rate; Scottish landholders were, in general, rather less well off than their counterparts in England and considerably worse off than their counterparts in France or the Low Countries), but where is the value of having money if you do not spend it? The household of an earl or great lord or the kitchens of a monastery, abbey or cathedral were very likely to spend large sums on expensive imported luxury goods. Their custom would help to achieve economies of scale that could not be supported by the burgh community alone.

The most profitable area of commerce was the import trade. The range of products to be found in Scottish markets was rather larger than we might expect. Spices, particularly cumin, ginger and pepper, appear regularly in rentals, clearly indicating that these products were readily available.[24] What is not so clear is why these items should be chosen as a means of expressing rents in what was unquestionably a cash economy. The expression 'peppercorn rent' no doubt has its origins in similar arrangements, and the nominal value of the rents – generally of the order of 'one pound of cumin (or pepper or ginger or galengale) valued at 2d' – would seem to indicate that such rentals were not genuinely commercial arrangements, though it is true that the value of a produce rent such as pepper or cumin given in a charter may reflect the value of money and goods at the time the charter was granted. The penny and twopenny rents that appear in the Edinburgh sheriff's records of 1335–36 (the first year in which rents for individual properties in Scotland are recorded in large numbers) mostly refer to rentals set 200 years previously and should not be accepted as any indication of current prices and values. The spice industry was lucrative and dependable, but the 'big money' business was probably the wine trade. Long before the days of William Wallace, a large and sophisticated commercial structure developed to supply Scottish markets with considerable quantities of wine, financed mostly by the export of wool. The cloth factories of the Low Countries may have been supplied principally from English sources, but the Scottish wool crop was substantial enough to support a positive balance of trade and provide Scottish kings with a significant revenue from customs.

One area of commerce that is likely to have seen a considerable expansion once it became apparent that war with England was a real possibility is the arms trade. Arms and armour were certainly produced in Scotland before the Wars of Independence, but the quantities are unlikely to have been large, since the market was small and wars were a rarity and tended to be brief. Men had military obligations and needed arms to fulfil them, but through most of the thirteenth century most of the martial activity in Scotland probably consisted of chasing brigands. In 1296, the most recent Scottish military operation had been the annexation of the Isle of Man, some twenty years previously. The Man expedition did not involve a very large force, nor was the campaign long or challenging, so the experience gained was marginal in itself, as well as being twenty years out of date. All the same, men needed arms and the Scots who were beaten at Dunbar in 1296 do not appear to have been noticeably ill-equipped, though it might well be the case that their equipment was rather old-fashioned – but then, a society unaccustomed to war was unlikely to invest a great deal in arms and armour if they were never required to do more than chase bandits. Arms could be bought; an entry in the plea rolls of Edward I's army in Scotland in 1296[25] refers to the theft of swords from a Scottish shop. Indeed, the Scottish name 'Lorimer' means armour or harness maker, but for fashionable, state-of-the-art equipment, Scottish nobles probably had to purchase weapons and armour of foreign manufacture. Throughout the Wars of Independence, most of the imported arms came from the Low Countries or from France, though repeated demands from English kings that Irish and English merchants should refrain from exporting arms to Scotland suggests that commercial considerations could be more important than patriotic ones.[26]

A career in the Church would generally require some sort of outlay from the family resources, either by purchasing a living in a monastery or through parish patronage rights. When a lord gave land for the construction of a church and the support of the priest, he might well retain the right of 'advowson': the power to appoint a new incumbent should the old one die or move on elsewhere. Such patronage was a saleable commodity; a position as a parish priest, or other forms of benefice, could be purchased from the holder of the advowson. Military service by Scottish clergymen seems to have been something of a rarity, though not unknown; the rector of Pencaitland served in the Plantagenet garrison of Edinburgh Castle in the 1330s with a tiny retinue of two men-at-arms.[27] Those clerics who came from noble families (and that would have been the vast majority of them) would have had the same sort of education as their peers; military, judicial and hunting duties would have formed a considerable part of that education. The family property would descend to the eldest son, and it might seem redundant that his younger brothers should have the same sort of education and training, since they would not become the head of their branch of the family; however, an eldest son might die before having an heir of his own, particularly in wartime, and a younger brother would need the practical skills required of a landholder should he happen to inherit the family property.

For most people today, the concept of family property has little, if any, significance, but in medieval Scotland it was of prime importance. The family property was not merely the home and source of income of the head of the family, but the source of support for members of the family through generations. Portions of the family estate would be granted to various relatives to provide for them and their families. Should someone inherit property while their mother was still alive, a portion of the land – nominally a third and known as a terce – would usually be granted to the mother of the heir to provide her with an income for the rest of her life, at which point it would revert to the family estate. Had William Wallace made a conventional career, he might have spent his days as a very minor member of the political community, holding a slice of his brother's estate in liferent. On his death, that slice would be restored to the main property, so Wallace would have to have made provision for his own sons or see his branch of the family decay in status. Most agricultural land in Scotland was tenanted, even the estates of relatively trivial landholders, so Wallace might never have put his own hand to the plough, but as the dependant of a very minor landholder it would be rash to assume that he enjoyed a notably better standard of living than his more successful tenants. The preponderance of farms would seem to have been held by groups rather than individual tenants. The root of multiple tenancies probably derived from a need to collectivise labour and plant in the form of draught animals, to achieve commercially viable farms. Demesne farming, lands retained in the lord's hands and under his own (or his grieve's) management, though highly developed in England, does not seem to have been a widespread commercial practice in any part of medieval Scotland. The numerous example of farms bearing the name 'mains', a corruption of 'demesne', would seem to indicate the sort of arrangement more commonly called 'home farms' in England: a means of providing produce for consumption rather than for sale. The Scottish nobility of the thirteenth and fourteenth centuries were essentially a class of rentier landlords with military and legal obligations; the Wallace family formed a tiny part of that class.

The noble status of the Wallaces was not sufficiently exalted to give them entry to the upper reaches of political society. Although they may have been members of the same class as the earls and great lords, the Wallaces were as much removed from the senior aristocracy as they were from the poorest of villeins. This would have a considerable effect on the career of Wallace. His attainment of power was achieved through successful military leadership, not through his social position. So long as that leadership continued to bring results against the occupation, Wallace could retain political leadership as well. Once he had been defeated his influence started to wane almost immediately, due to the fact that he had no customary body of support within the political community as a whole and, crucially, no network of sympathisers within the senior aristocracy. This might have been offset had Moray not died in the weeks after Stirling Bridge. Moray may not have been in the first rank of Scottish magnates, but he was well known and wealthy. The magnate class might have been rather more willing to accept the leadership of Moray (Murray), a senior baron, rather than Wallace, the younger son of a minor laird.

CHAPTER THREE

The Roots of the War

Throughout the reigns of Alexander II and Alexander III, Scotland and England had enjoyed a stable and generally peaceful relationship. Although Scottish trade continued to be chiefly with France and Flanders, commercial and cultural activity between the two countries would seem to have increased steadily through the thirteenth century.

Following the death of his son and heir, Alexander remarried in 1285; he was still only in his early forties and could be reasonably hopeful of fathering another son and living long enough to see his son grow to adulthood before inheriting the throne. On 19 March 1286, despite the entreaties of various Crown servants and officers who suggested he should wait overnight for a storm to pass, Alexander decided to make his way to his wife. Unfortunately for all concerned, he never arrived, but was found dead at the base of a cliff near Kinghorn in Fife. The queen claimed that she might be pregnant, and matters stalled for a short while before it became clear that she was not. This meant that Alexander's heir, his granddaughter Margaret, was the heir to the throne. Margaret's mother had been queen of the late king of Norway.

Despite her tender years, Margaret's marriage had already been a matter of discussion between Alexander III and Edward I. It had apparently been broadly agreed between them that Margaret should marry Edward's son (Edward of Carnarvon, later Edward II of England), thus bringing about an eventual union between England and Scotland under the rule of Edward and Margaret's son, assuming that they had one. This proposed union does not seem to have been an unpopular plan. Scotland and England had been at peace for most of the preceding century and there was no strong tradition of antipathy between the two nations. A number of issues had to be addressed – in particular, guarantees for the traditions of Scottish law and the preservation of ecclesiastical independence for the Scottish Church – but it would seem that a dynastic union was not seen as a threat by the Scottish political community. Margaret's death en route from Norway to Scotland destroyed any possibility of that union, and the Scots were left with the thorny problem of selecting a new king. There was no shortage of candidates; on the other hand, who exactly was going to make the decision?

The council of Guardians, originally set up to rule on behalf of Margaret during her minority, has been roundly criticised by Scottish historians for approaching Edward I at all, but in fact their choice was both practical and inevitable. Edward's reputation as a 'second Justinian' is largely the product of Victorian wishful thinking, but is not wholly unjustified. He was a jurist of repute and ability, but was not above radical reinterpretations of legal practice when it suited him. Perhaps more significantly, he was the king of Scotland's only geographical neighbour; he was likely to be acceptable to all of the claimants; he had had a good relationship with Alexander III and, though Scots would deny it, he had, in his own view at least, certain 'rights' in relation to Scotland. Edward's 'right' stemmed from a number of occasions when Scottish kings had accepted the overlordship of English kings: generally, if not invariably, as a result of military defeat. Henry III made some attempt to resurrect that type of relationship when Alexander III came to the throne, and Edward I made a similar attempt when, on his own accession to the throne of England, Alexander came to perform homage for the various properties he held in England. Like his predecessors, Alexander held extensive lands in England, just as the king of England held extensive lands in France. In each case, the homage and fealty requirements of landholding presented a problem for the superior and the inferior. For the inferior, there was the issue of whether their prestige as a king was undermined by giving homage, or to what extent, if any, their homage for lands in a foreign kingdom affected the sovereignty of their own kingdom. For the superior, homage might afford an opportunity to gain prestige by accepting homage from a king, or to 'stretch the envelope' of the homage commitment to extract a political advantage. Homage and fealty had to be renewed at the death of either party, so the issue arose fairly regularly.

After Edward I became king in 1272 he naturally wanted the homage and fealty of all of his barons, including Alexander III, who held extensive land rights in Tynedale and elsewhere. During the ceremony, Edward tried to insert a measure into the formula which would mean that Alexander would have accepted him as his superior and lord, not only for his English properties, but for his kingdom of Scotland. Alexander refused, saying that he held his kingdom from God alone, and Edward chose not to press the point, effectively accepting that he had no legal position in respect of Scottish kingship.

As far as the Scots were concerned, any rights that English kings might have enjoyed in Scotland had been extinguished by the Quitclaim of Canterbury in 1189,[1] when Richard I of England had sold any and all English Crown interests in Scotland for the sizeable sum of 10,000 merks (one merk, or mark in England, was equivalent to two-thirds of one bound: thirteen shillings and fourpence), but effectively the Scots could hardly avoid asking for Edward's help; not only was he a noted jurist, he was the king of Scotland's only neighbouring country and a mighty prince. If his help was not sought, he might well impose it anyway. That help was forthcoming, but only on Edward's terms. As a precondition of participation in the contest, all of the claimants had to accept Edward's right to conduct the court and his superiority. Most of the claims were, superficially at least, relatively frivolous. Those with no expectation of outright success were looking for opportunities. If, for example, the new royal line should fail, there might be a new competition, and anyone who had failed to make their case in the first contest would be unlikely to be accepted into a second. Furthermore, those whose claims were unlikely to bear fruit directly might be able to profit from lending (or selling) their support to one or other of the more serious candidates; also, the Canmore line of the Alexanders had failed, so why not the Balliol or Bruce line? If the new Scottish king should happen to die without an heir, the whole business of the Scottish succession might have to be examined afresh. Men who had been passed over for the Scottish throne might be able to extract some concession or advantage from a second 'competition', but only if they had declared an interest at the outset.

The two most significant claimants were Robert Bruce of Annandale, a prominent lord and grandfather of the Robert Bruce who would eventually become king, and John Balliol. Each of these men was descended from the royal house, and in very similar degree. A third candidate, Sir John Hastings, claimed that the kingdom of Scotland was a fief of the English Crown and, as such, should be divided equally between himself, Bruce and Balliol, just like any other Crown fief inherited by females. Hastings's plea was rejected by Edward I on the grounds that, as a kingdom, Scotland was not a divisible inheritance. The court was conducted between 1291 and 1292. A total of 104 auditors were appointed. The selection of auditors reflected the political realities of the situation. The Balliol and Bruce camps appointed forty each, the balance being selected by Edward I. The eventual decision to appoint John Balliol has been seen, by Scottish medievalists particularly, as an indication that Edward perceived John to be a more malleable person than Robert Bruce. This may have been true, but the evidence does not indicate that Robert would have been any less amenable to Edward's influence. John, in common with all the other competitors, had accepted Edward's superiority as a condition of being accepted as a claimant at all, and was in any case already a homager of Edward for several properties in England, a distinction he shared with Robert Bruce.

Edward may have chosen John, but he was determined to make clear to him that he reigned under Edward, not independently of him.[2] Within a year or two, Edward was demonstrating his suzerainty by undermining John I's government. In medieval societies the role of the king as the final judge of appeal was very important, both as a matter of judicial practice and as a demonstration of the king's ability to exert lordship. Edward made it clear that he was willing to hear appeals against the judgements of John, just as if he was any English baron. In fact, it seems more or less certain that Edward encouraged at least one person, Roger Bartholomew, a Berwick merchant, to bring a case before Edward which had already been heard, and rejected, by John. Naturally, such behaviour undermined John's prestige and authority and led to resentment of Edwardian interference. Not content with interference in appeals procedures, Edward decided to demand military service from the king of Scotland as a vassal of the king of England. Whether Edward actually expected to gain troops by this measure is unclear, though since various Scottish lords had campaigned with Edward in France, Wales and Palestine, he may have expected the support of a few. It is more likely that he was simply trying to force John into a reaction that would allow Edward to depose him and to annex Scotland.

It is by no means certain that Edward had had that intention since the demise of Alexander III, but it can hardly be denied that he was willing to make an opportunity for intervention from the earliest days of John's kingship. John's refusal of service and his repudiation of his homage to the king of England provided Edward with, in his view, excellent grounds for war. Although his summons to the Scots for military service had failed, Edward was still able to take advantage of divisions among the Scots. There is some doubt about the stability of John's government even before his defiance of Edward. English chroniclers tell us that a council of twelve prominent men had been erected to govern the country on John's behalf. The chroniclers may have been confused about the Guardianship that existed between the death of Alexander III and the installation of John I and concluded that that council of worthies had either continued to rule, or recovered their power, during John's kingship, or there may indeed have been such a council of government; however, it is not inconceivable, though highly unlikely, that the council was simply an invention of Bruce propaganda in the fourteenth century, aimed at undermining any vestiges of respect for the Balliol dynasty. The Bruces would in fact maintain that John had never really been the legitimate king of Scotland, merely an appointee of Edward I; charters of Robert I describe Alexander III as 'our immediate predecessor as King', thereby denying the very existence of John's kingship.[3]

John's defiance in 1295, and his commitment to a treaty with France against England, prompted Edward to mount a Scottish invasion in the spring of 1296. The Scottish nobility as a whole had accepted Edward's leadership during the 'Great Cause', and several influential men, for a variety of reasons, chose to serve Edward against John I. A number of Scottish lords probably had real doubts about what exactly was the ethically 'correct' position to adopt. John may have been their feudal superior but Edward was John's feudal superior, so which level of command should take precedence? On a purely practical level, there was the question of military competence. The Scots had not been at war for more than thirty years, and there had been very little fighting then. The English on the other hand had a well-established military system and a great deal of relatively recent military experience. Some Scots were in fact active in support of the Plantagenet cause. The Bruces adopted the Plantagenet cause through a mixture of antipathy to John Balliol, whom they resented because he had won the position that they felt was rightly theirs, and, perhaps, hope that Edward would depose John and replace him with Robert. John Balliol's army would inevitably be much weaker than Edward Plantagenet's, and the defection of the Bruces and others would weaken it even further.

Inexperienced, divided among themselves and, apparently, in the absence of their king, the Scots raised an army and mounted raids into England in support of the commitment to the French, but the amateur nature of their approach to war achieved little or nothing. Cross-border raiding was likely to make no real impression on Edward, but the claim that the Scots had set fire to a school at Hexham and burned more than 200 young scholars to death probably did his cause no harm in the propaganda battle, though it is extremely unlikely that a place like Hexham would have a school with anything like 200 students. While the Scots made ineffectual raids in Northumberland, Cumbria and Westmorland, Edward's army advanced on Berwick. Initially the town made a stout defence, but the defences of the town were not adequate to the task of keeping out a strong and well-motivated enemy. The town fell to storm and was sacked with enormous loss of life; apparently the dead were so numerous that they could not be buried and the bodies had to be thrown into the sea.

This was not the full extent of Scottish resistance to Edward's army, however. The castle of Dunbar was held against them and there was a Scottish army mustered nearby at Caddonlea.[4] However, the two armies did not clash. At the end of April 1296 a portion of the Scottish cavalry encountered one of the four English cavalry formations and were quickly routed. It is very unlikely that the Scottish force comprised all or even a large proportion of the men-at-arms in the Scottish army. It would have been very bad practice indeed for the entire armoured cavalry element of the army to be detached from the rest of the force without a very clear and attainable goal and for an operation for which the chances of success were very high and the potential damage from success or failure would be negligible. Medieval armies, like modern ones, depended on the effective combination of various arms to achieve victory, so the loss of the heavy cavalry would compromise future operations and put the main body of the army at risk. The impact of a sharp reverse on the morale of the army was probably another significant factor in convincing the Scots leadership that there was no point in continuing the fight, but to do so with no mobile force under command would have been suicidal. The men-at-arms element of the army could operate, under certain conditions, without the immediate support of infantry, but the infantry would be near-helpless without the cavalry if they were confronted by a force of all arms.

Dunbar Castle was surrendered almost immediately and the English pressed on to Edinburgh. Already a well developed fortress, Edinburgh withstood five days of bombardment before surrendering.[5] Assuming that the castle was adequately stocked with supplies and that the garrison was large enough for the task, it might be reasonable to ask why it should have surrendered so quickly; however, all of the strongholds that fell to Edward in 1296 shared a common problem. They might be able to withstand a siege for some time, weeks or even months, but without relief they must all surely fall eventually; Stirling Castle was left in the care of the gate porter, the rest of the complement having decided to return to their homes, presumably in the hope of avoiding any recriminations in the wake of Edward's victory, and because there was no realistic hope of rescue. In the aftermath of the fight at Dunbar and the subsequent disintegration of the Scottish army, where was such a relief column going to come from? A considerable portion, at least 200 men, from the class that provided the traditional source of political and military leadership had become prisoners of war in the spring and summer of 1296, and the bulk of the rest of the Scottish political community, particularly in the southern and eastern counties, had accepted Edward's lordship by the end of August that year, under the terms of the Ragman Roll and/or in personal submissions.[6]

Who, in any case, could claim the authority to demand the military service and financial contributions that would be necessary if the Balliol cause was to make a recovery? John had been deposed and was hardly in a position to appoint a Guardian to further his interests. The Scots had, of course, been confronted with this sort of problem in the past. When Alexander III died unexpectedly in April 1286, a council of Guardians was quickly appointed to administer the country and look after the interests of the Crown. When Margaret died in the winter of 1290 there had been no clear heir to the throne, but the political community had arranged for the business of the country to proceed; however these two situations were very different from that in 1296. On the previous occasions the country had not been at war, did not have an occupation government and army to deal with and, crucially, there was no division between those who had accepted the rule of the Plantagenets and those who had not.

Edward spent the summer of 1296 making a progress through the eastern seaboard counties as far as Elgin, accepting homages and fealties from magnates, minor nobility and burghs. Content that he had essentially dealt with the 'Scottish' problem, he returned to more pressing affairs, specifically his conflict with France. His confidence that his lieutenants could be trusted to finish the job of annexation was misplaced. Within a year, Edward was being informed that, of all the counties in Scotland, only Berwick had a proper structure of administration in the Plantagenet interest.[7] Not only were the other counties outside English control, but the Scots had started to appoint sheriffs and other government officials on behalf of the Balliol cause. The source of this information was Hugh Cressingham, Edward's chief administrator in Scotland and, as such, a man likely to have a pretty clear idea of the extent and effectiveness of the Plantagenet occupation. One of the reasons for Edward's failure to turn his defeat of the Scots into annexation probably lay in the fact that he did not fully appreciate the sheer size of the undertaking. Map-making was not yet an exact science, or even a particularly well developed art. Edward almost certainly did not realise that he had in fact traversed only a portion of Scotland. He had been able to extract homage and fealty from a large body of the political communities of the southern counties, but had made little progress in the north and west. The Ragman Roll exercise had brought about 300 people from Lothian alone into Edward's peace, but only three from the entirety of Ross.[8]

It seems very likely that Edward had no plans to change the general administration of Scotland, only to replace John and his officers with himself and men of his own choosing. He may in fact have expected that there would be little or no reaction to this change of dynasty among the Scottish political community: why should a different head under the crown make any great difference to the lives of the subjects? Certainly his initial dispositions of troops were hardly major deployments. When he first appointed a sheriff for Edinburgh, during the succession dispute, Edward allocated ten men-at-arms to form the sheriff's retinue. This was probably in line with, if not identical to, the size of complement that had been maintained under Alexander III[9] and may indicate a policy of promoting an image of 'business as usual' in local government; however, his garrisons may have been established with a view to discouraging unrest between the Scottish political factions. Even a very tiny token force would be an indication to ambitious Scottish magnates to refrain from trying to improve their position through force; if they wanted to seize royal castle they would have to dislodge Edward's men, an action that would provoke Edward into a reaction that was likely to be both swift and violent. It should not be assumed that ten men-at-arms was the sum total of the force theoretically available to the sheriff of Edinburgh. Like his predecessors under King Alexander, the sheriff would have the authority to demand the customary military service of the local political community. The lairds, lords and the more prosperous burgesses of Lothian, like those of other counties, had an obligation to discharge military service, generally as men-at-arms, for a fixed period, probably forty days. Presumably these men were 'rotated' so that a number of them were available at any given point in the year.

The most fruitful sources of material relating to military service are government records: garrison muster rolls, victualling arrangements, pay rolls and the valuation of chargers. Men on active paid service in Plantagenet armies and garrisons were usually (though not, apparently, universally; see Dr Ayton's *Knights and Warhorses* for a thorough examination of cavalry service in the armies of the three Edwards) entitled to have one of their horses valued for replacement costs by Crown appointees. Men giving customary service were not paid wages, nor were they normally entitled to 'restauro' payments for lost horses; their forty days' service, with an adequate mount, was part of their land rental. Failure to provide that service could lead to forfeiture and, in the absence of extensive forfeitures among the Scottish minor nobility in 1297, we must assume that a fair quantity of the due service was in fact discharged. The men in question had little choice. In areas where King Edward's government was functioning effectively, it would be almost impossible to avoid compulsory, customary service obligations without incurring the displeasure of the government.

This does not mean that Edward did not face opposition. A considerable number of men were forfeited and then restored to their properties in 1296–98.[10] To what extent this was the product of continued activity against the Plantagenet government after Dunbar and to what extent these restorations indicate men accepting Edward's kingship in the light of defeat in the summer of 1296 is impossible to say, but clearly Edward felt that there was every chance of effecting a relatively painless annexation of Scotland, and that existing sources of leadership and influence could be persuaded to accept his authority. In theory, at least, the Ragman Roll and other submissions should have helped to secure Edward's position in Scottish affairs. The men and women who declared their allegiance to Edward represented the class of government in its widest sense – not simply the great lords, but the class of minor landholders, lairds, who carried out a great deal of the actual business of government, particularly judicial and military activity. If they could be induced to accept Edward, and to remain in his affinity, he should have had little to fear from insurrection. Each of these men and women had bound themselves personally to Edward's cause, after all. The problem was, how reliable were these declarations? Even men who had joined Edward's army in 1296 could not always be relied on to toe the party line. Robert Bruce (the one who would become king in 1306) had committed himself to the Plantagenet cause, campaigning on Edward's behalf in 1296, but by the summer of 1297 had defected to the Scots.

Quite what moved Bruce to align himself with Andrew Murray and William Wallace against the Plantagenet cause in that year is open to question; Murray and Wallace were unreservedly committed to the Balliol kingship, whereas Bruce had unquestionably been Edward's 'man' for years. He had appended his seal to the Ragman Roll, his grandfather had accepted Edward's suzerainty over Scotland, and his father was sufficiently in favour with the English king to serve as his sheriff of Carlisle. Should a revolt against Edward lead to the restoration of King John, any ambitions the Bruce family held in relation to the Scottish crown would be stopped dead in their tracks. Worse than that, a restored John might take exception to the fact that the Bruces had refused to serve in his army in 1296, turning out for Edward instead. If the Balliol cause seemed like a hopeless venture in 1297, one must question Robert's involvement: what did he hope to achieve? Alternatively, if the Balliol cause was looking quite promising, how did he hope to reach an accommodation with King John in the light of Robert's service to King Edward?

One possibility is that Robert did not in fact consider the Balliol cause a viable proposition in itself, but believed that the English were incapable of permanently acquiring Scotland. If that were the case, he might be well advised to ensure that he was seen as a force in the struggle against King Edward, particularly if he retained his ambition for the crown. If Scotland were to become an independent country again, he would have little influence in the post-war settlement if he had not been involved in the struggle. Conceivably, Robert may have been trying to exert political leverage on Edward I. If Edward's administration proved unequal to the task of assimilating Scotland, it might be more in his interests to install a Scottish king once more, as he had done in 1292. No doubt Robert would have been more than happy to accept kingship at Edward's hand, but he would first have to demonstrate that he was a powerful figure in the Scottish political landscape, who would be capable of keeping his subjects under control should he gain the throne and an unequivocal allegiance to Edward I. Edward, of course, was no fool, and would have been well aware that to reconstitute Scottish kingship would be a hostage to fortune. He might be able to keep a sub-king in order, but would his descendants be able to do so?

Given that Bruce and Wallace were both at war with England in 1297, it might be reasonable to ask why Wallace did not choose to support a Bruce bid for kingship. First and foremost, Balliol was the legitimate king whereas Bruce would be a usurper. In the diplomatic arena, John could reasonably be described as a duly constituted king who had been deprived of his realm by a neighbour. There would probably be more popular sympathy with the cause of John Balliol, a king deposed, than there would be for Robert Bruce, an earl with ambition. The Balliol name would have been better known than that of Bruce outside Scotland. As an earl, and, after the death of his father, the holder of the extensive lordship of Annandale, Bruce would have had significant financial and military resources and a position of some prominence politically, but he was only one of a dozen or more men of similar status in Scotland. Had Wallace decided to support a Bruce bid for kingship, he would have alienated several leading magnates who preferred the 'legitimist' succession of the Balliols. In any case, a Wallace-Bruce partnership would have had to depend on the willingness of Robert to nail his colours to the mast. As long as he could claim to be acting on behalf of his liege lord, King John, Robert could retain a realistic hope of making his peace with Edward, should that become expedient. Were he to claim the throne in his own right, he would lose any prospect of an accommodation with Edward I other than by outright military victory. Even with the unquestioned support of the entire political community of Scotland, that would have been, to say the least, a daunting task. Far from being sure of that support, Robert could reasonably rely on the outright opposition of a considerable body of opinion within the 'patriotic' party, let alone from those who had accepted Edward I's kingship before the Strathord armistice. It would seem much more likely that Bruce offered to bide his time, presumably waiting for Edward I to die, before making his move. His 'bond' with Bishop Lamberton, which was made at Cambuskenneth Abbey at about the time of Edward I's siege of Stirling Castle in the spring of 1304, required him to find the sum of £10,000 – a fortune which would probably have been well beyond the resources of either party – should he undertake any 'arduous business' without consulting the bishop first.[11]

In addition, if Wallace were to endorse Robert as king he would utterly compromise his own position. Very few political figures in any period of history have willingly given up a position of great authority. Wallace's Guardianship was completely dependent on his success as a military leader, a fact clearly demonstrated by his loss of the Guardianship immediately after his defeat at Falkirk. It is reasonable to assume that he did not intend to be defeated and that he planned to carry on as the principal figure of authority in Scottish political life. Had he helped Bruce to become king, he would have had to surrender his own power immediately. This would obviously have been the case had Wallace succeeded in restoring John I to the throne; however, he could be reasonably confident that John would reward him suitably, whereas Robert might well think it desirable to marginalise Wallace in the interests of confirming his own authority, and to suppress any suggestion that his kingship was dependent on the efforts of a man from a minor lairdly family.

There is no suggestion from contemporary accounts to suggest that Wallace ever entertained the possibility of helping to erect a Bruce kingship; he seems to have been totally committed to the Balliol dynasty. Of course, while Wallace was crucial to the Balliol cause, the Balliol cause was crucial to William Wallace. Without his affiliation to, and acceptance by, the Balliol party, Wallace's actions in 1297 would have been acts of brigandage rather than of policy. In peacetime there was no real possibility of a man from Wallace's background rising to a position of national prominence; senior political leadership was very much the province of the magnate class. Oddly, however, the relatively junior status of Wallace may conceivably have helped to make him acceptable, as a temporary measure at least, to the more senior members of the community that embraced the Balliol cause. A man of Wallace's station had no claim, however tenuous, to the throne, nor would he ever be able to develop the kind of power base that might enable him to bid for the throne by force of arms. So long as his commitment was to the Balliol kingship – a loyalty in which he never wavered so far as is known – Wallace did not represent a long-term threat to the prominence of the magnate families, though perhaps, had he been successful in effecting the restoration of King John, he might reasonably expect to have been rewarded sufficiently well to enable him to join their ranks.

In all medieval European kingdoms it was expected that service should bring rewards. A king could be given no greater service than the restoration of his kingdom. If successful, Wallace could reasonably expect to receive grants of land, money and office and/or a very advantageous marriage through the offices of a grateful monarch. The latter was obviously preferable from the point of view of the king; it cost nothing of itself, and though if the marriage was seen as 'disparaging' to the bride that would reflect badly on the king, it would have been obvious that Wallace would have to be rewarded suitably or *he* would be disparaged – still a poor reflection on the king. It is unlikely that a man who had achieved such a project would be willing to return to obscurity and life on the farm, or that anyone would expect him to, but the restoration of the king would inevitably mean the loss of Guardianship and would call for action on the part of the king to secure a position within the senior aristocracy for Sir William Wallace as compensation, as well as out of gratitude and a desire to keep Wallace firmly in the Balliol camp should King John regain his kingdom.

CHAPTER FOUR

From Gangster to Governor

T he information relating to William Wallace before his rise to military and political prominence in the summer of 1297 is scarce almost to the point of invisibility. His birth date is unknown and his birthplace unverifiable. Although Wallace has traditionally been associated with Elderslie in Renfrewshire, there is precious little in the way of evidence to substantiate the claim. James MacKay has made a case for associating William Wallace with Ellerslie, Ayrshire, a small village and colliery that disappeared in the middle of the last century.[1] Most of the early exploits of William Wallace seem to have occurred in and around Ayrshire, and there was a relatively high incidence of the Wallace surname in the sheriffdom.[2] A good deal had been made of the absence of William and his immediate family from the Ayrshire entries of the Ragman Roll; however, two Ayrshire Wallaces, Alan (Aleyn) and Nicholas, did append their seals to the roll, thereby acknowledging the sovereignty of Edward I. Alan is one of a relatively small number of homagers described as 'king's tenants', sometimes described as Crown tenants by historians. In the strictest sense, everyone was either a tenant or subtenant of the Crown; however, most people who held property directly from the Crown did so on very easy terms indeed. The lesser nobility who appear as minor 'in capite' tenants do so in groups described as being 'of the county of' Fife/Aberdeen/Dumfriesshire as appropriate; the 'king's tenants' are clearly differentiated from the 'county' homagers, though there was no social or economic divide between the two groups. It would seem safe to conclude that the 'king's tenant' rentals were more economically realistic than those due from 'County' homagers, but the two groups were not separate entities; several men and women appear in both categories – often, though not always, in the same sheriffdom. As a king's tenant, Alan Wallace would have had the same social, legal and military obligations as his neighbours, but would probably have paid a great deal more rent, however, the chief difference in their tenures was whether they were heritable. King's tenancy landholding was, therefore, more ministerial in nature and was probably the more traditional form of land tenure. These properties probably had their origins in the thanage and drengage tenures of ninth- and tenth-century (if not earlier) Lothian and Northumberland, many of which had been converted to knight service tenures in the early twelfth century to provide Scottish kings with the weapon of choice of the later medieval period, the man-at-arms.[3]

The significance of Alan Wallace may be greater than one might suppose. In the Mitchell Library in Glasgow[4] there is an imprint of both the obverse and reverse sides of the seal of William Wallace, Guardian of Scotland. Apparently made in 1912 by one P. Sinclair Rae, the lettering has been identified by Professor A.A.M. Duncan as reading 'William son of Alan'. There are several possibilities: it is perhaps just conceivable that the piece is a forgery, in which case it would be reasonable to expect that the forger would avoid anything that might lead to controversy – there would have been no need to include the name of the principal's father. It is also a possibility that the seal-carver simply made a mistake; Alan and Adam are fairly similar names, after all. However, the great importance of seals for all sorts of administrative, financial and personal business and the care required to cut the seals would surely means that seal-makers were likely to be painstaking individuals. Even if they were not, even if the carver had made a mistake, there is no reason to assume that nobody else would have noticed – William Wallace, for example. It is of course possible that when he took delivery of his new seal as guardian that he did not think to examine it; had he done so he would surely have noticed if his father's name was wrong and would just as surely have demanded a replacement.

Another aspect of William Wallace's seal (as guardian: it is quite possible, even likely, that as a young man of no great social or political significance he would not have invested in a seal of his own, but would have made use of the seals of others for those odd occasions when he needed one) is of course the image of an arm holding a bow. A number of writers have taken this as evidence to support the statement of the Lanercost chronicler that Wallace had been an archer and/or leader of brigands, and that he made his living by 'the bow and quiver'. How he would have made a living as an archer in Scotland before the war is not clear. There was little if anything in the way of employment for a military archer, and hunting was the sort of thing that people did themselves for entertainment: they did not hire others to do it for them. The motifs used on seals, like heraldry, might contain a 'pun' on the name of the owner, but that would be the exception rather than the rule. Most seal emblems are quite arbitrary, as much a reflection on the imagination of the owner and the talents of the carver as anything else. A person might have a pigeon engraved on their seal without having any particular fondness for, or association with, pigeons.

The seal image has drawn more than one Wallace biographer to questionable conclusions about the source of the experience that made Wallace a 'military genius'. It is quite possible that Wallace was a bowman of some skill and that his prowess as an archer was the inspiration for adopting an archery theme in his seal artwork; however, there is no evidence at all to lead us to believe that Wallace served Edward I in Wales in the campaigns there before 1296. We might question the validity of describing Wallace as a 'military genius' at all. He was certainly an effective battlefield leader as the commander of a body of men-at-arms conducting hit-and-run operations against the English, and he was able to lead a large raiding force through the north of England, but the targets he found in Scotland were not primarily military ones so much as administrative operations. Wallace participated in only two large battles, Stirling Bridge and Falkirk. At the first of these the Scots took advantage of English indecision and disorganisation during a river crossing. The decision to attack may have rested with Wallace, but it may just as easily have been Andrew Murray who forced battle on the enemy. At his second battle, Falkirk, Wallace seems to have been caught by the unexpected approach of the English; he certainly seems to have had no clear plan for achieving victory over them.

If we are unsure of William Wallace's family, we are on even softer ground with some of his companions. Blair, the writer of the manuscript from which Blind Harry claimed to have made *The Wallace*, seems to have no provenance whatsoever as a historical figure, though that is hardly evidence of his non-existence. The same applies to Marion Braidfute; just because there is no contemporary record of her life does not mean that she did not have one, though the absence of any other Braidfoots in the record material of the time would suggest that, if she did exist, her family was probably of very low status, low enough to avoid registering on the Ragman Roll. Alternatively, if Marion Braidfute never existed, it would not have been beyond the skills of a Scottish writer to invent her.

One of the few things we can safely say about William Wallace was that he was steadfast in his support of King John and the continuation of Scottish kingship independent of England. The fact that Wallace was able to furnish himself with armed support extensive enough to challenge the administration of Edward I within a matter of a few months of its establishment is indicative of more than an ability on the part of Wallace to motivate men. It suggests that there was a body of public opinion that was more than just receptive to appeals on behalf of the Balliol dynasty, but that was prepared, or even eager, to take up the fight. It is easily forgotten that although the 1296 campaign had effectively been decided by the battle at Dunbar, the action had not been an extensive one. Only the Scottish noble cavalry, the men-at-arms of the army, and very probably only a proportion of those, had been engaged. There had been no great battle resulting in thousands of casualties among the infantry, the bulk of the army, which had simply disintegrated after Dunbar. The outcome of Falkirk may have made it harder for Scottish armies to recruit (though the evidence is hardly conclusive), but in 1297 the Scots had yet to experience a general engagement. Since most of the army of 1296 had not seen action, there is every reason to assume that many of them had retained the arms they had borne in that campaign and they had no reason to believe that the English could not be beaten in battle and ejected from the country.

Why exactly they should have chosen to enlist in the armies raised by Wallace, Murray, MacDuff of Fife or the 'Noble Revolt' of Bruce, the Stewart and Bishop Wishart at all is a complicated matter, and is addressed elsewhere, but the fact remains that Wallace was able to enlist men in considerable quantity.[5] His success in the minor actions that characterise Anglo-Scottish conflict in 1297[6] was undoubtedly a factor in attracting men to his banner, but, to some extent at least, there must have already been men who were willing to be lead; Wallace was their leader of choice, but we should not assume that they would not have been active in the Balliol cause had Wallace never existed. It is hardly likely that Wallace was able to single-handedly motivate large numbers of men to join in his venture if there was not already a body of opinion that was prepared to take action in favour of a restoration of the Balliol kingship, or, at the very least, the expulsion of the Plantagenet government. Nor is it likely that Wallace was the only man in Scotland trying to exert leadership in that direction, only that he was the most successful man of his station to do so. In the north-east, the fight against the occupation was taken up by a man of more exalted rank, Andrew Murray; in the south-west, by prominent magnates and prelates. In central Scotland, though, it was William Wallace who provided military leadership in the summer of 1297.

The earliest recorded operation of William Wallace was the murder of the sheriff of Lanark, Sir Wiliam Haselrigg,[7] allegedly in revenge for the murder of Wallace's mistress.[8] By May of 1297 he was the leader, with Sir William Douglas (father of the great Sir James, the original 'black' Douglas), of a group of men-at-arms, probably very small in number, that made a descent on the Plantagenet justiciar, William Ormsby, just as he was opening his court session at Scone, Perthshire. Ormsby escaped with his life, but there was no longer any question that a revolt against the occupation was under way.

In August 1297, at much the same time as Edward I was leaving England for Flanders, confident that he had dealt with the Scots, Wallace combined his army with that of Andrew Murray. As Dr Grant has observed, Wallace and Murray are among the small number of Scottish nobles that can be clearly identified as constant supporters of the Balliol cause and, in the case of the Murray family, with the continuation of the struggle under the Bruce party after 1306. Murray was a man of far greater status than Wallace, a man more in the tradition of noble political leadership, though not perhaps quite of the first rank. Murray had been made a prisoner of war in 1296,[9] presumably either at the Dunbar engagement or at the surrender of Dunbar Castle, had subsequently escaped from captivity in an English castle and made his way north to raise men to fight against the occupation. His chief ally in the area was Alexander Pilche, a burgess of Inverness. Pilche has been seen as an example of the willingness of Scots of humble station to take up arms in the cause of independence; however, Pilche's status as a burgess was considerable. Only a very tiny proportion of the inhabitants of a burgh enjoyed the privilege of being members of the merchant or burgess guild which effectively provided the government of each burgh.[10] The high incidence of marriages between the families of lairds and burgesses is a clear indication of the social status of the latter.

Co-operation between the forces of Murray and Wallace had numerous clear benefits, both for their shared objectives and for the leaders as individuals. Obviously, the greater the force that could be raised and committed to operations against the occupation, the greater the chances of success; also, the fact of their co-operation would be likely to lend each a degree of credibility that they would not enjoy as separate operators. As the unchallenged commander of a large force and as a popular leader gaining a dramatic reputation, Wallace would have been a most attractive ally to Murray; as a prominent member of the Scottish political community, Murray might bring Wallace a degree of acceptance among the great and powerful men whose active support would be required if the occupation was to be defeated.

The majority of recruits were not in any sense experienced military men; the very low incidence of military activity of any kind in Scotland in the preceding fifty years meant that the opportunity to learn the skills and techniques of war, as opposed to personal ability at arms, had been, to say the least, limited. The most recent Scottish military operation had been the conquest of the kingdom of Man, an undertaking that had not stretched the capacities of even the very tiny Scottish military establishment, insofar as there was one at all. Without doubt, almost all of the men recruited by Wallace or Murray in 1297 served as spearmen and virtually all the remainder, though a small number, served as archers. Historians of the period, for the best part of 100 years, have been quite clear that there was a distinction between Scottish and English archers: the English used longbows and the Scots the less effective short bow.[11] To date, no actual evidence has been put forward to support this contention; if it was the case that Scots used the short bow, no medieval writer would seem to have noticed it, and it is certainly the case that the Scottish army operating in France in the 1420s included a large body of men armed with the longbow. There is a similar issue relating to the areas from which archers were recruited for Scottish armies. Contrary to a belief popular among medievalists, it was not the case that archers were drawn solely, or even particularly, from the forest of Ettrick. Several charters from the reign of Robert I or before specify the service of archers rather than men-at-arms. One of the heaviest military burdens in the whole of feudal Scotland outside the great lordships was an obligation to provide thirty archers for the king's army from the barony of Kilsyth.[12]

There was of course a great difference between an archer and a man who happened to be armed with bow and arrows, and there is no doubt that archery was more popular in England and enjoyed greater social status, at least in some areas. Men from Cheshire whose status would, in other counties, compel them to equip themselves and serve as men-at-arms can be identified serving as archers in France, Flanders and Scotland. Since there were a great many archers in English armies the level of ability of each individual was not of greater importance; archery in battle was much more a matter of achieving high concentrations of missiles shot into a relatively small area than of marksmanship. The relative scarcity of archers in Scotland is probably more a reflection of the sizes of the respective populations. A very large English army in the late thirteenth or early fourteenth century might be as strong as 20,000 men. Of these, as many as 3,000 might be men-at-arms, another 2,000 less heavily armed and less well mounted cavalry. The balance of 15,000 would comprise spearmen and archers, mostly spearmen. The first English army to treat the bow as a primary line-of-battle weapon was the one lead by Edward Balliol and Henry Beaumont to Dupplin Muir in 1332. There was certainly a sizeable contingent of archers in the English army defeated by Robert I at the battle of Bannockburn, possibly as many as 3,000 or 4,000 out of an army of perhaps 15,000, but there does not seem to have been anything that we could think of as a 'usual' or 'traditional' approach to the deployment of English armies until the adoption of massed archery as part of fundamental English practice in the 1330s and 1340s. Even the English armies that were consciously planned around the longbow seldom exceeded an archer strength of more than 4,000-5,000. Since the population of Scotland was a fraction of that of England, it is not surprising that the archer strength of their armies should be of the same order.

The same consideration applies to men-at-arms. The incidence of knight service or man-at-arms service does not seem to have been radically different to that in England relative to the populations. The small scale of cavalry service in Scottish armies can be very misleading, however. For one thing, men-at-arms, knights and lords might dismount to fight, depending on the tactical situation; Sir Edward Keith may have led a force of 500 mounted, armoured soldiers at Bannockburn, but that does not mean that King Robert's army was limited to 500 men-at-arms. Several of the most prominent Scottish knights of the day fought on foot there, including the Earl of Moray, the Stewart, Sir James Douglas, Angus Og MacDonald, Sir Neil Campbell and of course the king himself.[13] There was of course a political dimension to King Robert's choice to fight dismounted, the implication being that he would take his chance along with everyone else. The same applies to his declaration – according to Barbour – that he would refuse to be ransomed; Shakespeare ascribes a similar sentiment to Henry V on the eve of Agincourt.

None of the prominent Scottish nobles fighting on foot at Bannockburn would have been alone among the common spearmen, but would have had a party of friends, relatives and tenants fighting alongside them. There is a widely-held belief that Scottish men-at-arms either could not or would not acquire the quality of mount or armament that their English counterparts enjoyed. If that was the case it was a matter that went unnoticed by English writers of the day, notably Sir Thomas Grey, who, like his father before him and his son after, made a career of army service in Scotland for Edward III and Edward Balliol.[14] By the time of Bannockburn, Scotland and England had been at war with one another for nearly twenty years, so it would be surprising if the Scots had not sourced the quality and quantity of equipment necessary to meet the English in battle and defeat them, but the horses and arms were available in Scotland in 1297; when Wallace and his followers raided Scone they were, so we are told, 'well-mounted', a phrase completely associated with men-at-arms and knights. Record strongly supports this; considerable numbers of Scottish men-at-arms and knights served in the Plantagenet garrisons wherever they existed, not just in the south and east as E.M. Barron implied.[15] They served on the same operational conditions as knights and men-at-arms from England or anywhere else, and were expected to have adequate mount and arms for heavy cavalry service.

Clearly the Scottish armies of the late thirteenth century could not field a force of men-at-arms as large as those raised by Edward I or his officers, but this was not simply a reflection of the larger and wealthier population of England. There was never a time when Wallace could call on the service of the entire political community of Scotland, which was the chief source of men-at-arms. In England or France the cavalry element of an army consisted of the retinues of the magnates. These retinues might be combined to form a number of stable formations for the duration of the campaign. A similar structure operated in Scotland, but not, perhaps, to the same extent. A very large part of the political community in Scotland consisted of relatively minor 'in capite' tenants, men who held their estates directly from the Crown rather than through an intermediary lord. There were, of course, very many people who did owe service to a superior lord, and these men formed the retinues of Scottish magnates on a similar, if not identical, pattern to their English counterparts. It would seem more likely than not that the minor 'in capite' tenants would have effectively fallen under the command of men with retinues, but it is possible that they were formed into units under officers appointed by the king or by the local sheriff. However temporary the command arrangements might be, they must still have existed. The administration of a large body of men and horses would inevitably be something of a challenge. Maintaining an army is not simply a matter of keeping it fed, and even if it were, it would be virtually impossible to administer even that most basic function without some degree of articulation within the army – a means of dividing it into smaller formations than simply 'the army'.[16] The tactical need for a system of subdivision to allow manoeuvre on the battlefield is obvious, but would be necessary for the day-to-day existence of the army. The vital functions of gathering and distributing food and providing sentries and work parties would be very difficult carry out without a means of apportioning suitably sized bodies of men to the tasks in hand.

The chronicler Walter Bower gives William Wallace the credit for introducing an articulated command system to the forces that he and Murray raised in the summer of 1297, but it would seem very unlikely that there had been no comparable system in the past. It could be argued that the previous system, if any existed, would have been discredited due to the Dunbar campaign of 1296; however, the Scottish infantry had not been engaged at Dunbar at all – it had not failed in battle. Whether the approach to command and control was good, bad or indifferent, it would at least have been fairly familiar to the men who joined Wallace and Murray. The arrangement described by Bower does seem to be a little fanciful, giving a very large proportion of the army some degree of authority over their peers (see below, 'Wallace and Bower'), but it is not impossible. However, it is probably more realistic to assume that the structure was simpler, at least in lowest ranks, and that it pre-dated the army that fought at Stirling Bridge.

CHAPTER FIVE

The Battle of Stirling Bridge

The first question to be asked of any battle is 'why should it have occurred at all?' From the perspective of Edward I, the threat posed by Wallace and Murray to the English occupation was a challenge that could not possibly be ignored. Had Edward abandoned his Scottish ambitions, he would have had to abandon his garrisons and his adherents in Scotland, thus damaging his prestige as a soldier and a king and, in all probability, his financial situation – never a strong point with Edward I, since he would have faced a great deal of unrest from people who had been disadvantaged through their support for the Plantagenet cause. Due to preparations for his expedition to the continent, Edward was not in a position to lead a force into Scotland himself in the summer of 1297, but even had he been able to do so, it is possible that he would still have left the operation in the hands of his lieutenants.[1] Had he been faced by a wider segment of the senior nobility obviously acting in concert, it might have been a different matter, but to react in person to the actions of a small group of magnates and two 'popular revolts' – one under a northern baron (or rather the son of a northern baron), Sir Andrew Murray, the other under the younger son of an obscure Ayrshire knight – could have given his enemies a certain credibility that might be denied them if all of the 'revolts' could be dealt with quickly and effectively through subordinates.

Edward had reasonably good cause to believe that that would be a safe course of action; the Scottish nobility had already been humbled at Dunbar, little more than a year before, and he had no special reason to expect that the infantry element of a Scottish army would prove to be any more effective an opponent than the cavalry had. The Scottish men-at-arms at Dunbar had no real experience of war in 1296 and were easily outmanoeuvred and routed accordingly, but the majority of the man-at-arms class would seem to have escaped the battle unscathed.[2] The Scottish infantry had not been engaged at all at Dunbar, but had disintegrated in the wake of the rout of the cavalry and the surrender of Dunbar Castle. No doubt many of them abandoned arms and armour to facilitate a faster escape, but it would be unrealistic to assume that they all had, particularly those with a great distance to travel through a disturbed land to get home. It would be even more unreasonable to assume that any resulting shortage of arms could not have been made good in the period between Dunbar in the spring of 1296 and Stirling Bridge in the late summer of 1297.[3] Wallace, and probably Murray as well, felt sufficiently short of men to enforce military service with the threat of the death penalty,[4] but the majority of the men who followed either of them probably did so of their own free will. In the sense that all governments draw their power from the consent of the people, it is probably fair to say that Wallace and Murray represented the most popular of the various groups competing for authority in Scotland by the mid-summer of 1297 – Edward Plantagenet and the 'noble revolt' leaders Bruce, Wishart and the Stewart being the others.

The 'noble revolt' fizzled out in negotiations at Irvine, much to the detriment of the reputation of the men involved and the Scottish nobility in general. There are several issues to be considered, however. English chroniclers of the time seem to have believed that Bruce and Wishart stretched out the Irvine meeting as long as they possibly could to allow Wallace and Murray the best opportunity to assemble and train their men. It is certainly reasonable to assume that the number of men-at-arms that could be raised by Bruce, Wishart and the Stewart would have been very much smaller than that available to the Earl of Surrey. On the other hand, if Surrey had enjoyed a great superiority of numbers he could have forced battle on the Scots and undoubtedly have won the day. The fact that he did not suggests a number of possibilities. He may not have had an advantage in numbers, or not enough of an advantage for forcing battle to be a wise policy. Even with a substantial advantage, combat might not have been a desirable option. An English victory might not be successful in dissuading Scots from joining the Balliol cause if the English losses were comparable with the Scots, and an English defeat would probably help to dissuade Scots from actively supporting the Plantagenet government even if it did not encourage them to join the Balliol party. Even a sharp English victory might be counter-productive; it could harden attitudes among the Scots, particularly if it was followed by harsh retribution towards the participants. Perhaps most importantly, it may have been contrary to his instructions to bring about an engagement at all if he could avoid doing so.

Edward was well aware of the advantages of bringing the Scottish political community into his peace. As men who had exerted authority in their different regions, they were known to the community, the people were accustomed to accepting their leadership and, most importantly, they knew how the business of government was conducted in their locality: they would not inadvertently cause offence to the community by changing local practices. Moreover, in the short term at least, it would have been very difficult to maintain an administration at all without bringing some of the noble estate 'on board'. If none could be persuaded to uphold Plantagenet kingship, they would all have to be replaced if Edward's Scottish plans were to be made a reality. Although there were doubtless plenty of men who would have been willing to undertake the role of laird, knight, baron or earl, there would have been very few with the necessary background to carry out the work properly, and many, probably most, of those people already had extensive estates elsewhere. They were hardly likely to abandon their properties in England in order to concentrate on making a reality of Scottish lordships granted by Edward, when the entire fabric of the Plantagenet government in Scotland might well be defeated.[5] If, however, they were to make a worthwhile contribution to the administration or profit by Edward's grants – and the latter was obviously dependent on the security of the former – they would have to spend time in their new Scottish possessions to make good their lordship and to establish their authority with the tenants of the estates, a challenge in itself and a hopeless undertaking in areas outside Plantagenet control. By the summer of 1297, Edward had been made aware that only a very small part of Scotland had been secured for his government; more importantly, the Scots had restored pro-Balliol (or at least anti-Plantagenet) sheriffs and other officers in most of the counties that had been lost. Recovering those counties was likely to call for a huge investment in men, materials and money. The first two might be acquired through compulsion, though Edward was already less than popular at home, so demands for troops and supplies might not be a good move; as for the financial element, Edward was broke. If he could induce the Scottish nobles in the southwest to end their revolt without a clash of arms, his status as a wise and magnanimous lord would very probably be enhanced; there would be no need to raise any more troops for service in Scotland. Better still, he would have brought several Scottish magnates out of the enemy camp and into his own; he would have no need to install sympathetic leaders in the areas affected by the noble revolt, since they would now be his lords, not John Balliol's.

Regardless of whether the nobles made the Irvine negotiations a lengthy business for the benefit of Wallace and Murray (it is difficult to see what other cause they could have for doing so, and English writers seem to have been quite sure that they were taking their time), that was part of the outcome. That Wallace and Murray were able to raise troops at all seems to have come as a surprise to several historians, though not, seemingly, to observers at the time. They mention the activities and success of the Scots, but do not seem to have been at all surprised that a revolt had broken out, nor that the Scots were re-establishing government in the name of King John. Self-evidently, Wallace and Murray were able to recruit men in considerable numbers, and, presumably, had embarked on a training programme more or less immediately, if only to help establish their authority; it would be rash to assume that they were the only men engaged in resistance to the Plantagenet government. Historians have seen that resistance as foolhardy in the face of Edward, the 'Hammer of the Scots', but in 1297 it was by no means clear that Edward was the 'hammer' of anybody other than the English nobility. His conquests in Wales were not yet completely secure, his wars with the French had hardly been an unalloyed success and his administration in Scotland was already close to complete collapse. The only clear battlefield victory that Edward had achieved was over those English barons who had continued to adhere to Simon de Montfort after Edward's own defection to his father's cause nearly forty years previously.[6] Since the Scottish infantry had not fought at Dunbar, they had no reason to believe that they could not be victorious against the English; even if there had been extensive fighting in the period after Dunbar, and there is no evidence to suggest that there was, there had certainly not been any major confrontations in the period from then to Stirling Bridge. Despite the fact that there had been war for more than a year, there had been no great general engagement, only a clash between elements of the cavalry of either side and an unknown number of minor skirmishes that probably owed as much to private enterprise – the line between political activity and banditry was a slender one – as anything else.

At some point in the summer of 1297, Wallace and Murray clearly came to an agreed policy with regard to the English. Instead of effecting a union of their armies at Stirling, they could have chosen to disperse the bulk of their troops and retain small mobile forces to harass the enemy until the problems of supply, pay and desertion forced him to withdraw.[7] Their decision to seek a confrontation suggests a number of issues that might have influenced them. The first is that they had come to the conclusion that they could win a battle if they could dictate the circumstances: if they had no confidence that their army could win a battle they would not have been willing to let the enemy come within striking range in the first place, but would have withdrawn. This does not imply that the Scottish commanders were sure of victory, or even that they were eager to offer battle at all, just that they believed that their force was competent for the purpose, should a good opportunity present itself. The army itself may well have exerted pressure in favour of combat; if Wallace and Murray were the inspirational leaders of tradition there would surely have been a highly-charged and excitable element in the army that was desperately keen to fight.

The political situation certainly called for firm action, and combat must always be borne in mind by commanders as an option, however unpromising the immediate situation, but it would be unsafe to assume that the Scots were committed to accepting battle, let alone offering or forcing it. The Balliol party had made a remarkable recovery in 1296–97, but was still very vulnerable.[8] Most of Scotland north of the Forth was in Balliol control, or at least outside Plantagenet control, but the advent of a large English army might have been enough to undermine the credibility of the Balliol administration. If Wallace and Murray could prevent the English from crossing the Forth they would afford protection to the growing Scottish administration, but they did not necessarily have to give battle to achieve that end. An opposed river crossing has never been considered the easiest of operations to carry out. As long as the English could be denied adequate facilities for crossing the Forth at Stirling or below, their only real avenue to approach the Scots was to move upriver to find good fords, where, assuming the Scots matched the English movements, they would probably have to fight to effect a crossing, almost inevitably providing a good opportunity for the Scots to attack on advantageous terms.

The advantages that were likely to accrue from a success on the battle-field were substantial for either side. If Wallace and Murray could prevent the English from destabilising the Balliol administration, their stock as political entities would be very much enhanced; if they could actually defeat an English army, so much the better. Both Wallace and Murray were acting in a capacity more usually the province of kings and magnates. Murray was a relatively substantial lord, but Wallace was a political non-entity; he had neither lands nor office nor extensive experience of senior leadership. Although Wallace and Murray evidently enjoyed the confidence of the army – they had raised the men, after all – they had yet to establish themselves as a credible source of authority in a civil or political setting. On the eve of Stirling Bridge they could be described as the commanders of the Scottish army, but they were not yet acceptable to the bulk of the political community as the lieutenants of King John.

For the English commanders, combat was the only serious option unless the Scottish leadership was prepared to disband their army and throw themselves on the mercy of Edward I. The Scots might well be able to withdraw quickly enough into the north to avoid battle in the short term, but if Edward I was prepared (or could afford) to keep an army active in Scotland indefinitely, Wallace would have to give battle eventually or have his army melt away to nothing through a mixture of disillusionment and the demands of an agricultural economy – sooner or later, the men would want to go home to their families, farms and businesses. Achieving complete victory over Wallace and Murray had a social and political significance for Edward I. A negotiated settlement with a small number of disaffected lords could be 'managed' with face-saving devices on both sides; a revolt of thousands under leadership that could be construed as a challenge to the traditional political order was a different matter. If Edward's administration were seen to be actively negotiating with Wallace and Murray, his prestige might be undermined; the great lords could claim to be acting in the interests of their country as the traditional representatives of their regions and in their traditional capacity of advisors to Scottish kings. Neither Wallace or Murray was a magnate; therefore their actions could be seen as undermining the authority of the magnates of Scotland as well as undermining the occupation government of King Edward. Additionally, the Balliol party had already made very rapid progress in installing an administration, and Wallace and Murray were obviously men capable of motivating thousands to join the struggle. If they, and the Balliol party generally, were not dealt with quickly, they might prove very hard to dislodge. Moreover, if they were successful in ejecting Edward's garrisons, his position at home might be undermined: his kingship was not particularly popular domestically with either the nobility or the commons of England. If the Plantagenet government was driven out of Scotland it might prove very difficult indeed to raise the men and money for an attempt at re-conquest, which, given that the Scots were now rather better organised for war, would probably be a much more difficult undertaking than the campaign of 1296. The English, then, were under some pressure to seek battle, and, in general terms, could be reasonably confident of the outcome; they had beaten the Scottish nobility at Dunbar and had encountered no serious opposition from the balance of the Scottish army through the following summer. There was very probably an element in the English army that doubted if the Scots would be prepared to fight at all.

The geographical location of Stirling has made it a focus for military activity throughout recorded history. As the first point at which the Forth could be crossed easily, possession of Stirling, or, strictly speaking, control of the bridge there, gave a great deal of control over access to Scotland north of the Forth. There were, and still are, several points above Stirling where the river could be crossed relatively easily on foot or horse, but few places which would allow passage by wagons. For an army to pass into northern Scotland it was necessary to secure a bridge crossing, so much so that Edward I commissioned a pontoon bridge to ensure that he would be able to effect a crossing even if he did not have possession of the bridge at Stirling.[9]

Although it has found a place in Scottish history books as the first great victory of the Scots over the English in the Wars of Independence, there was nothing inevitable about the process. Wallace and Moray united their forces to confront the English; whether or not they intended to offer, let alone provoke, battle is another question. They may have been looking for a confrontation, but that does not mean that they actually wanted a major engagement at all. If the English could be manoeuvred into a position that offered no good opportunities for attack, sooner or later they would be obliged to abandon their operation so long as the Scots stood fast. Stirling offered just such a situation. If the Scots could maintain their position on the left bank of the Forth overlooking Stirling Bridge, it would be a very difficult proposition for the English to dislodge them. Given adequate logistic and financial support the English army could, in theory, wait for the Scots to grow tired of the business and drift off home. Unfortunately for the Earl of Surrey and Hugh Cressingham, this was not an option, even if he had wanted to adopt it. The financial position of Edward I's government was never really very good, but by the summer of 1297 it had been heavily burdened for many years and keeping a large army in place against the Scots was more of a burden than could be easily carried. Money and food are always important issues for commanders, but they were not the sum of the challenges facing Cressingham. Virtually all medieval armies suffered from chronic desertion, the natural consequence of low pay, poor conditions and unpopular compulsory foreign service in a country from which one could make one's way home without having to board a ship. If desertion was high in English armies serving in France or Flanders, it must almost inevitably have been more of an issue for those serving in southern Scotland. Most of the men serving in Scotland for the Plantagenet cause in 1297 were recruited from the counties of northern England; making the journey home on 'unauthorised leave' was not such a daunting project for a Durham soldier in Lothian or Roxburghshire as it would have been for a Cheshire man serving in France. Both might have to travel through hostile countryside, but the man deserting from army service in Scotland could at least walk home.

The spectre of desertion and the pressing difficulties of supply and pay were not the only factors that pushed the English to a combat option. Edward I was not going to be at all impressed if Cressingham failed to force battle on the Scots, particularly in the light of the successful negotiated settlement that had just been made with the leaders of the 'noble revolt' at Irvine. Having taken an army to meet the enemy, it would have been very detrimental to Edward's regal prestige if there was no significant victory to compensate for the costs. If the English failed to engage at all, it would undoubtedly give a moral – or perhaps morale – advantage to the Balliol cause while simultaneously undermining the credibility of the occupation government, whose authority rested solely on success in war. For the Scots, then, battle was not strictly necessary for victory. If they could confront the English army at Stirling for long enough without giving battle they could achieve a tactical and political victory without any loss whatsoever. This was presumably clear to Cressingham, an intelligent and experienced political operator.

In addition to the political imperatives that made battle a preferred policy, there were practical martial issues. As well as having to weather the reaction of Edward I to a failure to carry the war to the Scots, if Cressingham decided to take his army home the desertion rate would very likely rise rather than fall. Men would be inclined to feel that their personal contribution was not going to make any difference to the situation and that they might as well make the journey home faster rather than slower, thus weakening the army at a potentially alarming rate at a point when it was being shadowed by the Scots. Wallace and Murray might be prepared to let the English depart in peace, but it is surely much more probable that they would take every opportunity to harass the English retreat, and might even be able to inflict a defeat on Cressingham's army during its return to England. If Cressingham's own estimate of the strength of his force is to be accepted at face value then he only had 300 men-at-arms in an army of 10,000,[10] a very weak mounted element for an army on the march. The Scots would have been able to match a man-at-arms element of that stature without much difficulty, though traditionally that was a weak aspect of Scottish armies throughout the Middle Ages. Cressingham's assessment of his numerical strength was not, however, made at Stirling, but at Roxburgh, more than a fortnight before the battle. His command had almost certainly been weakened by desertion and disease over the intervening period.

At least one writer has suggested that Cressingham's army could not have amounted to 10,000 foot, partly on the grounds that Edward himself led a smaller army on the continent and partly due to exaggeration on the part of Cressingham; however, there was no advantage to be had in telling King Edward that his army was greater than it actually was. The greater the army, the more Edward would expect his lieutenant to achieve with it; if anything, it would have been in Cressingham's interest to understate his strength rather than overstate it. The size of Edward's army is, in any case, completely irrelevant to the size of Cressingham's force; they were two different armies raised for different theatres. Desertion may have reduced the infantry element of the English army, but probably had little impact on the men-at-arms. It was by no means unknown for men-at-arms to desert, but it was certainly very much less common, chiefly because they were easier to identify and therefore prosecute when the opportunity arose. Because of the rather better pay and conditions and because of the cultural *mores* of the late thirteenth century, men of rank and status were expected to pay for their privileged position in society through service to the Crown, but it was also something of a social imperative. In a society which liked to think that it adhered to the values of chivalry, fighting was a natural part of social, political and cultural identity.

The 300 men-at-arms that Cressingham had under command at Roxburgh may not have been the extent of his cavalry arm. Scottish nobles and burgesses who had appended their seals to the Ragman Roll and had remained in Edward's peace owed exactly the same level of military obligation to King Edward as they had to King John or to Alexander III. No record has survived relating to the service of Scottish men-at-arms serving Edward I at Stirling Bridge, but it is highly probable that the occupation government would have made some effort to call on that service. Not only was the service itself desirable, but activity on behalf of the English Crown had a political dimension. If the Scots nobility could be induced to fight for Edward I, that would deny their service to the Balliol party, a useful objective.

Superficially, Cressingham was in a very advantageous position. The collapse of the 'noble revolt' had removed one threat to the occupation; a successful operation at Stirling would very probably undermine the other fatally. With a little good fortune he would be able to destroy Wallace and Murray and then penetrate northern Scotland. In practice, Cressingham really had little choice other than to fight. Had Cressingham chosen to withdraw, he would have faced the prospect of what would inevitably have been a very difficult interview with his king. Edward had no great opinion of the Scots generally, and would not be impressed in the slightest by the issues faced by his lieutenants in Scotland; Edward wanted results, and quickly, before the Scots could establish their authority at home or attain any degree of international political credibility. Practically, his situation was rather more precarious. He has been criticised, and rightly, for failing to take advantage of local knowledge which might have allowed him to make a flanking move on the Scottish position, but that would be rather dependent on managing to make a crossing farther upstream. It might have been possible for Richard Lundie, a Scottish knight who had defected to the English at Irvine in his disgust at the ineffectiveness of the Scots, to take the 500 men-at-arms he asked for across the river at Drip fords or elsewhere, but it was not guaranteed; he might well have had to make an opposed river crossing in the face of superior numbers. His proposal may not have been a practical proposition anyway. If there were as many as 500 men-at-arms in the English army they must have come from other sources beyond the army that Cressingham had mustered at Roxburgh, since Cressingham was clear that he had only 300 men-at-arms in his command there. It is quite possible that this was the case. As we have already seen, Scots in English peace who had a military obligation would have been under some pressure to discharge their obligation to the 'new administration' of Edward I just as they had been under Scottish kings, so there may have been a contingent of such men from those counties most securely held by the English: Lothian, Roxburghshire, Lanarkshire, Berwickshire, Peeblesshire and Dumfriesshire.

It is not clear whether Cressingham's force of 300 men-at-arms present at Roxburgh included the force that Clifford and Percy had commanded at Irvine, but it must be considered unlikely. Clifford's force had been enough to dissuade the 'noble revolt' leaders into seeking terms. There is no reason to assume that he led a particularly large force at Irvine, but it must surely have been a body powerful enough to convince the Scots that battle was out of the question. Although the 'noble revolt' did not attract many of the great lords of Scotland, it is ludicrous to imagine that the leaders of the revolt were prepared to even consider a confrontation with the English unless they too had a significant force.

The pressure on Wallace and Murray to give battle was not as well developed as that on Cressingham, but it was still an issue. Although their authority would be bolstered if Cressingham withdrew, they must have been aware that a battlefield victory would be better for their political and military status than any other outcome. The men who joined the armies of Wallace and Murray did so in order to fight and win, not to stand on the Ochils waiting for the enemy to march off home. If the campaign of summer 1297 failed to achieve significant results under the leadership of Wallace and Murray, they might find it very difficult indeed to recruit an army for the campaign of 1298: what was the point of giving military service if it did not bring easily recognisable benefits? Wallace and Murray had to protect their credibility as leaders. In one sense at least this was more of a difficulty than it was for Edward, since he had the benefit of kingship, a matter of status as well as of political power. Edward inherited authority, whereas Wallace and Murray had to acquire it, and in August 1297 their status as leaders was completely dependent on maintaining the military initiative. It was not crucial for them to offer battle in the short term, but wars are seldom won without trials of arms. Sooner or later they would have to fight unless Edward was willing to abandon his ambitions in Scotland, a very unlikely circumstance.

The popular perception of the battle, unusually, is not far removed from the reality; even some of the more dubious assertions of the chroniclers may in fact be fundamentally sound. The initial activities of the day as recorded by Walter of Guisborough would seem to beggar belief, but are not perhaps quite as unlikely as they would appear. According to Guisborough, the English army initiated two premature crossings of the bridge before the battle proper began. The first formations to cross did so at dawn but were quickly recalled, due to the fact that the other significant English commander, the Earl of Surrey, was still in his bed. Though not impossible, this has to be considered rather suspect. Even if true, his fondness for his sleep would not have been a good reason to recall the men who had already crossed. Since the troops started to cross at dawn, it is perfectly possible that the business of waking troops and putting them into march order before first light had not been a great success, leading to a bottleneck at the bridge itself but also, very probably, to a good deal of general confusion among the English army. With the majority of the army still being marshalled on the south bank of the river, the balance of the army on the north side would be very vulnerable to a sudden Scottish attack. Even if the Scots were heavily outnumbered, and there is no great weight of evidence to indicate that they were, they might well be able to achieve local superiority on the north bank while the rest of the English army looked on ineffectually from the south bank.

The second alleged crossing commenced rather later in the morning, but, again according to Guisborough, was recalled because of the arrival of some Scottish magnates in the English camp, bearing news that Wallace and Murray were prepared to negotiate. An agreed settlement would have been an attractive proposition for Cressingham. Even if he were to inflict a massive defeat on Wallace and Murray there was no guarantee that they, or others, would continue to oppose the Edwardian occupation; however, if the Scots could be induced to disband their army he would have achieved a political victory that might go some way toward disarming the Balliol cause more generally. He may have believed, with some justification, that this was exactly what had already occurred at Irvine, with very positive results for the administration: Robert Bruce and the Stewart were now in the Plantagenet party, so why should Wallace and Murray not be brought into Edward's peace? If they were, the leadership and credibility of the Balliol cause would be dealt a major blow and, assuming that Wallace and Murray did disband their army, Cressingham would be able to lead his army across the Forth and into northern Scotland, where he could set about dismantling whatever was left of the Balliol administration without fear of serious opposition.

Cressingham might have been prepared to consider negotiations, but it is not at all clear that Wallace or Murray were interested in the slightest. Cressingham would never have been willing to entertain the notion that he could withdraw his army and abandon the remaining administrators and garrisons (King Edward would not have given him the authority to do), so really he had nothing to offer to the Balliol party other than terms for their surrender or battle. None the less, if there was any possibility of agreement Cressingham would have been unwise not to pursue it. If Guisborough's assertion that the Stewart approached Cressingham with an offer of discussions at a point when only part of the English army had crossed the bridge is true, he might well have felt that it was preferable not to leave a portion of his army exposed to the possibility of a sudden attack from the Scots; the situation would have been very similar to that which had already (according to Guisborough) occurred earlier in the day.

Although negotiations would have held some attraction for Cressingham, he did have good cause to believe that combat would be to his advantage. The Scots were evidently very weak in men-at-arms and in any case, since the fight at Dunbar the previous spring, English commanders generally had little reason to be impressed by the performance of Scottish cavalry. The Scottish command consisted of two men – in itself a situation traditionally considered unwise – neither of whom had, so far as we are aware, any extensive experience of making war, and the Scottish army was largely comprised of men who had never seen a major action. The level of experience among his own troops may not have been very much greater than that of the Scots, but Cressingham still had good cause to believe that his army was the superior, in quality certainly, and probably in quantity as well.

The Scottish cavalry had been routed easily and quickly at Dunbar and the Scottish infantry had yet to meet the English in battle at all.

A good deal has been written about the nature of the relationship between Wallace and the nobility, one writer going so far as to assert that the Wallace/Murray plan for battle was '…largely improvised, and was the work of men of a different mentality from the lords' but neglecting to inform the reader about the manner in which Wallace and Murray differed from the rest of the members of their class. Wallace's early actions all seem to carry the hallmarks of traditional and conventional military practice of the day: he led a party of men-at-arms. That was, however, only part of the tradition of medieval war. The belief among historical enthusiasts that the infantry were not thought to be an important part of the structure of an army seems very curious indeed, considering that very few medieval armies of manoeuvre were anything less than 70 per cent infantry, and more usually of the order of 80 or even 90 per cent. If the infantry were insignificant, why were they recruited at all? Wallace, Murray, Edward I, Cressingham and Surrey all seem to have been convinced that a strong force of infantry was a vital part of the structure of their armies.

The course of the engagement at Stirling Bridge is not the subject of any great amount of historical controversy, which is in itself something of a rarity in medieval war studies. Cressingham's decision to cross the river cannot be seen in any other light than an attempt to force battle on the enemy. The Scots kept to their position until a body of the enemy army had effected a crossing, before making a rapid descent on them from the area to the west of the Wallace monument. There would appear to have been no requirement for manoeuvre, though at least one recent commentator has decided, for reasons that he has not chosen to divulge, that the Scottish army made an oblique manoeuvre in the course of advancing to contact. Such a movement would have been very difficult to achieve, as well as unnecessary if the Scots had adopted a position that would prevent an English force from advancing northwards after crossing the river.

Naturally, it is reasonable to assume that Wallace and Murray made a deliberate choice to attack: their enemy was, after all, in a very vulnerable position. However, it is always possible that they in fact had to make the best of a bad job. Some portion of the Scottish army is likely to have been very keen indeed to get into action, and, if Guisborough is correct in his description of the English army as making three separate attempts to cross the bridge, there must have been a degree of excitement among the troops: they had seen the enemy cross and retire twice. When the English made their third attempt it is likely that Wallace, Murray and their subordinates would have been struggled to prevent a general advance even if they had wanted to. The opportunity was, however, far too good to miss, and whether the Scots made a precipitate and unauthorised advance or whether Wallace and Murray gave the order for it is not too important: what mattered was the outcome.

The area into which the leading English units debouched when they crossed the bridge was not very extensive. The 'buckle' of the Forth (see Illustration 10) meant that they had deployed into a near-circular area bounded by a river too fast, too wide and too muddy to cross, with a very narrow 'neck' from which the English would have to advance on the Scots. The problem of course was that the Scots did not wait to be attacked, but made a descent on the English which effectively blocked up the 'neck', denying the English the space to deploy properly and forcing the English back on their supports. Due to the narrowness of the bridge, the English could not join the fight.

As ever with a medieval battle, it is difficult, if not impossible, to come to any realistic conclusions about casualties. The Scottish chroniclers are very clear that Scottish casualties were very light indeed, but that is of course to be expected. The lack of a great list of prominent gentlemen killed or taken prisoner should not be seen as an indication that the Scottish army was unscathed by the battle. The most significant casualty on the Scottish side was, of course, Sir Andrew Murray. He was not killed in the action, but died of his wounds some weeks later. Self-evidently Murray had taken part in the battle, as had Wallace. Personal combat by commanders was part of the nature of medieval battle, and Stirling Bridge was not exceptional in that regard: Moray was fatally wounded, Cressingham was killed and William Wallace no doubt behaved as gallantly as chroniclers would have us believe. Personal prowess at arms was an important aspect of medieval leadership; example was considered important, but the efforts of one man, however strong, brave, skilled and determined, are still only the efforts of one man. The William Wallace who took part in the battle of Stirling Bridge bears little, if any, resemblance to the giant warrior beloved of popular writers. A recent writer tells us that Wallace cleaved his way through the English wielding the vast sword that can be seen today at the Wallace monument. Apart from the fact that two-handed swords the better part of 6 feet long were not a feature of the medieval arsenal generally, the sword in question is a much later artefact, probably from the late fifteenth or early sixteenth century, and therefore has no connection with William Wallace's life whatsoever. Wallace the warrior, casting about him with a great cleaver, scattering the English before him in a welter of amputated arms, legs and heads, may be an attractive romantic picture, but not a useful one. There is no reason to believe that William Wallace was given to fighting in any mode other than the one he grew up with, that of a conventional armoured, mounted soldier of the late Middle Ages – a man-at-arms. In close combat, the life expectancy of a man-at-arms without a shield would have been very short indeed and it is extremely difficult to see how a man could use a two-handed sword and a shield at the same time. The two-handed sword only became viable for men-at-arms when body armour had developed to a degree that made a shield more of a burden than it was worth[11] and was in any case an option for dismounted action, not for fighting on horseback.

The outcome of the action was certainly dramatic, probably exceeding the very best hopes of Wallace and Murray. They probably had little doubt about the prospect of victory once battle was joined; the tactical situation suited them well and they must have had some confidence in their troops, otherwise they would have avoided the risk of a major engagement, but the political results were as significant as the military, possibly more so. With a major success behind them, Wallace and Murray could not be ignored as political figures. To what extent the Guardianship was entrusted to them and to what extent they simply assumed the role is impossible to say; unsurprisingly, the magnates of Scotland did not leave any record of their reaction to the political advancement of a minor baron and an obscure member of the lesser nobility. Stirling Bridge had seriously undermined the security of the occupation government and proved that the English in arms were not invincible, but it had also brought a prominence to Wallace and Murray that was rare for men of their station in society.

If victory on the battlefield brought political advancement for Wallace and Murray, it did not bring the war to a close, and the new Guardians would have to establish their authority and prove that they were worthy of their office. Murray's role in government was of course very brief; he died of his wounds a few weeks after the battle, leaving Wallace to carry on as sole Guardian. For a short while at least, Wallace was probably able to proceed as he saw fit without any great amount of consultation or consideration of the peacetime political community, but it is hard to accept that he was able to carry on the business of government without the support of a considerable portion of that community; their participation in the administration of justice and the collection of issues and military service was a vital prop to any party aspiring to power. Although there is very little in the way of documentation showing the Wallace government at work, there can be little doubt that there was plenty to do. The management of the war must surely have taken priority over civil issues, but the latter could not be ignored. As a substitute for the king, Wallace would have been the recognised source of authority in the Balliol camp, and as such he would have had to fulfil the functions of kingship other than war. After 11 August 1297, William Wallace the soldier had to become William Wallace the politician.

His ideological position was not a complicated one. As Guardian his responsibility extended into every sphere of the life of the community: war, justice and the economy. To a considerable degree, his interest in the last of these was related to the first. Wallace and Murray's letters to German merchants at Hamburg and Lubeck[12] did have a political/diplomatic dimension: Wallace was looking for international recognition of the existence of a Scottish polity and of his rule within that polity, but the economic aspects relating to the war were pressing issues. Although arms and armour of all kinds could be, and were, manufactured in Scotland,[13] it is reasonable to assume that the demand for arms had increased dramatically in 1295–96 as relations between England and Scotland deteriorated, and that the existing Scottish manufacturers and suppliers could not hope to satisfy that demand. The repeated instructions from English kings to their own subjects (and, through their fellow-rulers, to the subjects of others) to refrain from exporting war materials generally, and arms and armour in particular, to Scotland is a clear indication that the arms trade into Scotland was exceptionally profitable – sufficiently so for merchants to feel it was worth risking their ships, not to mention the extreme displeasure of their king, in the search for a fast return on investment.[14]

Naturally, arms had to be paid for, and the purchase of foreign arms meant the export of goods to finance arms procurement. To what extent, if at all, Wallace's government bought arms for distribution to their soldiers is not known. The normal practice of war throughout Europe called for the personal ownership of weapons, armour and horses; however, that does not preclude the possibility that 'munition'[15] weapons were acquired so that more infantry could be enlisted. In 1332, during his first attempt at gaining Scottish kingship, Edward Balliol's army apparently uncovered a cache of spears, variously reported as 800 or 4,000.[16] The second figure would represent a huge arsenal, but even the lesser one would have been a substantial investment. These spears may have been bought by the Crown either for issue or for sale to the troops, but they were certainly bought against the eventuality of war; there is no reason to assume that the Wallace government was not capable of doing the same thing.

Apart from the conduct of the war generally, there were other issues that required Wallace's attention: primarily, reducing the garrisons of the

occupation government and replacing the Plantagenet sheriffs and bailies
with men of his own choice, and also campaigning for the allegiance of areas
that remained in English control. A good deal has been written in the past
about the letters Wallace sent from Haddington to Lubeck and Hamburg,
but little about the circumstances that took Wallace to Haddington in the
first place. The strong castles of Lothian made the business of maintaining
an occupation government there less of a challenge than in other parts of
the country. It has long been the opinion of many English and Scottish
historians that the Lothian community was actually perfectly content with
English administration (though the evidence to support that position is, to
say the least, thin on the ground) and there is no doubt that in comparison to
most other Scottish counties in 1297–98 Lothian was held relatively securely
for the Plantagenets. This may not have been quite so clear to the English
administration there at the time. At least three Lothian castles[17] had been
recovered from the English before the battle of Falkirk and in November
1297 Wallace had led his army into what was – supposedly – an area where
the English administration was intact.

Marching into Lothian was an operation with several dimensions. As the
Guardian, Wallace had to give some proof of his commitment to eventually
recovering the entirety of Scotland for King John, not just the parts of it
from which the English could be dislodged easily. One aspect of that was
simply the business of carrying the war to the enemy: the Lothian campaign
certainly did that. Another was to establish his lordship among the Scots
generally and in Lothian itself in particular. In short, the 1297 campaign
was a mixture of flag-waving, sabre-rattling, crowd-pleasing and a less than
subtle threat to the Lothian political community. By marching through
the country in force, Wallace demonstrated his power to friend, foes and
falterers alike. People sympathetic to the Balliol cause could be encouraged
in their loyalty by the visible presence of a Scottish army; those inclined
toward the Plantagenets were likely to be discouraged by the fact that
Wallace could march his troops around the country with seeming impunity,
and the people of Lothian were likely to become rather focused on their
own futures. Wallace's arrival in Lothian was a boost to his supporters, but
it was also an indication that those who sided with the occupation might
have to explain their actions to a restored Balliol king at some point in
the future, possibly quite soon.

The success of the Lothian campaign was quite limited however.
The castles that fell to the Scots may well have been turned over to the
forces of William Wallace by their garrisons or just plain abandoned; there
is no evidence to indicate that they fell to siege or storm. The central

establishment of the English administration in Lothian, Edinburgh Castle, does not seem to have been threatened at all. Although the garrison was small, the castle was very strong indeed and was unlikely to fall without a protracted siege. The presence of Wallace's army would have deterred the garrison from mounting operations against the Scots and, temporarily, from fulfilling the other roles of such installations – gathering rents and other dues and maintaining law and order – but Wallace was not able to put his own officials in place with any confidence. He might be able to lead an army into Lothian and march it out again without intervention by the English, but he had not brought Lothian back under Scottish control for King John. That does not mean that the Lothian campaign was a failure; in all likelihood Wallace did not expect to recover the sheriffdom in one operation. Even if he had been able to win the unswerving allegiance of all of the Lothian communities to the Balliol cause, he did not have the material or expertise to conduct one conventional siege, let alone invest all of the smaller strongholds held for the Plantagenet cause throughout the sheriffdom.

Wallace's offensive into Lothian would have brought some recruits to the Balliol party through demonstrating that the issue of independent Scottish kingship was not a lost cause, but he could not afford to enforce his authority through the sheriffdom by military power. If he kept his army in Lothian he would have to feed it from the resources of the county, a burden that would almost inevitably draw local sympathies to the Plantagenets. Nonetheless, if William was to keep a force in being through the winter, it would have to be fed. Obviously it would be better for William's reputation if he could maintain the army without imposing on Scottish communities other than for manpower, and it would be better for the army if it was kept busy with worthwhile operational activity rather than idling in billets through the winter, a sure-fire recipe for disorder. These considerations made an invasion of England an attractive proposition militarily, but there was an important political dimension as well. Wallace's prestige and credibility as Guardian rested firmly on his success in arms against the English. If he did little or nothing for even a few months, the lustre of his achievements was liable to fade quickly, possibly leading to competition for the Guardianship from men of greater social rank. A successful foray south of the border would go a long way toward confirming his political position among the Scottish hierarchy and maintaining his popularity and authority in the army.

CHAPTER SIX

From Victory to Ignominy

I f Stirling Bridge gave Wallace power, it also gave him responsibility. He was not the king, but he did have the authority – given or assumed – to wield the royal prerogative. His political role the king's substitute would have involved a great variety of activities, but military affairs naturally formed a significant portion of his duties. The greatest priority was obviously the army. In the winter of 1297 he led his army into England. Unlike Edward I's invasion of Scotland, Wallace's invasion of England was not mounted to secure territory, but to undermine the authority of Edward I and to enhance his own prestige as Guardian.[1] It also gave him the opportunity to feed his army at the expense of his enemy. His approach was not revolutionary; at the beginning of hostilities in March 1296 the Scots had mounted a series of raids into northern England, presumably to demonstrate that a state of war existed and thereby fulfil the commitment of John I to his treaty obligations with Philip IV of France. These operations do not seem to have had any very specific military objectives: no English castles or towns were seized and English landholders were not pressured to give their allegiance to King John. The achievements of the Scots in England in 1296 were limited to the diplomatic obligations of the Scoto-French treaty of 1295[2] and some indiscriminate looting and burning.

After Stirling Bridge Wallace set himself to the task of pressing on with the war; the fact that he could do this would seem to support the possibility that he had either been able to assume control of the Scottish administration, which was already recovering and appointing officials by the summer of 1297, or that he had effectively been adopted by the active elements of the political communities of Scotland as an acceptable leader in the absence of the king. He was of course active in spheres other than warfare. On 11 October 1297 Wallace was at Haddington, with sufficient force to deter the English garrisons of Lothian from confronting him.[3] The garrison commanders may have been aware that Wallace intended to move on quickly from Haddington and therefore may have been unwilling to risk any operations at all if Wallace was about to leave their area of responsibility. They may have simply been keen to avoid a fight; the English had, after all, been beaten at Stirling just a few weeks before. Wallace was unable to seize Edinburgh, town or castle, but it would be unrealistic to assume that he simply ignored the English garrisons in Lothian, Lanark and Roxburghshire as he made his way to England. Although he could not have had many men-at-arms to spare to counter the garrison forces, the garrison complements were not large,[4] and could probably be contained within their establishments by relatively small numbers of men. He evidently was not too concerned about the garrisons in Scotland since he was prepared to undertake an invasion of England.

Under normal circumstances, mounting an operation into England would have been a very risky business, but the circumstances were not normal. The knights and men-at-arms that served in the English army at Stirling Bridge would have been drawn from the political communities of the north of England, particularly Northumberland and Cumbria.[5] Since a large number of these men were either dead or captives of the Scots or were serving in Scotland anyway, the English military establishment of northern England was deprived of a significant portion of its armoured cavalry strength and, perhaps more importantly, it's political and military leadership. These men were not just the striking arm of the northern English army, they were the men who would normally ensure that military service was being discharged, both by the other members of the political community and by the rest of the population. In a sense, their skills and experience were secondary considerations. What was important was that the community knew who they were and that they held the appropriate authority. Naturally the men who had been killed or captured at Stirling Bridge had sons or brothers to take their places in military activity, but the mere fact that there were a lot of new faces would not have been an encouragement to any forces raised to oppose the Scots in the autumn of 1297. The situation was, perhaps, similar to that in Scotland in the spring and summer of 1296. The actual number of men killed or taken prisoner at Dunbar was not particularly large, but it did include a significantly large proportion of the leadership of the Balliol party.[6]

The absence of any realistic attempt to confront the Scots in October and November 1297 is not adequately explained by the casualties at Stirling Bridge. The political communities of Westmorland and Northumberland had been damaged, but not those of the other northern counties. The military tenants of Lancashire, Cheshire and Yorkshire had not taken part in the Stirling Bridge campaign. The fact that they had been on active service in Scotland before that[7] did not, however, excuse them from their obligation to serve against invasion, yet there seems to have been no co-ordinated effort to raise a force of men-at-arms from these counties. One explanation may lie in an unwillingness to abandon home and hearth, thus allowing the Scots to penetrate into these counties unopposed. The plight of the people of Northumberland might not seem so critical to Yorkshiremen if there was any chance at all of a Scottish army turning up outside York.

If there was no co-ordinated plan among those responsible for military leadership in northern England, it would seem that there was no real agenda among the Scots either. Colm MacNamee has put forward the possibility the Wallace did not in fact instigate the invasion of England at all, suggesting that Scots acting on their own initiative were active in Northumberland by 13 October 1297, though Wallace himself had still been at Haddington two days before. Whether he directed an assault on northern England as a matter of policy or whether he assumed control of a situation that he could not prevent, Wallace does not seem to have been able to exercise much control over his men compared to the discipline that Robert I was able to impose on his armies in similar circumstances a generation later, but, like Robert, he seems to have lacked the resources to mount an effective siege. He approached Newcastle and Carlisle, but made no attempt to take either, though he may have been able to contain the garrison at Carlisle and prevent them from hindering his operations in the area.

The Scots would seem to have been perceived as a threat, if not yet a reality, by 15 October, when the local clergy voted money for military preparations[8] and in London orders for a muster were issued, though it was not to take place until 6 December, some six weeks distant.[9] Although communications were slow in the Middle Ages, and administrative functions sometimes cumbersome, six weeks does not seem to indicate any sense of urgency on the part of the English government. It would surely have been possible to give suitable authority to an officer of the Crown and entrust that person with making an appropriate response to the Scots; however, the timing of the muster may have been a conscious policy decision based on an estimate of the resources available to William Wallace, rather than on those available to the English Crown. By the time an English army assembled on 6 December, Wallace's army would have been operating continuously for much longer than the traditional forty days' service owed to the Crown. Service in Scotland could be extended, in

theory anyway, almost indefinitely, since there was an obvious threat to the
security of the country as long as there was an English military presence.[10]
Service against the English outside Scotland may have been a rather harder
proposition to 'sell' to the Scots as part of their customary obligation. With
any luck – from an English point of view – by the time the army was on
the march Wallace's force would have dwindled in quantity, and probably
in quality as well. The men whose service was most vital to the Scottish
cause were the men who could afford to invest in appropriate horses and
equipment; however, to a considerable extent these were inevitably the
men whose presence was most needed on the 'home front'. They were
the farmers, minor landholders, merchants and craftsmen on whom the
economy rested. The men who were willing to serve continually were
more likely to be men with little in the way of means other than the army
or prospects other than plunder.

William Wallace led his men around northern England for five weeks
before returning to Scotland. In a sense it was an aimless exercise, a mean-
dering around Northumberland, Cumbria and Westmorland, doing very
little beyond ruining farms and villages, but achievements of the 1297
campaign were real, if transitory. The Scottish army had been maintained
for several weeks on the enemy's territory and had taken large quantities of
plunder and provisions back to Scotland in a year of poor agricultural yields
all over northern Europe.[11] Scottish morale would certainly have been
improved by news of a successful foray against the English, and the prestige
of William Wallace as Guardian of the realm would have been enhanced
accordingly; all the same, no blow of political significance had been landed.
To an extent, the Scots could regard that as a victory in itself: they had
invaded the king of England's realm, despoiled it, and returned home
unscathed. More realistically, the English political position was untouched.
The Scots could not force Edward to the negotiating table by burning
the homes and farms of his northern subjects. Wallace could not keep his
army in the north of England indefinitely. Once the land had been swept
of movable goods and standing crops and byres fired, he had to move on,
but he could not afford to move any further south for fear of having his
return journey barred by a force raised in his rear. By Christmas Wallace
was back in Scotland and the English were already mounting a recovery in
Berwickshire and Roxburghshire,[12] thus relieving any immediate pressure
on the Plantagenet administration in Lothian.

Preparations for a major invasion to restore the fortunes of the English in
Scotland were not undertaken until the return of Edward I from Flanders
in March 1298. It had become all too plain that the Scots would have to be

taken seriously, and the army raised for the purpose would have to be the product of a major effort. The force commanded by Cressingham at Stirling Bridge had not been insignificant, but it had obviously not been adequate to the task. The man-at-arms element had been small and the army does not seem to have been well organised. The army of 1298 was larger, better resourced and, perhaps most importantly, was led by King Edward himself. The army he summoned was a powerful one: writs were issued for the enlistment of over 10,000 men from Wales and a further 1,000 each from Cheshire and Lancashire.[13] The other northern counties, Northumberland, Westmorland, Cumbria and Durham, were not called upon to provide contingents of infantry, though several knights and men-at-arms from those communities joined the army as it passed northwards. To some extent this may have been a recognition of their sufferings of the previous year; however, it also meant that there was a reservoir of manpower in those counties should Wallace manage to evade Edward and cut his communications or make another foray into England. The heavy cavalry element of the army amounted to something over 2,000 men-at-arms[14] and knights, of whom slightly more than 50 per cent were serving for royal wages, the balance being provided by the retinues of the magnates attending the king. Even for the wealthiest of the great lords and earls, leading a retinue in the king's army was an expensive business. Some portion, possibly a very large one, of the men in his command would have been discharging the obligations attached to their landholdings, or would have been provided at their expense if they could not serve in person; others, however, would require wages and indemnification for loss of horses and perhaps for losses incurred by being captured and ransomed. All would expect to be shown some sign of appreciation during or after the campaign.

King Edward arrived at York with the household element of the army on 16 May 1298. On the assumption that there would be a brief campaign, Edward moved his seat of government to York as a temporary measure to ease the administration of the war. It would continue to be the principal seat of his government for the next six years while he tried to bring the Scottish war to a satisfactory conclusion. From York he marched to Durham, arriving on 12 June and resting there some time before moving on to Newcastle. By the middle of July he was at Temple Liston, waiting for supplies and mounting relatively minor operations against the Scots, such as detaching the bishop of Durham, Antony Bek, to recover three castles in Lothian lost to the Scots over the preceding year. King Edward was in a difficult situation in July 1298. His supply arrangements had broken down badly through a mixture of unseasonable weather conditions and a shortfall in promised shipping. There can be little doubt that desertion was already an issue in the army; if Edward could not feed the troops it would increase. When supplies were eventually landed and delivered to the army, matters went from bad to worse: the chief part of the delivery was wine and within a short time a major riot broke out between Welsh and English infantrymen.[15]

Although his army was a demonstration of his power, it was also a sign of his weakness. If he could force battle on the Scots – and win – he could expect to force them to a negotiated settlement, but if he failed to engage them, all the propaganda in the world about the cowardly nature of the Scots in refusing battle would not hide the fact that he had failed, despite great effort and expense, to overpower a smaller and weaker neighbour. Evidence that it was possible to defeat the English might have very severe repercussions in Ireland and Wales, particularly in those areas only recently annexed by King Edward, and it would do no good to the prestige of his kingship at home, at a time when there was already serious discontent over taxation, requisitions and increasing demands for military service.

The picture was less bleak for Wallace, insofar as he could hope to win a victory of sorts without actually committing to battle at all. If he could confront Edward but not fight, Edward would eventually have to leave Scotland and disband his army. That might not do a great deal of good for the political career prospects of William Wallace, but it would not do them any harm. The longer he could maintain his position of prominence, the more entrenched he would be in his authority, as people became increasingly accustomed to having a very junior member of the political class as the head of government. There is no evidence to indicate that Wallace had any intention of actually confronting Edward across the battlefield. No one could have been more intimately aware of the shortcomings of the Scottish army than Wallace himself. As far as we know, William Wallace only ever witnessed two battles, Stirling Bridge and Falkirk, but he must have been aware of the disparity between Edward's force and his own. Frightening the county communities of northern England was well within the capabilities of the Scottish army, but they were not very well provided with men-at-arms and archers. The only realistic plan for Wallace to adopt was one of avoiding combat with the English army, waiting for it to start breaking up and harassing it on its return journey to England. If he could achieve this he would be able to preserve the army, the basis of his political power, and retain the Guardianship, at least until the next crisis. If Edward could be induced to leave Scotland without making any mark on the political situation, the remaining English garrisons would probably become compromised. The men serving in the garrisons would become less confident of eventual victory, or even of being relieved in the event of a siege, and the credibility of the administration as a whole would be undermined. If at all possible, Edward wanted to take the combat option; Wallace surely did not.

Wallace was nearly successful in his aim. Edward was becoming concerned that the Scots would slip away from him, when he was brought news at Kirkliston. Wallace was on the south side of the river Forth, near Falkirk, a distance of about 8-10 kilometres. His army was deployed for battle in four (David Penman, *The Scottish Civil War*, suggests three) circular formations, with archers dispersed around them and a small body of men-at-arms drawn up in the rear. If Edward could close with the Scots quickly enough he might be able to force battle on them, if not in a place of his own choosing exactly, certainly not in theirs. Large armies of spearmen had secured victories in the past, and would do so again, but only when they could give battle on terms that suited them: constricted battlefields, firm, level ground for the attack or elevated ground for the defence, and a viable response to archery. A more conventional army, one with a greater strength in men-at-arms and archers, was a more versatile beast by far. Its practice could be adapted to suit different conditions with relative ease and efficiency. The move to Falkirk would take the army all day, but it was not a great deal to ask; failing any unexpected developments Edward could reasonably hope to have all of his army gathered under his command in the vicinity of the enemy by the end of the day, with a view to locating him and bringing him to battle the following morning. In this he was entirely successful. By mid-morning the Scots had been located on a hillside, probably overlooking the Westquarter burn. The position was a strong one, but not particularly so. To the front of the army was the burn, which passed through a boggy area. This had been dismissed as a factor of the Scottish position; however, it would, at the very least, slow down and probably disrupt any general advance by the English army if it deployed from the Linlithgow–Falkirk road. It would seem that Edward had gained a march on the Scots. With Edward's powerful cavalry force on hand, Wallace could hardly expect to extricate his army without interruption. His army would be extremely vulnerable in anything other than carefully selected circumstances, so he really had little choice other than to fight.

The leading cavalry formation, under the Earl of Lincoln, possibly supported by the Earl of Surrey, approached the Scottish right flank with the Falkirk road to their left, where they encountered a marshy area around the Glen burn, forcing them toward the right. The cavalry formations of the king and the bishop of Durham moved on the left of the Scottish army, crossing the upper reach of the Westquarter burn and meeting stiff resistance.

Neither attack could make much impression on the Scots, however: horses can be persuaded to do many things, but not to throw themselves bodily into hedges of spears. The solution to the problem lay at hand; Edward committed his archers to the fight and the dense Scottish schiltroms was decided. The Scottish archers, greatly outnumbered, could offer no worthwhile resistance to their English counterparts. Many were killed and the rest left the field; the Scottish cavalry had already done so. A lot has been written about the abject failure of the nobles to engage, but it is difficult to see what sort of contribution they could have made. Even when the Scots were not divided among themselves, or at least no more so than was normal in a medieval country, they would have struggled to ever put a force of anything like 2,000 men-at-arms in the field, but the Falkirk army was not, in any case, a conventional 'national' army raised for a great battle, but a force held in being to confront the enemy until he decided to retire. Also, the country was not united; a significant part of the political community, from whom most men-at-arms were drawn, was in the peace of Edward I, and a considerable portion of the remainder were prisoners of war in England. The Scottish cavalry force at Falkirk probably did not exceed 300 and was therefore in no position to inflict a serious blow on the English cavalry; on the other hand, if the English cavalry brought them to battle, the Scots would assuredly be completely destroyed. The withdrawal of the Scottish cavalry may not have been glorious, but it was the only sensible course to pursue.

The Scottish nobles were not alone in abandoning the fight. Seeing that the battle was lost, William Wallace and his immediate companions fled the field; there was really very little else they could do, other than find a pointless death in a battle where more than enough Scottish people were going to die anyway. As ever, contemporary estimates of casualties are of little value, but there had been a hard business for both sides. Little evidence survives to give any suggestion of casualties. Horse valuation rolls show that more than 100 horses lost in the campaign had to be accounted for. Not all of these claims would actually result in a payment from the Crown; the king might provide a man with a horse in order to have his services. Thomas Lillok, a Roxburghshire man,[16] lost a charger that had been lent to him 'of the king's grace'. Thomas had served King Edward in 1296 as the *socius* of Sir Richard de Horsburgh, and would therefore probably be known to someone in the king's household who could help procure a position for him in the king's household cavalry; however, he may have been serving for his lands in Roxburghshire and have been obliged to borrow a charger from the king's stable so that the king could avail himself of his services.

For Edward, Falkirk was a fine victory over his Scottish enemies. For Wallace, it was the end of his career as a senior political figure. His assumption of leadership had been the product of military success and his loss of it a consequence of military defeat. If he was no longer acceptable to the traditional political and military leadership of Scotland, we should not assume that he had retained his popularity with the people as a whole. It is reasonable to assume that Scottish casualties at Falkirk had been heavy, which can scarcely have endeared Wallace to the community. By imposing his rule, he had raised a great war against the English which may have been very popular indeed in the aftermath of Stirling, but perhaps much less so in the days after Falkirk. William Wallace resigned the Guardianship by his own choice, or so Fordoun and Bower tell us, on the banks of the Forth shortly after the battle, but there was little else he could do. If he was no longer an asset for recruitment and no longer had the confidence of the rank and file of whatever was left of the army, it was time for him to step aside, even if the magnates had not obliged him to do so, which they undoubtedly would have done.

Victory at Falkirk had immediate benefits for Edward I. He had inflicted a significant defeat on the Scots and had undermined the credibility of William Wallace, but it did not change the course of the war, and, having procured a victory, what exactly was he to do next? Several of his senior 'in capite' tenants had served throughout the campaign without wages and were keen to return to their homes and estates. The financial situation was, in any case, more than just difficult. Edward could hardly find the money needed for the men who had enlisted for pay in the first place, let alone offer wages in the hope of retaining those who had served as volunteers. For a fortnight he stayed at the Dominican priory at Stirling, recuperating from a kick he had received from his horse on the eve of the battle, before moving to Edinburgh and then making his way across the county to Ayr in search of Robert Bruce. Bruce, unlike his companions in the 'noble revolt', had not adhered to the terms of Edward's peace after the Irvine negotiations, despite promises – unfulfilled – that he would surrender his daughter, Marjory, as a hostage for his future good behaviour. Edward was able to take Lochmaben Castle, but a contemplated operation into Galloway had to be abandoned because of a shortage of manpower.[17]

Edward returned to England before the end of the year. His prestige as king had been enhanced by a signal victory on the battlefield, but he had failed to make any real political progress. Some of the Scottish nobility had entered his peace, but not enough to indicate a general shift in Scottish attitudes, and, as the Lanercost chronicler put it, wherever the bodies of the Scottish lords might be, their hearts were 'with their own people'.

The resignation of Wallace could certainly be seen as a positive out-come from Edward's viewpoint, though even that may not have been as significant as historians have tended to believe. When Wallace assumed or received the office of Guardian in the summer of 1297, the traditional political leaders in Scottish society were either powerless to intervene or were prepared to accept his leadership. Several were of course prisoners of war and therefore had a very limited influence anyway, but it seems much more probable than not that Wallace had effectively been endorsed by the nobles of the Balliol party. By the late summer of 1298 the situation had altered considerably. A number of the men who had been prisoners of war or who had been obliged to perform military service for Edward in Flanders in 1297 had now achieved their release and were, not surpris-ingly, anxious to re-establish themselves in the political arena.[18] It would be uncharitable to suggest that men like John Comyn, Lord of Badenoch, John Comyn, Earl of Buchan and Robert Bruce, Earl of Carrick spent the summer of 1298 waiting for Wallace to meet a disaster, but they were certainly ready to step into his shoes when the opportunity arose.

The willingness of the Lord of Badenoch and the Earl of Carrick to take up where William Wallace left off is a strong indication that Edward had not really had a successful campaign in 1298. If the Scottish cause had seemed hopeless to them, there would have been little point in accept-ing the appointment. The Bruce and Comyn families were the two most significant elements of the Balliol party. The Comyns had come to promi-nence through a long tradition of service to Scottish kings;[19] their rise to a position of extensive political influence was based on Crown patronage, so it would have been no surprise that they favoured the continuation of an independent Scottish monarchy. Robert Bruce's decision to join the Balliol party as a Guardian of the realm on behalf of King John was a more complicated matter. If the Balliol party was successful against the English, King John would be restored, a prospect that was highly desirable from a Comyn perspective but obviously rather less so from that of Robert Bruce. It was no secret that Robert had ambitions for the crown, so why should he support the Balliol cause? Naturally the Bruce cause would have been rather closer to his heart, but Robert could not afford to have the politi-cal entity of Scotland disappear into the domains of Edward I. If Edward could successfully impose his rule in Scotland for any length of time, the sympathies of the Scottish populace might veer away from the cause of independence toward the cause of peace and stability. If Robert was ever to become king he would need to ensure that Scottish nationhood had not become a thing of the past.

CHAPTER SEVEN

Exile and Defiance

Wallace left Scotland at some point in the late summer or autumn of 1299. His defeat at Falkirk had undermined him militarily and politically; for the foreseeable future he had no major contribution to make to the Balliol cause in Scotland, and may even have been regarded as more of a liability than an asset. On the other hand, he could not be ignored or disparaged: to do so would give another propaganda coup to Edward I. There was nothing for him to do in Scotland other than join the ranks of the men-at-arms. If he happened to be killed in action he would join the roll of dead Scottish heroes and be a glorious figure in death, but if he was captured who could know what the English might be able to make of the situation? Leaving the country was a sensible option, so Wallace made his way to France. What exactly he achieved, or hoped to achieve, during his sojourn in France is difficult to say. Enthusiastic biographers have suggested that he was active in diplomatic affairs, that he served Philip IV as a soldier, that he spent his time with Duns Scotus, a prominent Scottish scholar living in Paris. One possibility that does not seem to have been considered is that Wallace was in France because he had made Scotland too hot to hold him. The new Guardians, John Comyn and Robert Bruce, probably felt that they could manage without having Wallace in the background; with his credibility as a military leader destroyed, there was little Wallace could offer other than his personal service as a man-at-arms. It is unlikely that he had anything much to offer the Scottish diplomatic effort. He may well have been an educated man in the sense of being literate, numerate and having a reasonable knowledge of Latin if, as Blind Harry tells us, he was preparing for the priesthood, but he had no experience of the ways and means of international diplomacy.

As far as we are aware, he had had no experience of soldiering before 1297 either but made a good fist of it, so it could be argued that he might have learned about making diplomatic offensives as he had military ones, but the argument is not sustainable. It is conceivable that he had seen service in the Welsh wars of Edward I, though surely someone would have noticed such a gift to English propaganda. Even if he had seen service, it would be exceedingly unlikely that he would have been party to the command processes of the army unless he had been a person of some stature socially and politically, in which case he would have been a 'weel-kent' face to plenty of English soldiers of the 1290s: medieval armies were quite small affairs. It is also possible that he served in the retinue of a major Scottish noble as a man-at-arms – indeed, it is more likely than not that he would have done so at some point in his upbringing – but, again, that would hardly have made him accustomed to command. It is clear that baronial war was not a normal part of medieval Scottish society; there had been no 'national' or 'kingly' war waged by Scots for a generation, and what there had been – the annexation of the kingdom of Man – was scarcely a major military event.

Peacetime soldiering is a very different business from wartime soldiering and it is a commonplace of history that men – and occasionally women – come to sudden prominence in wartime through a particular gift or have it thrust upon them by circumstances. Since the requirements of peacetime and wartime soldiering are so radically different, it is impossible to know which of the senior officers of an army will actually make good field commanders in the event of war. Wallace's military, and therefore also his political, career was founded on his personal ability: the skills and strength of a big man with a sword. By attracting an increasingly large following of similar men, he was effectively promoting himself in military rank through recruitment. Men joining his band of adherents were looking to receive leadership, not to exert it, so he would have faced little competition for authority as long as he was successful militarily.

The diplomatic world did not offer that sort of opportunity. By the time Wallace arrived in Paris, the Scottish diplomatic 'team' of Baldred Bisset, William of Eaglesham and Wiliam Frere, Archdeacon of Lothian, had developed its own policies and practices, it was *au fait* with the procedures and traditions of the European political arena.[1] There was no role for Wallace to perform, other than perhaps that of a heroic figure who could be shown to the French as an example of Scottish determination and chivalry. The problem with that, of course, was that sooner or later everyone of any importance in Paris would have seen or met with William

Wallace and started to question his importance. If he was such a fine soldier and man-at-arms, what was he doing in France? Why was he not fighting in Scotland?

After Falkirk, the Guardianship had passed to Sir John Comyn of Badenoch and Robert Bruce, Earl of Carrick,[2] but theirs was a difficult relationship, to say the least. In August 1299 they had been conducting operations from Selkirk forest when a fight erupted between them during a council meeting at Peebles. The report of an English agent received by Sir Robert Hastang, the Plantagenet sheriff of Roxburgh, and therefore Edward's chief military officer in the vicinity, shows the tension in the Scottish camp and is worth quoting in its entirety:

> At the council Sir David Graham demanded the lands and goods of Sir Wiliam Wallace because he was leaving the kingdom without the permission of the guardians. And Sir Malcolm Wallace, Sir William's brother, answered that neither his lands or goods should be given away, for they were protected by the peace in which Wallace had left the kingdom, since he was leaving to work for the good of kingdom. At this the two knights gave the lie to each other and drew their daggers. And since Sir David Graham was of Sir John Comyn's following and Sir Malcolm Wallace of the earl of Carrick's following it was reported to the earl of Buchan and John Comyn that a fight had broken out without their knowing it; and John Comyn leaped at the earl of Carrick and seized him by the throat, and the earl of Buchan turned on the bishop of St Andrews, declaring that treason and lesemajestie were being plotted. Eventually the Steward and others came between them and quietened them. At that moment a letter was brought from beyond the Firth of Forth, telling how Sir Alexander Comyn and Lachlan were burning and devastating the district they were in, attacking the people of Scotland. So it was ordained then that the bishop of St Andrews should have all the castles in his hands as principal guardian, and the earl of Carrick and John Comyn be with him as joint-guardians of the kingdom. And that same Wednesday, after the letter had been read, they all left Peebles.[3]

Evidently Wallace was still in Scotland in the summer of 1299, but was no longer at the centre of political or military decision-making. We should not assume that he was not active personally, but it seems that he was not at Peebles with the main body of the Scots. His departure was evidently imminent, however: hence the claims of Sir David Graham. Graham's attack on William Wallace may be an indication of the level to which the former Guardian's prestige had sunk. If Wallace had still been a popular heroic figure it would have been rash indeed for Graham to make a move on Wallace's lands and goods. It is of course possible that there was a perception that Wallace had done very nicely personally out of the Guardianship and that Graham was articulating a resentment shared by others. As a younger son, possibly a third son, Wallace would have had little prospect of acquiring land of his own that he could pass on to a son 'in heritage'. Any portion of the family estate that came into Wallace's hands would be much more likely than not to be a life interest that would return to the main body of the estate on his death.[4]

Graham's claim was surely motivated by the political agenda of his patron, Sir John Comyn, or was at least acceptable to Comyn, but attacking Wallace would have been a risky undertaking. Even if the former Guardian had become so unpopular that a move to acquire his property was unlikely to be opposed among the nobility or by the wider community, he was still a force to be reckoned with on a personal level. Graham might be able to procure a political decision in his favour, but that would not prevent William Wallace from killing him.

How Wallace spent his time in exile is a matter of debate. He certainly received a letter of credence from Phillip IV, in which the king asked his officers at the curia to give whatever help they could to his dear and trusted knight, William Wallace of Scotland.[5] Whether he actually managed to arrange an audience with the Pope is not known, though he obviously would have had little to discuss other than the political condition of Scotland. It has been suggested that he would have met with John Balliol, who was released to papal custody in 1299, but there is no evidence that he did so. By 1303 Wallace was back in Scotland, possibly at the request of William Lamberton, but not in the capacity of a significant leader. The war had continued in his absence, and the Scots had enjoyed a deal of success. No great victories had been won, but there again no great defeats had been inflicted in the period 1299–1302. The military situation had not stabilised, insofar as the Scots could neither prevent nor even confront major English armies, but the gains made by Edward's expeditions tended to be lost to the Scots once the army was dismissed. Edward was making progress; he was able to arrange for the construction of 'peles' at Selkirk and Linlithgow,[6] and was endeavouring to make another at Dunfermline. These peles were not castles, but army establishments. Their function was to provide a number of centres of operation for mobile columns of men-at-arms who could impose Edward's rule throughout the vicinity. The forces of his 'permanent' administration were not up to the task of extending his rule throughout the country, but the Scots were incapable of dislodging them. The absence of battles of great stature did not mean the presence of peace. The nature of the war was largely a business of demonstrating local superiority in order to be able to exert lordship, and was almost exclusively conducted by small parties of men-at-arms, a milieu in which William Wallace would have been perfectly at home, and which he doubtless joined on his return from France.

The Guardians had not been able to expel the English from the whole country, but they certainly had more control over more of Scotland more of the time than the Plantagenets. The vital castle of Stirling had been recovered after the battle of Stirling Bridge and remained in Scottish hands until after the Strathord agreement of 1304. The economy was functioning, sheriffs and judges carried out their normal duties and the war was being conducted in an effective, if unadventurous, way.[7] The course of events during the absence of Wallace had proven that he was not indispensable to the Balliol party: the former Guardian was now just one of many men-at-arms and knights serving the cause of King John.

The loss of the Guardianship, and perhaps his prolonged absence overseas, undoubtedly took the shine off Wallace's reputation to some degree, but he was still probably capable of attracting the adherence of men of a similar station and outlook, if only on the basis of his personal prowess as a fighter – which was, of course, the foundation of his rise to power in the first place. He was no longer a senior figure in the command structure, but he does seem to have had a following of his own and to have been active against the English, though not, perhaps, really under the command of the Balliol party. He does not appear to have been involved in their operations to any great extent, though that may be more a reflection of the survival of record material than of the level and intensity of his activity. He was not, for example, present at the battle of Roslin in February 1303, though it was precisely the sort of action where the Scots had most need of men of his status, but he was in action against a substantial force under Sir Aymer de Valence at Earnside in September 1304.[8] By this time, however, the political situation had changed radically. In July 1302 the French had been badly beaten by the Flemings at Courtrai, and Philip IV had been obliged to make peace with Edward. Until this point Philip had been able to insist on the inclusion of the Scots in any truce arrangements: Philip's weakness was Edward's opportunity. He was at last able to have peace with France without abstaining from war in Scotland. The Scots had struggled to contain Edward when he was at war with the French; they had little chance of defeating him unaided, and in February 1304 the Balliol party came to terms with Edward's representatives at Strathord.[9] The relatively lenient terms allowed to the Scots in general did not extend to certain specified individuals. William Wallace, no longer referred to as a knight, was carefully excluded. No man was to accept him into Edward's peace on any terms other than unconditional surrender.[10]

Part of the price the nobles of the Balliol party paid for acceptance into Edward's peace was, naturally, the acceptance of an obligation to uphold the law and to persecute the enemies of the king.[11] Wallace was not the only man to have been excluded from the Strathord agreement, but he was certainly one of Edward's most urgent priorities. Quite why Wallace chose to remain in Scotland at this juncture is something of a mystery. A man of his evident talents as a combatant would have been able to find reasonably lucrative employment overseas. While patriotic fervour was surely part of his motivation, he may have felt, and probably correctly, that he would not be able to have a secure future wherever he went. Edward was obviously bent on procuring Wallace for trial if he possibly could, but there is no reason to assume that he would not have settled for his murder if all else failed.

The capture of Sir William Wallace at Glasgow in 1305 by Sir John Menteith can hardly have come as a surprise to anyone, including, perhaps especially, Wallace himself. Although he must still have been able to motivate men and women to assist him in his struggle, once the Balliol party had made their peace at Stathord, Wallace must have been aware that his days were numbered. The men who had served the Balliol cause – nobles, burgesses, clerics and commoners – were now in the enemy camp and were obliged to do everything in their power to bring an end to Wallace's operations. From the moment King John accepted Philip IVs change in his policy toward Scotland (though he probably had no choice in the matter and little interest in recovering his kingdom anyway), the Balliol cause was finally and fatally compromised. The Scots could not rationally continue a war to restore the king if the king did not want to return to Scotland. Edward I's administration was beginning to achieve effective lordship in an increasingly large portion of the country, and the people were exhausted. Wallace and men like him – there were probably others who, for whatever reason, had been effectively excluded from the peace agreement – were not an effective source of authority or a realistic focus for recruitment. In the summer of 1297 Wallace had been able to raise men in large numbers relatively easily, initially through his personal abilities as a man-at-arms and a leader, later by virtue of the fact that he had enjoyed some success in battle. An important factor in the recruitment of Wallace's army in July and August 1297 was the fact that it existed at all;

it provided a vehicle for political – which under the circumstances almost inevitably meant military – activity. At some point that summer, William Wallace's force made a transition. It ceased to be a retinue of men-at-arms making attacks of opportunity on isolated elements of the occupation and started to become, by medieval standards, a large army with much more sophisticated needs. It also became a political institution, one made for the purpose of liberating the country from the Plantagenet occupation; as such, it was a focus for men who were willing to fight.

By the summer of 1305 there was no Scottish army, just the odd handful of men who would not or could not be reconciled to the Edwardian rule that now extended to their fellow Scots. Whatever sympathy there may have been for William Wallace in the political community or in the society of Scotland generally, there must have been many who felt that 'enough was enough' and that it was long past time the business was settled. The Balliol cause was discredited, thousands of people had been killed, ruined and imprisoned and the economy was deeply damaged; furthermore, Wallace had a price on his head. There would be rewards for the person who captured Wallace, but there would also very likely be sharp treatment for anyone who sheltered him. Wallace's standing in among the wider community of Scots may not have been quite so healthy as the chroniclers and historians suggest. His period of personal rule had come to an end after the battle of Falkirk; Fordoun, Bower and Blind Harry all blame the treachery of the Comyns and/or Robert Bruce for the Falkirk disaster, but at the time Wallace must have carried the responsibility in the eyes of most people – he was the commanding officer. Scottish chronicle writers of the later fourteenth and fifteenth centuries had something of a shared agenda: animosity to English expansionism and the glorification of heroes long dead. There was no mileage for them in telling readers anything that might throw any doubt on the esteem of the common people of Scotland for William Wallace, but after Falkirk his name may not have been a good advertisement for the Balliol cause.

Wallace's survival in Scotland from the Strathord agreement until his eventual capture does indicate that he was either still well thought of by a substantial part of the community, who were willing to risk life and limb to support him, or that he had sufficient military strength in his following to demand whatever he needed. Had he been entirely reliant on violence to provision his men and horses, his remaining popularity would have evaporated quickly and English propagandists would have been quick to recount his depredations, but it is most probable that he drew aid both from the willing and the unwilling. Increasingly, however, his position was untenable. He could no longer attract large numbers of men to his banner, and even if he did, what was he going to do with them? In 1297 he had enjoyed enough support in the political community to allow him to assume the Guardianship. The recovery of the Scottish administration in 1297 was not the work of William Wallace alone; if anything, it is possible that Wallace, as a proven leader, was as much adopted as accepted by those members of the Balliol party of the Scottish political community as were at liberty. Without the support of the political community, there would have been no Scottish administration to carry on the business of governing the country, thereby allowing Wallace to get on with the war. In 1304 that community had accepted the lordship of Edward I; as Edward's officers and as prominent figures in society, they had an obligation to capture Wallace, and it was inevitable that they should do so. In August 1305 Wallace was captured by Sir John Menteith at Glasgow, and was sent south to face trial.

William Wallace's trial was never intended to be a demonstration of justice, just the recitation of a formal litany of charges presumed to be true by the fact that they had been made. There was no question of a defence. There was no defence Wallace could make that would change the outcome of the trial, but it would have been redundant anyway, in the sense that to defend his position would be a recognition of Edward I's right to hold him for trial at all. Wallace was accused of treason, but he had never given his allegiance to King Edward and had fought him tooth and nail as the aggressive invader that he most certainly was. The point of the trial was not to assess the guilt of William Wallace, but to demonstrate the power and majesty of Edward I, to show clearly the Scottish war was at an end, to show what happened to people who resisted his kingship, to give a symbol of vengeance achieved to the subjects of England and to provide a great entertainment for the citizens of London.

Executions continued to be a public spectacle until well into the nineteenth century; indeed, their removal from public view was more a matter of the changing tastes of the ruling class than of any apathy on the part of the community. Hangings were relatively commonplace, though by no means a daily occurrence, but ritualistic killings and dismemberings were a great rarity and were welcomed as spectacular entertainments. William Wallace made the journey to the scaffold dragged on a hurdle behind a horse for about four miles around the City of London. It would have been a slow business, unlikely to have taken less than two hours and very probably much longer, since the streets would have been crowded by Londoners keen to see a rare spectacle. Considerable damage could be inflicted on the body by drawing it through the streets, and it would seem that it was not uncommon for the accused to be wrapped in hide, to protect them sufficiently to ensure that they would still be alive when they reached their destination.

Dragged from Westminster to the Tower, then to Aldgate and finally to Smithfield, Wallace was given to executioners to hang by the neck, but not until death. While he still lived he was cut down, and, still conscious, had his torso split open so that his organs could be removed and burnt on a brazier in front of him. At length – and the fame of the executioner rested on his ability to make the death of the victim slow as well as agonising – his head was removed for display on London Bridge and the four quarters of his body sent to Newcastle, Berwick, Perth and Stirling: a trophy for the people of Northumberland after their sufferings at the hands of William Wallace, and a warning to the inhabitants of Berwick, Stirling and Perth.

Edward's determination to ensure the complete destruction of William Wallace must have been apparent at the time, and it is worth giving some thought as to why the king of England, having successfully brought the Scots into his peace, should have been so relentless in his pursuit of a man who, though he had been of great stature at one time, was now 'yesterday's man'. For reasons of personal prestige, it was important that someone should be seen to pay a dire penalty for the trouble to which the king of England had been put. A failure to ensure that the people were aware that he had utterly suppressed the Scots might be construed as weakness, or at least lead to resentment that the cost in blood and money that the English had borne in Scotland had not resulted in a clear victory. In order to procure a settlement in February 1304, Edward had had to offer very lenient terms to the Balliol party, largely because he had come to the conclusion that he could not secure Scotland without the acceptance and active support of the political community. Had he seized and executed one or more of the Balliol party leaders – the Earl of Buchan for example – he would have compromised any prospect of gaining the confidence of the rest of the nobility. He might have liked very much to have taken action against several of them, but not if he wanted to reach an early settlement. The Scots had effectively been abandoned by their own king, but they were not finished militarily and it might yet be a major struggle to overcome them. If Edward was to have peace without waging more campaigns that he could not really afford, he would have to pay a price; he would have to settle for Wallace as the focus of his vengeance.

Edward not only wanted peace, he wanted it in a hurry. He was no longer a young man, nor so hale as he had been in the past, and would have been eager to see his projects completed before he died. If he could manage to make his rule acceptable in Scotland he would have extended the scope of the kingship he had inherited, a very natural ambition for a medieval monarch, and he wanted men to think well of him when he was dead. If Scotland was at peace and under his rule when he died – an event that could not be many years distant – he would have been a 'success' within his own frame of reference. Even if his son were to 'lose' Scotland in the future, the loss would reflect on his failure to maintain Edward's legacy, not Edward's failure to provide a secure and stable patrimony.

The men who joined Edward's peace do not seem to have been particularly committed to the capture of Wallace, given that he remained at large for nearly eighteen months, but some of them at least were probably not unhappy to hear of his demise. If the Strathord agreement was to be effective, men like Wallace would have to curb their enthusiasm for the Balliol cause; if it was to be a temporary expedient, a lull in the hostilities rather than a final accord, the activities of Wallace would be less than desirable. As long as they kept fighting, Edward would maintain garrisons in Scotland capable of mounting operations and imposing his government. Like the 'Real' and 'Continuity' IRA splinter groups of recent years, Wallace, and men like him, may have been seen as an obstacle to progress, even by the most sympathetic observers. William had provided leadership for the Scottish cause for a critical period in 1297–98 and had doubtless served his prince assiduously thereafter, but his capture may have come as something of a relief to the people of Scotland in 1305.

CHAPTER EIGHT

But What Was It All *For*?

Never one to miss an opportunity, Edward I was able to manipulate the various claimants to the Scottish crown in the Great Cause of 1291–92 into accepting him as their feudal superior. Over the following three years, he goaded the successful candidate, King John I, into 'rebellion' through consistently undermining the authority and therefore the prestige and credibility of his kingship by hearing appeals from John's courts and eventually, in 1295, demanding military service from King John and a number of Scottish magnates for his campaign against the French. King John made his defiance to Edward, repudiating his acceptance of Edward as liege lord on the grounds that it had been given under duress and that Edward was acting beyond the bounds of reasonable behaviour. Conscious that they could not readily withstand Edward on their own, the Scots needed to find allies and formed an offensive and defensive alliance with the French. None of this impressed Edward in the slightest and he invaded Scotland in April 1296, destroyed the Scottish cavalry in battle at Dunbar, deposed John, took the allegiance of a great swathe of Scottish noble, clerical and commercial society, led his troops as far north as Elgin, installed his own administration and made his way to Berwick, where he called a Parliament at the end of August.

His remarkable progress through the east of Scotland was a *tour de force* of conventional military practice; towns and castles surrendered on his arrival and there was no sign of resistance on the part of the Scots when Edward returned to his other affairs in England and on the continent, leaving several small garrisons to secure his occupation. If he assumed that he had dealt with Scotland, he was much mistaken. Within the year he faced the opposition of a Scottish administration which soon controlled virtually all of Scotland north of the Tay and was making steady progress in reducing English power through the rest of the country.

The extent to which the entire period between 1286 and 1307 is seen as little more than a backdrop to the careers of Scotland's most cherished heroes – William Wallace and Robert Bruce – is proof positive of the remarkable success of Bruce propaganda,[1] constructed both in his own lifetime and in the works of Barbour, Fordoun, Wyntoun and Bower in the following century and a half. They, and their successors right down to the twentieth century, tended to portray the efforts of the Scots in resisting Edward I as a vehicle for the heroism and martyrdom of Wallace and a delaying action to keep the English at bay until the right circumstances developed for Robert Bruce to seize the throne just a few months after Wallace's betrayal, capture, trial and execution.

We can be confident that the situation was not seen in that light by the participants in and supporters of the various Guardianships[2] which endeavoured to maintain Scotland's status as a sovereign country with a sovereign lord, King John, even if he was a captive in a foreign land. In theory, and certainly in practice during the early years of the conflict, the Guardian administrations were committed to the restoration of the Balliol line rather than the recovery of Scottish independence by any means, although the latter stages of the conflict were perhaps more a question of holding out for good terms of surrender. Had Edward wished to do so, he could have restored John to the Scottish throne at any time, on the same basis as John's previous kingship. The extent to which that could be considered 'independence' is perhaps open to question from a twenty-first-century perspective, although, having been deposed once already, it would not be surprising if John refused to be reinstated. He apparently made a deposition to an English notary public to the effect that he had encountered nothing but trouble among the Scots, and intimated that he had no desire to have anything much to do with them in the future. John's refusal would have utterly compromised the position of those fighting the Plantagenet occupation: they would have had no cause to fight for.

If a Balliol restoration was a course of action Edward ever considered there is no record of it, and the Scots continued to fight in the name of King John, though to what extent the conflict developed into a war of national identity, and how quickly, is impossible to say. It is clear that by 1304 at the latest some men were quite prepared to carry on the king's fight even without a king to fight for, but that does not mean that they would be willing to do so forever. Although medieval monarchs were, in many ways, rather closer to their subjects than contemporary ones, they were seen as the ultimate source of authority and enjoyed a certain amount of awe that would be denied a mere officer of state, even one so exalted as a Guardian of the Realm.

The Guardians exercised the power of the king, but with the authority of the Community of the Realm, or at least with the assent of the political community.[3] With the sole exception of William Wallace, all of the men who served as Guardians for John I's kingship were men of great standing in their communities and of some prominence nationally. The most junior of them, other than Wallace, was Andrew Murray, a man of baronial rank, of considerable wealth and very well connected throughout the noble community of the north, particularly to the Comyn family.

The Scots had some experience of non-regal government. During the reign of Margaret of Norway, throughout the Great Cause, and possibly in the reign of John Balliol himself, Scotland had been ruled by Guardians.[4] These Guardians were drawn from the uppermost ranks of what medieval society perceived as the most valid representation of the Scottish people, the Community of the Realm.[5] With the exception of Murray and Wallace all of the Guardians were magnates, whether temporal or ecclesiastical; they were men accustomed to wielding authority in their own sphere of power and had been entrusted with regal powers by their peers; they could be just as easily undermined as supported by noble interest groups and were therefore vulnerable to threats of disobedience, defiance or even defection if they offended other members of the aristocracy.

By the standards of medieval political structures, the willingness of the Scots to accept non-regal government, particularly the willingness to accept government by committee on behalf of a minor, and a female minor at that, indicates a remarkably sophisticated political consciousness. The Community of the Realm was the practical expression of the 'political identity or nationhood'[6] of the Scots over and above the institution of monarchy. The Community of the Realm may have been dominated by the most powerful alignments of the nobility, but it represented the 'totality of the Kings free subjects' and 'the political entity in which they and the King were comprehended'.[7] The practical need to carry on the kings' government when there was, effectively, no king at all was perfectly understood, and the authority of the Community of the Realm was seen as adequate for the provision of government during a royal minority or as a forum in which to address a specific problem, such as a succession dispute, but it was not considered an adequate permanent substitute for the personal rule of a monarch. Like any other medieval monarchy, to make Scotland's government 'complete' she needed a king, so the primary objective of all the Guardians (including Robert Bruce) from 1297 to 1304 was to bring about the restoration of King John.

In order to achieve this, the Guardians would have to procure his release from English (then papal, then French) custody,[8] and in order to do that they would have to establish and maintain a secure Scottish sovereignty.[9] In order to achieve administrative credibility at home and diplomatic credibility abroad, the Guardians needed to establish a Scottish administration in direct competition with that of King Edward, and the main focus of that administration would have to be the successful pursuit of the war, leading to the ejection of the occupation. The speed with which such a government was erected would suggest that the views of the Guardians were not at odds with the sympathies of the population as a whole, and the Guardians were able to exercise effective power in all the departments of medieval government – judicial, legislative, diplomatic and, above all, military – with the authority conferred on them by the Community of the Realm. To what extent Wallace had these powers conferred after the battle of Stirling Bridge and to what extent he simply assumed them is impossible to say. It seems clear that he and Murray had the benefit of a considerable degree of support from the traditional sources of political leadership, and Wallace certainly seems to have had the wholehearted enthusiasm of the army, so it would have taken a very confident person to contest his authority.

If the Scots were fighting for the reinstatement of King John, what were they hoping to achieve if they were successful? The constant themes of the Scots in their negotiations with the English and their petitions to the papacy, other than the return of the king, is the demand for the reintroduction of the laws and customs of John's reign, the acceptance by Edward I of Scottish sovereignty and the removal of English garrisons. The restoration of the king may not have been quite so unlikely a prospect as it might seem; the Scots were remarkably successful in their diplomatic campaigns from 1297, until Philip IV was obliged to abandon his Scottish allies through the defeat of his army at Courtrai, an event that effectively removed Phillip's capacity, if not his willingness, to carry on his conflict with Edward. The transfer of King John to the custody of the Pope and then to King Philip of France must have been an encouragement to the Scots generally. One man for whom it was not good news was Robert Bruce, Earl of Carrick and Lord of Annandale. The restoration of the Balliol line would seriously compromise any prospect of a Bruce succession to the Scottish throne. Bruce might be prepared to fight under the Balliol banner as a vehicle for his own career ambitions, but not if the return of King John was to become a reality: Bruce made his peace with King Edward and joined the occupation. The defection of Robert to the

Plantagenet cause has been a difficult topic for Scottish and English writers; it undermines Robert's patriotic credentials. However, as with most people, Robert's chief priority was himself and his dependants. Bruce may have fought for King John in his absence, but he had not been prepared to turn out for the Balliol cause in the summer of 1296, a choice which he might have cause to regret should John be restored.

Resentment of the occupation generally was undoubtedly a factor encouraging resistance, so it is worth giving some thought to the aspects of King Edward's rule that engendered that resent. The clerical community of Scotland was broadly supportive of the campaign against the English. Part of their interest lay in the unusual relationship between the Scottish Church and the Holy See. As a 'Special Daughter' of the Papacy, Scottish prelates were free of archiepiscopal supervision. If Scotland were to be annexed by England, the Scottish Church would sooner or later be made subject to either Canterbury or York, which would have serious repercussions for their financial position and for their powers of patronage and, of course, their own career prospects.[10]

The nobility faced a similar problem. The distribution of offices under the Crown (and, of course, the ability to influence its wearer) would be adversely affected – in their view – by a change not only in the ruling house but in the actual seat of government. Scottish nobles may not always have been in full accord with their kings, but at least the king was reasonably accessible. The expense of attending the king in London or Winchester would have been enormous, and cutting a dash among the English aristocracy would have been beyond the financial capacity of all but the very richest Scottish nobles. Like the clergy, the nobility feared the 'intrusion' of outsiders into positions of authority. The networks of lordships and offices through which the great families of Scotland furthered their interests and protected their adherents would be destabilised by the appointment of people with no interest in the domestic politics of the Scots. In a sense, the Wars of Independence could be described as an issue about whether the great and good preferred to be the big fish in a small pond or, relatively, rather less significant fish in a much larger pond. The choice was not a simple one: the assimilation of Scottish kingship into English kingship would certainly mean that access to the king would be more difficult and costly and that there would be greater competition for patronage, but the power and prestige of English kings was very great indeed, and the potential for advancement from English monarchs was very much greater than anything Scottish kings could offer, including the possibility of profitable service overseas.

The noble classes were not alone in their concerns. The gentry, burgesses and wealthier tenants were faced with the likelihood of higher taxes and increased obligations of military service. In practice, very little was demanded in the way of military service[11] beyond customary man-at-arms obligations on the nobility and the more successful members of the mercantile community, and taxes are resented whether they are increased or not, regardless of whose name they are raised in. Whether or not Edward's occupation was very onerous was not necessarily the issue: it was perceived as being more burdensome than the government of Scottish kings had been and it was thought that things would probably get worse rather than better the longer it continued – or at least that was the claim of the Scots in the surrender arrangements of 1304.

The Community of the Realm did not, of course, represent the whole of Scottish society, nor was it intended that it should; it only directly represents those with an obvious stake in the country. The labouring classes may have paid their rents and served in the army, but their views are unrecorded. It is reasonable to assume that in the main decisions of allegiance were the province of the landlord classes, but it would be rash to assume that the lord would not take account of the opinions and interests of his subordinates. Further, if called upon, the tenant was obliged to fight under his lord, but he might choose to fight anyway – Wallace was able to raise troops without the support of the nobility.[12] Given the popularity of Wallace's campaigning, it is not inconceivable that some nobles, in order to show 'good lordship', may have had to support the Guardians against their own inclinations.[13] If Wallace's rising involved a measure of social discontent[14] a wise lord might be obliged to take care to retain the confidence of his people; on the other hand, the lord as an individual might be captured and persuaded or forced to serve Edward and find himself on the opposite side of the battlefield to his tenants.[15]

Alongside the social and personal issues, the Scots fought out of injured pride and xenophobia, and they fought for what they saw as a national interest – there was a widespread sympathy for the concept of national 'liberty', in the sense of political independence, and they fought against 'the kind of intensive government which they were quite unaccustomed to, and which contrasted greatly, with a touch of rose-tinted nostalgia, with life under the King of Scots'.[16] If we acknowledge the consistency with which the Scots seek the restoration of their country's autonomy, and the frequency with which we encounter expressions of and reference to nationality, we must accept nationalism as a force in medieval Scotland[17] and therefore as one of the issues for which the Scots fought between 1297 and 1304.

Traditionally, historians have been less than generous to the leaders of Scottish resistance to Edward, with the exceptions of Moray and Wallace. The early death of Moray made him an impeccable patriot; he did not have time to do anything of a questionable nature (such as changing sides) or to be associated with any disasters. Wallace's death made him a hero, but his power in the Community of the Realm rested solely on his success as a military leader, and he lost his position as Guardian shortly after the defeat at Falkirk.[18] Wallace's term of government lasted for little more than a year and, by the later stages of the war period of 1296–1304, he was no longer in a position to come to terms with the English administration. His successors, John Comyn and Robert Bruce, stand accused of self-interest, duplicity, manipulation and both the threat and the reality of physical violence. It should come as no surprise that all of these criticisms are perfectly valid. If the new Guardians were careful of their interests, we should bear in mind that they did have an awful lot of interests to be careful of and that, without the strength and prestige afforded them by these interests – land, patronage, Crown offices, alliances and allegiances – it would not have been possible for them to govern. Duplicity and manipulation is the very stuff of political life in any society, and the violence of Bruce and Comyn is perhaps shocking, but surely not surprising.

The tension between the two Guardians – Comyn, premier baron in the realm, head of a family with a strong tradition of Crown service,[19] and irreproachably patriotic, and Bruce, whose wholehearted commitment might be questioned, given his regal ambition –was sufficiently strong to make the appointment of a third Guardian necessary. The political community chose Bishop Lamberton, to keep his colleagues from one another's throats. The government of the Guardians was less effective than it might have been because of internal dissent, but Scotland was not always easily governed by kings in peacetime let alone by regencies or guardianships in wartime. If we assume either 'altruism' or 'self-interest' on the part of the Guardians, we assume too much, and must remember that the interests of the great and powerful were not necessarily inimical to those of the society as a whole. Most people, most of the time, prefer peace and stability to any other condition, and the various Guardians were endeavouring to achieve just that. Under the circumstances prevailing in Scotland in 1296–1304, keeping any kind of an administration afloat was quite an achievement in itself.

The factors that brought the Scots to the negotiating table were largely external rather internal. Diplomatic isolation, resulting from the Anglo-French peace agreement of May 1303[20] and in particular the reduced likelihood of King Philip allowing King John to return to Scotland, turned a hard struggle into an impossible task. The position of the Scots was not promising before this turn of events: Edward was able to pay a great deal of attention to the military and political situations in Scotland in 1303–04. His foreign and domestic problems eased sufficiently for his to pass that winter at Linlithgow on Lothian, supervising operations against the Balliol party and preventing them from recovering their position through the winter months, a pattern that had developed over the years since 1296.

By the close of 1303, the inability of the Guardians to provide a king and the physical and economic exhaustion of the country overcame the will of the community to continue the fight. Due to the shortage of documents, it is impossible to develop a clear picture of the Scottish administration, other than to assume that the institutions of the state continued in much the same fashion as they had under King John; otherwise, what indeed were the Scots fighting for?

Regardless of *how* exactly the Scottish government functioned, the fact is that it *did* function. The Guardians were able to exercise the power necessary to call parliaments and councils,[21] collect rents and military service, hold courts and conduct a vigorous diplomatic campaign, while waging war against a vastly better-resourced opponent. Neither the war nor the diplomacy would pay for themselves, so revenue must have been raised, with all that that implies for the existence of chancery[22] and exchequer[23] and the willingness of the community to accept the authority of these institutions. The only part of the administration that might be expected to support itself from its own income was the judiciary,[24] which goes some way to explaining the determination of the Scots to speedily provide sheriffs in the counties they recovered, although the use of the sheriff's position as a visible evidence of the power of the government was also an important consideration. As the chief financial, judicial and military officer, whose appointment lay in the hands of the Crown, the sheriff, assuming he could exert his authority effectively, was a useful focus for the sympathetic and a deterrent to the unsympathetic.

The Balliol party maintained their struggle against Edwardian occupation for a period of more than seven years, and though they failed to achieve the restoration of King John or the political independence of Scotland, they were never overwhelmed by their opposition. An indication of the success of the Scots can be found in the terms of their eventual surrender. The rather lenient terms that Edward agreed with almost all of the Scots, as individuals and as representatives of their cause, do not suggest an abject surrender, and although Edward's commitment to the laws and customs of King John's reign was obviously open to question, he was not above dealing with problems in his Scottish domain by referring to the practices used in 'the days of the King of Scotland'. The continuation of established practice was not a sop to Scottish sentiments; it was in line with Edward's general policy toward Scotland. He had no great interest in changing the way in which Scotland was governed, only that it should be governed strictly in his own interest. Had he been successful in the conquest of Scotland, then no doubt over the succeeding years Scottish legal, commercial and military practices would have gradually fallen into line with those in England, but that would really be incidental to Edward. What he wanted from Scotland was a secure northern border, money and military service, and the recognition and reality of his kingship throughout the British Isles.

Of course, whether or not the survival of an independent Scottish government should be viewed as an achievement is dependent on a particular point of view. There was nothing particularly natural or inevitable about the development of a Scottish nation, and there was nothing inevitable about its surviving Edward's attempt at annexation. The Community of the Realm did not of course represent all Scots: some were actively engaged against the 'Patriotic' cause, and for a variety of reasons – the search for stability, peer pressure, the fact that one's life and livelihood were in an occupied zone or that one had homage obligations to Edward I. Most importantly, resented or not, the occupation did gain an increasing acceptance in the community, if raising revenue can be taken as a measure of the effectiveness of the government.[25] Such growing acceptance does not necessarily imply intimidation on the part of the English or despair on the part of the Scots; it is more a matter of the Scots adapting to a new order. The nascent nationalism to be found among some Scots was by no means universal; for some, the importance of homage given – even in the rather questionable circumstances of 1296 – was of greater significance, or was at least taken seriously enough to deter casual defections.

Over and above the threats to life, limb and property risked in resisting Edward (and it was obviously rather easier for the people in the bosom of a Scottish administration to be patriotic) it was, as Fiona Watson has pointed out,[26] difficult for people to be sure what constituted the correct ethical response to conflicts of allegiance. Promises extracted under duress could in theory legitimately be repudiated, or allegiance could be refused by the strong-hearted, but either was a risky undertaking in the volatile environment of medieval Scotland. Acceptance of Edward's rule could have very real attractions: for the nobility, who would obtain protection for their life and possessions, for the clerics, who would ensure the security of their appointments, and, potentially, for quite ordinary people like the 'King's husbandmen',[27] who petitioned King Edward for greater security in their tenancies. The careers of Malise, Earl of Strathearn and his eldest son (also Malise) clearly show the problems of divided loyalties among the magnates. Malise the elder could reasonably claim that his initial submission to Edward in 1296 was made under duress, but with his two younger sons hostage in England, he can scarcely be said to have had freedom of action. Malise left Edward's peace to support the Guardians after the battle of Stirling Bridge, by which time his sons had become members of Edward of Caernarvon's court. After the surrender at Irvine he served Edward I and then Edward II faithfully until captured at the fall of Perth, but his son served Robert I throughout his career. He apparently defied his father out of 'purely nationalist sentiment',[28] but the pragmatic value of being assured of having a family member on the winning side was surely obvious to all concerned.

The greatest achievement of the Scots in their kingless years was simply the maintenance of a Scottish kingdom without the supposedly vital component of the king. The Community of the Realm, as represented by the Guardians, acted in what it perceived to be the interests of the country, and the government worked through the traditional agencies of the country. The same offices and officers of state endured in the civil sphere, and although there is probably a considerable measure of truth in the view that Wallace's early success was based on a 'popular movement with a measure of social discontent in its make-up'[29] the forces employed in support of the Balliol government by MacDougall and Bruce in the west and by Moray in the north[30] were mustered by the 'normal' officers of the Crown, fulfilling their traditional roles as leaders in their local communities.

The ineffectiveness of these forces has as much to do with the generally demilitarised nature of thirteenth-century Scotland as defeat in battle at Dunbar in 1296. The development of an effective military strategy is the most significantly innovative area of the administrators' efforts,[31] and the ability of John Comyn to extract such reasonable terms as he did in 1304 speaks volumes for the partial success of the Scots in the field, even though their policies proved inadequate to the task of defeating the English in general engagements. The continual low-intensity war conducted by the Scots after the battle of Falkirk may have been unglamorous, but it was effective.

Fiona Watson prefaces her book *Under the Hammer* with a quotation from Edmund Burke: 'I venture to say no war can be long carried on against the will of the people'. This is surely crucial to our understanding

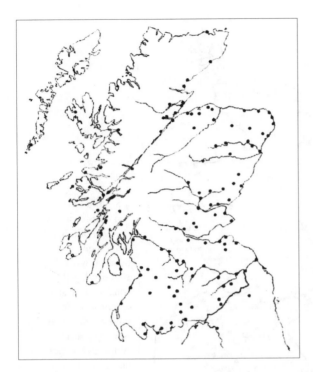

Clockwise from above left:
1 Scottish castles and fortresses. Scotland had little experience of war in the century preceding Edward I's invasion and there were relatively few major castles, most of those being royal establishments.

2 Seal of King Alexander III of Scotland. The unexpected death of Alexander III in 1286 followed by the death of his heir – his granddaughter Margaret – plunged Scotland into a succession crisis.

3 Parliament of Edward I. Edward's ambition of achieving a single kingdom in Britain was not initially shared by many of his subjects and he experienced considerable opposition from the English Parliament.

4 Scottish towns and cities, *c.*1300. At the time of Edward I's invasion Scotland was a well-developed administrative and commercial entity; however, the towns were very small. Although Froissart likened Edinburgh to the city of Tours, it is unlikely that any other Scottish town had a population in excess of 10,000.

5 Letter patent of John I. Letters patent were a normal instrument of government in England and Scotland throughout the later Middle Ages.

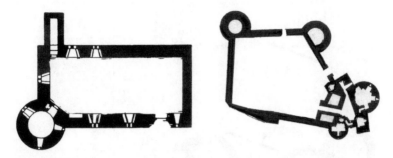

Above left: 6 Rait Hall house plan. Castles were relatively rare in thirteenth-century Scotland. Most of the minor aristocracy lived in hall houses like this one, possibly surrounded by a palisade.

Above right: 7 Dirleton Castle plan. One of only a small number of major up-to-date castles in thirteenth-century Scotland, Dirleton was a significant stronghold for the English occupation in Lothian.

Above left: 8 *Scalacronica*. Written by Sir Thomas Grey of Northumberland while he was a prisoner of war of the Scots in the mid-fourteenth century, *Scalacronica* is a particularly valuable source since it was written by someone who actually participated in the wars.

Above right: 9 The Wallace Monument. The monument was built in the nineteenth century and overlooks the site of the battle of Stirling Bridge.

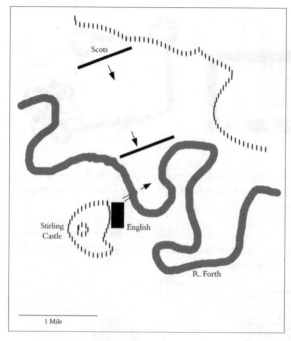

10 Sketch map of the battle of Stirling Bridge. The defeat of Sir Hugh Cressingham's army at Stirling in September 1297 confirmed Wallace's status as a significant leader in the struggle against Edward I.

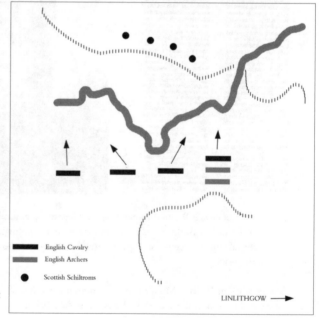

11 Sketch map of the battle of Falkirk. The defeat of Wallace at Falkirk undermined his political prominence, but heavy casualties and failure of supply forced Edward I to retreat after the battle.

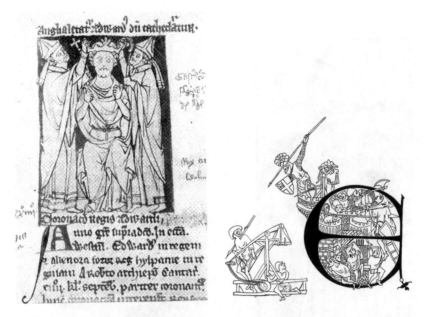

Above left: 12 The coronation of Edward I. Aware that he did not have much longer to live, Edward strove to achieve a settlement that would be acceptable to most of the Scottish political community, but the imposed 'peace' only lasted for six months after the execution of Wallace.

Above right: 13 Illustrated capital from Edward II's charter to Carlisle. Although it had been an important Scottish town in the reign of William the Lion, Carlisle was a crucial part of the defences of northern England against William Wallace and later against Robert I.

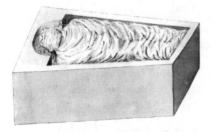

14 An eighteenth-century illustration of Edward I's body when his tomb was opened in 1774. The body was apparently well preserved.

Clockwise from above left:

15 Stone grave effigy of a soldier from the west of Scotland wearing a bacinet helmet – the height of military fashion at the close of the thirteenth century.

16 The arms of Edward I showing the three 'leopards of Anjou' that were the traditional symbol of English kingship. The leopard was considered to be a brave and noble beast, but prone to deceitfulness – highly appropriate for Edward I.

17 The enforced deposition of John I (John Balliol) in 1296 from a sixteenth-century Scottish armorial. The Balliol party fought for John's restoration from 1296 to 1304.

Above left: 18 The Stone of Destiny. Looted by Edward I in 1296 and installed in the Coronation chair at Westminster, it is now on display to the public at Edinburgh Castle.

Above right: 19 A particularly ornate example of a stone grave effigy. This is a good example of the convergence of Highland and Lowland cultural practice. The nature of the effigy is very Gaelic, but the soldier depicted could have served in any European army of the late Middle Ages.

Clockwise from above left:

20 The battle of Stirling Bridge. In the summer of 1297 William Wallace and Sir Andrew Murray raised armies in southern and northern Scotland and defeated the English under Sir Hugh de Cressingham.

21 Victorian illustration of the battle of Halidon Hill, 1332. Although Halidon Hill occurred a quarter of a century after the death of Wallace, the armour and weaponry depicted is in fact typical of those borne by the soldiers of Wallace and Murray's armies in 1297.

22 A typical late-thirteenth-century man-at-arms. Although plate additions were gaining in popularity, many Scottish and English gentry would still have served in simple mail suits of this nature. The lance would have been considerably longer – between three and four metres.

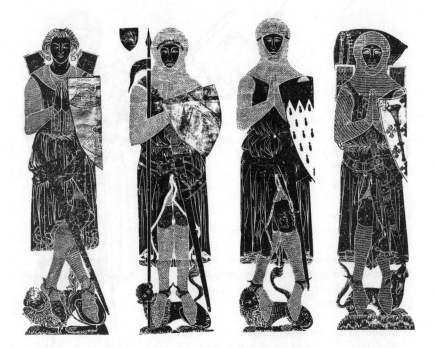

Left to right:

23 Sir Robert Setvans, an English knight who served Edward I in Scotland. The projections at his shoulders – ailettes – were a short-lived fashion of the later thirteenth and early fourteenth centuries. They were made from wood or stiffened leather and depicted the coat of arms of the owner.

24 A brass depicting Sir John d'Abernon, an English knight who served in Scotland under Edward I and Edward II. Sir John died in 1330, but his armour is typical of the late thirteenth and early fourteenth century.

25 and 26 Sir Robert Bures and Sir Roger de Trumpington. The devices borne on shields and trappings were of little value for battlefield identification other than to show that the wearer was a man of some substance and therefore worth holding for ransom if captured.

Clockwise from above:

27 Welsh infantry of the late Middle Ages. The archer is apparently carrying a short bow rather than the longbow associated with medieval Wales; however, since longbows were common to English, Scottish and Welsh armies this is probably an example of artistic licence.

28 Armour of the 'cyclas' period of the early fourteenth century. Armour of this style was worn by knights and men-at-arms throughout northern and western Europe.

29 A lightly armed Scottish spearman after the British Library MS 'Liber A'. The spear has been made much shorter than would normally have been the case – presumably to save space on the original manuscript.

Above left: 30 A bearded Scottish soldier. The sword was a vital part of a gentleman's armoury, but the spear and polearms were the primary weapons in battle.

Above right: 31 A Scottish man-at-arms of the thirteenth/fourteenth century. The padded garment – made of cloth tubes stuffed with raw wool – would probably have covered a chain-mail hauberk.

32 The capture of Wallace in August 1305 at last brought Scotland under the rule of Edward I, but only until Robert the Bruce seized the Scottish throne in February 1306.

33 Wallace's arrival at London as a captive. The artist has chosen to show Wallace in armour to denote his martial status, but with a totally anachronistic kilt – presumably to show his 'Scottishness'.

34 A sixteenth-century representation of London showing Westminster Hall, the location of Wallace's 'trial' in August 1305.

35 A dramatic Victorian depiction of Wallace at Westminster Hall. Wallace's 'trial' on 23 August 1305 was really no more than a statement of the charges against him, followed by a summary sentence of execution.

ANO EFTER KING ROBERT
YE BRVCE MARIIT YE
DVKE OF HVLLESTERIS DOCHTER

Above left: 36 A sixteenth-century depiction of Robert I and his queen, Elizabeth de Burgh, a daughter of the Earl of Ulster, one of Edward I's senior lieutenants.

Above right: 37 The great seal of Robert I, showing him armed for war, a typical device of royal seals of the late Middle Ages throughout Europe.

Below: 38 A margin illustration from Geoffrey of Monmouth's *History of the Kings of Britain* showing the city of London in the thirteenth century.

of the Scottish capitulation of 1304: after seven years the Community considered that the struggle had continued long enough, at least for the time being. The capitulation brought a close to hostilities between the 'official' Balliol party and the Plantagenet party, but some men, most notably of course William Wallace, were either excluded or excluded themselves from the terms of the agreement. Wallace remained active until his capture in 1305, but in the next year Bruce was able to raise forces to make an attempt on the throne. The men he enlisted may have been motivated by their support for the inheritance rights of a Scottish nobleman, but it is much more probable that the majority of the early recruits were motivated by potential gains of war and by nationalist, or at least xenophobic, sentiment, rather than by the technicalities of succession disputes. It would seem that the people, or a large enough portion of them anyway, were willing to carry on the war in 1306; whether that means that all of those people were solely, or even primarily, moved by their belief in the rights of Robert Bruce is a different question.

Were the Guardianships a successful experiment in maintaining the government of the country in a time of crisis? The answer has to be a guarded 'yes', assuming that the political independence of medieval Scotland was a laudable object. Although it is true that the Scots failed in their primary task and that in the final stages of their resistance the Community of the Realm were, essentially, holding out for 'reasonable' terms[32] while they still had sufficient military power to make their defeat a real challenge, they had established and maintained a Scottish government in the name of King John and had come close enough to reinstating the king to induce Robert Bruce's defection to Edward.[33] Though Robert the Bruce may not have been a particularly important figure at the time, his departure to the Plantagenet cause must have had a destabilising affect on the Scottish administration; however, it did not degenerate into a Comyn interest group but retained a broad support among the different factions and family affinities among the nobility and the burgesses. There has, perhaps, been a tendency to see the Guardianships as a temporary measure, to keep the Scottish cause alive until Robert Bruce was in a position to assume the Crown. The Guardians did not labour to preserve the country for King Robert, but for King John; their contribution to the kingship of Robert I was probably a vital one, but it was not intentional.

The practical reaction of the Scottish political community to the collapse of John I's rule in the summer of 1296 was both rapid and effective, bearing in mind the challenges presented by poor communications, an occupation government, internal political divisions and the absence of an extensive body of influential and powerful men who were passing their time as prisoners of war in English castles. Its political reaction puts Scotland 'amongst the most conceptually advanced nations of medieval Europe',[34] a far cry from the popular perception of Scotland as a wild and crude backwater.

The Scots fought to preserve their customs and traditions against one of the most powerful nations in Europe for seven years. For most of that period the Guardians managed to do without either William Wallace or Robert Bruce, but it is difficult to see how the Guardianship would have become a reality without Wallace, or how the Bruce kingship could have been established without the tradition of resistance developed by the Guardians. The range of factors that led individual Scots to accept or reject Balliol or Plantagenet (and, after 1306, Bruce) lordship was immense – a maze of social, familial, cultural, economic and political pressures – but for the majority of the men in the Plantagenet camp there was no conflict of personal issues: they were in Scotland to serve their king, Edward I of England.

Edward did not move on Scotland at random, and it is important to give some thought as to why he should have chosen to do so. There has been a tendency among English historians to assume that English kings tradition-ally aspired to making one kingship effective throughout the British Isles. It would be difficult to make a case that English kings prior to Edward I saw British unification as either a priority or a practical proposition, or even that they were terribly interested at all, though no doubt all of them would have been happy to accept the annexation of their neighbours had the opportunity presented itself. The opportunity did not exactly present itself to Edward: he manipulated the situation to give himself opportunities to intervene in Scotland. He may have obeyed the letter of his various commitments to the Scots during the succession dispute of 1291–92, but it is easy to obey the letter of the rule when you are the person who interprets the rule. For Edward to seek to extend his influence and sovereignty was no more than his duty, as it would be for any other medieval king. If he genuinely chose to believe that English kings were the feudal superiors of Scottish ones, he must have been very selective about the evidence he chose to disregard, but for him to advance his cause, and thereby, in medieval perception, his country, was a natural obligation.

The question remains, however: what did Edward want Scotland *for*? The ideological position of increasing the bounds of a kingdom because it was a 'natural' aspect of kingship cannot have been sufficient to persuade Edward to commit large armies and vast sums of money to the acquisi-tion of what, it would appear to us, would have been at best a domain that would only make a marginal contribution to the English Crown and at worst might become a theatre of war and a drain on the English nation for generations. The latter possibility may never have occurred to Edward. He probably expected that there would be some opposition to the deposition of King John, and some, perhaps more, to his decision to keep the government of Scotland in his own hands rather than granting it to a replacement client-king. He evidently did not think that he would face widespread revolt within a few months of his departure, or he would surely have taken measures to ensure the security of his administration. Edward's intention was to replace the Balliol kingship, not to alienate the Scottish political community. Essentially, Edward hoped to annex Scotland as a going concern, appoint a number of new managers and incorporate it into the structure of his kingship. Scotland was not to be held as a separate kingdom from England, nor was it to be held as a fief, like Edward's possessions in France. This does not answer the question of 'what was in it for Edward?'

In 1291 Edward visited Scotland in the approach to the Great Cause. He passed through the eastern counties as far as Perth, taking fealties from landholders, ecclesiastical institutions and royal burghs. What he saw may have given him a rather misleading picture of the Scottish economy, since the towns and counties he passed through were probably the most prosperous parts of the country. The landholders and burgesses of eastern Scotland were not noticeably poorer than their counterparts in northern England. Presumably Edward, or his officials anyway, made some study of the resources of Scottish kings during his 1291 progress, and that would, no doubt, have given them a better picture of the Scottish economy; if so, the information did nothing to discourage Edward from attempting the acquisition of Scotland should the opportunity arise.

In all probability Edward believed that he could annex Scotland successfully, and he must have believed that the effort of doing so would be repaid. In the very short term, Scotland did prove to be a source of revenue: Edward was able to send a subsidy of over £4,000 to the Count of Bar from the proceeds of his 1296 campaign. Scottish kings may not have been rich but they were certainly solvent, and, since Edward's government and household already existed, the funds previously spent on several aspects of the Scottish kings' normal expenditure, such as the royal household and diplomatic matters, would now be surplus to requirements and could find their way to Edward's pocket.

Edward perhaps hoped that Scotland could be added to his domains as a personal possession, separate from England. He might be able to impose his government there permanently, without having to seek and obtain support from family and regional interest groups, but to what end? The economy of Scotland was very much smaller than that of England, but it was, before 1296, a stable and productive entity. If Edward could annex Scotland as a sort of mammoth barony held by the Crown, he could expect an increase in revenue from rents and customs that was not subject to the interference of Parliament. The same might apply to military service. If the political community of Scotland could be induced to accept Edward's lordship, they would be liable for military service, just as they had been under Alexander III or John. Service based on land tenure did not generally extend to service abroad, but no doubt Edward would have been able to prevail on Scottish gentlemen to follow him on campaign. If he was their liege lord and was offering wages for service, there would be no reason why they should not give that service just like any other gentlemen in Edward's domains.

Since these men were already accustomed to the burden of military service and were already obliged to keep suitable arms, armour and mount, they could potentially supply a considerable body of men-at-arms to Edward's army. Research has indicated that some hundreds of land-holders and burgesses in Lothian alone were liable for man-at-arms service. Lothian may have had an unusually high incidence of such duties because of the high incidence of relatively minor landholders there. A great lord might, and almost invariably did, hold his estate for what was really a trivial amount of knight service; seldom more than eight or ten, even for a great lordship or earldom. The lord or earl might, in reality, be expected to bring rather more men-at-arms to the army than their due service demanded, as a matter of personal prestige and for influence in the army, but their formal debt was not heavy. A minor landholder with perhaps 1 per cent of the wealth of a great lord or earl and providing the service of one knight was providing the king with much more in the way of 'service per acre', so Lothian may not be a good example of a 'typical' sheriffdom; however, the amount of service available from other counties – Berwickshire, Wigtownshire, Roxburghshire, Lanarkshire and Ayrshire – does not seem to have been significantly different to that of Lothian when compared as acreages.[35]

The potential for raising substantial bodies of men-at-arms, and of course other troops as well, was quite good, but there were other military advantages to be derived from a successful conquest of Scotland. Although England and Scotland had been at peace for generations in 1295, there was no guarantee that this would always be the case. The alliance that King John made with Philip of France may have been a response to Edward's pressure – an abnormal situation – but any future Scottish king might choose to form a more aggressive alliance with the French, if they thought it might lead to the recovery of counties in the north of England that previous Scottish kings had ruled at one time and might covet in the future. The conquest of Scotland would not only provide an opportunity for recruitment, but by securing his northern border permanently Edward would be able to draw men from the north of England for service in France or Flanders in greater numbers than in the past, since he would have no fear of an invasion by the Scots.

Having made his move, Edward was committed to pursuing his objective to the utmost of his power. If he failed to bring Scotland into his domains, the damage to his prestige would be immense. Defeat by a great nation like France would be unlikely to have an immediate impact on affairs at home because an English army fighting against the French was almost inevitably going to be on campaign on the continent, not in England. Defeat at the hands of the Scots would be seen quite differently; for one thing, Scotland was hardly one of the great powers of medieval Europe, and for another, unlike France, it had a shared border with England. A successful Scottish army might not be able to impose its will on the king of England (too much of his wealth lay in areas beyond the reach of any Scottish force), but the failure of the king to protect his subjects would be detrimental to his image as a just and competent monarch. An ambitious king, and Edward was certainly that, needed to be able to attract the support of his subjects, or at least most of them, most of the time, to procure the money and manpower that his plans demanded. Edward may not have been much moved by the sufferings of his subjects in Northumberland and Cumbria, nor by that of his clients and adherents in Scotland, but he could not ignore them without compromising his reputation for good lordship.

CHAPTER NINE

Death and Immortality

Whatever else can be said about William Wallace, his place as a great hero, perhaps the greatest hero of the cause of Scottish independence, is secure. In part, his reputation rests on his solid and unquestioned commitment to the cause of John I and the political liberty and prestige of Scotland, in part his reputation as a 'bonny fechter'. As we might expect with a heroic figure of such stature, his reputation is further enhanced by a great deal of wishful thinking. Historians of a socialist or Marxist sympathy can be forgiven for their tendency to see Wallace as a man of the common people: in short, a 'working class hero' – in the terms of Lennon if not of Lenin. The roots of such views are easy to identify. Wallace was not a great lord; he was prepared to confront the magnates to further his political ambitions; and he resisted the king of England. A somewhat sentimental analysis of these facets of his life has endeared Wallace to political radicals since the days of the Chartists, if not before. Even the most cursory examination of the life and acts of Wallace in the context of the society in which he lived undermines any claims for Wallace as an egalitarian liberal. The bones of the premise are certainly very real indeed: Wallace did confront the traditional influence of the magnates and he most certainly opposed, perhaps even frustrated, the expansionist policies of Edward I by upholding the cause of the Balliol kingship and thereby the cause of the political independence of Scotland. However, it is crucial to bear in mind that Wallace was both a man of his times (as all men are, at the end of the day) and a man of the aristocracy, though of a very low degree.[1]

The 'gentle birth' of William Wallace made him a member of the governing class, not a servant of it. However humble in his degree of nobility, Wallace would probably have been quite prepared to take the head off anyone who had the temerity to suggest that he was not of noble birth. Throughout medieval Europe, such a suggestion to a man of his rank would have been 'fighting words' to say the least: more so, perhaps, because there was no great economic divide between the lower nobility and successful peasant farmers, let alone between the nobility and the burgesses. Despite a 'low' social status within the nobility, Wallace actually had more in common socially and culturally with aristocratic enemies of similar status among the Plantagenet party than with the average Scottish commoner. Almost all of the latter were field workers or low-status urban labourers; they had little common ground with the men of the privileged classes who provided administration – social, fiscal, military and judicial – throughout medieval European societies generally. The nobility on the other hand shared a great deal of common experience. Although the details of their rights and responsibilities varied from one individual to the next, let alone from one country to another, the extent of their duty and of their privilege varied more in degree than in nature, depending on their social, cultural, economic – and therefore political – status within the noble community.[2]

William Wallace has attracted a great deal of attention from interested enthusiasts, but surprisingly little from historians. Of the several biographies readily available at the time of writing, not one has been written by anyone with a background in medieval history generally, let alone with any scholarly understanding of the society in which Wallace lived. The lack of an understanding of the context has led to the easy acceptance of material that is at best questionable and at worst fraudulent. This is most evident in the film *Braveheart*. Not content with relying on Blind Harry's largely fictitious poem *The Wallace* as the sole source of material, the writer, Randall Wallace, simply changed the story to suit a script that made no sort of historical sense and has, in fact, deprived Scottish people of part of their history by effectively undermining the factual material. The benefit of the *Braveheart* phenomenon is of course the extent to which it has heightened interest in medieval Scotland: an important consideration in a country where there is no viable programme of history in schools. Although *Braveheart* did help to make Scots more aware of their past, the damage done to our perception of Wallace and of the early period of the Wars of Independence is incalculable. If it is true that a picture paints a thousand words, how damaging is it when the picture is a fantasy?

Many readers will have seen pictures of armoured knights being lowered on to their chargers by means of a block and tackle and a set of sheerlegs. The pictures may have been very well executed, but the premise is nonsensical. Armies did not carry large arrays of engineering equipment simply to enable cavalrymen to get mounted. Practical demonstrations of the ability of a middle-aged man, little accustomed to armour and only a little more accustomed to horses, encountering no difficulty whatsoever in getting mounted draw the defence that 'armour was heavier then', which is simply untrue: the weight to volume relationship of steel has not changed appreciably in the last 700 years. The same applies to the oft-repeated observation that an armoured man who had the misfortune to fall over would have been unable to stand without the help of an assistant. No one can realistically accept that men went into battle wearing equipment so heavy that they would be completely compromised if they should happen to slip.

The *Braveheart* film takes this problem to an extreme degree. The costumes worn by the Scots were, presumably, chosen by a design team with an extensive background in Brigadoon studies: they certainly bear no resemblance whatsoever to the clothing of medieval Scots. The same applies to other visual aspects of the film; it can only be presumed that the project was carried out without any of the benefits of historical research into the clothing, housing, social and political conditions or military practices of fourteenth-century Scotland and England. Mel Gibson was perfectly honest about the production values of the project; he described the film as being his 'fantasy' of William Wallace and his many adventures. This is a fair point – none of us would expect that a film about any romantic hero from history would necessarily have any great claims to historical validity. For one thing, a movie is not a documentary; for another, *Braveheart* was made before the current, and highly laudable, vogue for visually convincing sets and action, as exemplified by *Saving Private Ryan* or *Gettysburg*. All the same, unwittingly or otherwise, *Braveheart* has made an enormous contribution to a romantic 'kailyard' vision of medieval Scotland that historians find almost impossible to dislodge with mere evidence. Quite why it should have made so great an impression is impossible to say, though the involvement of a major Hollywood star in a heavily promoted production must surely be part of the explanation. What is harder to account for is the reaction of audiences. A medieval historian attending the film at Alnwick, Northumberland, was disconcerted when the audience cheered Wallace enthusiastically as he unleashed his men to sack and destroy… Alnwick, Northumberland!

Normally enthusiasm engendered by a history film dies out quickly, as the film recedes in public memory or as it is increasingly 'debunked' by students of the period concerned. For reasons unknown, *Braveheart* has lasted the pace more than most: in 2001 re-enactors attending an event at Bannockburn were astonished – and not a little put out – when they discovered that a man dressed as Mel Gibson (in the sort of costume he wore in the film, and complete with blue face paint) had put himself at the head of their procession. Given that most, if not all, of the re-enactors had taken a great deal of trouble to provide themselves with reasonably appropriate arms, armour, footwear and clothing, they were understandably rather less than impressed. When approached, this 'Mel Gibson' character was able to defend himself on the grounds that the makers of a film – expert professionals – were bound to be more thoroughly informed about Scottish medieval society than historians, none of whom, as he accurately pointed out, had ever '…taken Braveheart seriously as history'.

Inevitably there is a danger in writing history for the cinema or stage; the needs of the narrative do not always coincide with the parameters of recorded history. A similar outcome can be identified from other productions and from other artistic genres: the average person's view of the First World War is probably the product of the poems of a small number of middle-class poets, men from a privileged background with no previous military experience and a very insecure understanding of the strategic or tactical issues facing their commanders. The other 'popular' experience of the same conflict is the musical and film production *O What a Lovely War*. It is a fine work of art, but is of less than zero value as an insight into the 1914–18 conflict: not only does the picture fail to give a realistic view of the practical nature of the conflict on the Western Front, it ignores the other fronts entirely and promulgates an inaccurate (and fundamentally dishonest) representation of the commanders and their staffs as being universally incompetent, uncaring, ignorant, bloodthirsty and stupid. The only way to combat that lack of reality is to read the history of the period rather than the poems. The poetry of the First World War does constitute useful, even vital material, but it is only one strand of the experience, and in no sense a common one. The same principle applies to the life and career of William Wallace. The poetry and romance of medieval Scottish writers are a part of the history and historiography of the Wars of Independence, but only a part.

Unfortunately, the search for Wallace in the history section of the local bookshop, or even library, is unlikely to yield very much of interest, unless the reader is willing to undertake a fairly extensive programme of reading. Inevitably, since it is the only source to contain any extensive material, real or fictitious, relating to his early life, scholars and enthusiasts alike have been drawn to Blind Harry. Like Mel Gibson and Randall Wallace, Harry had his own agenda; each of these men has or had a shared interest in portraying Wallace as heroic beyond the normal behaviour of men. The chief difficulty in using *The Wallace* as source material lies in the indisputable fact that it is largely fictional. Sadly, several writers have chosen to disregard that aspect of Blind Harry's work, preferring Harry's confabulations 150 years after the death of his principal character to analysis based on reliable material from record sources. This should not come as a surprise to students of medieval history generally, or to Scottish medievalists in particular.

The tradition of presenting invented romance as informed research has a long and ignoble tradition both in Scotland and, distressingly, in the rest of the world too. This can be demonstrated easily by a swift glance at the titles on the 'Scottish History' shelf in virtually any bookshop that has such a section. There are many titles in print which describe, in considerable detail, the arrival of refugee Knights Templar, who, escaping from persecution in France, escaped to Scotland with vast amounts of treasure in a fleet of seven ships.[3] In gratitude for the shelter given to them by King Robert, these renegade Templars arrived en masse at the battle of Bannockburn to rescue the king in the nick of time, before heading off to build a mystical and mysterious chapel at Roslin and eventually turning themselves into Free Masons. These tales were first invented by a certain Father Hay, an eighteenth-century romanticist. There was, of course, absolutely no substance whatsoever to these stories, and they were comprehensively rebutted at the time, but they have been reheated and served up again and again by several twentieth-century writers in the guise of history. To what extent these literary efforts are fantasies, and evidence of a complete lack of understanding (or research) of medieval history on the part of the authors, and to what extent they show a desire to make a fast and essentially fraudulent buck is difficult to say. If there is a modern mystery about William Wallace it is to be found in the fact that none of the Templar novelists has – so far – decided that Wallace was a secret Templar, though perhaps it is tempting fate to put both 'Wallace' and 'Templar' into the same sentence.

It is difficult to see quite why there have been no academic biographies of Wallace, certainly none that are really adequate for use by serious students of the period. The volume that most frequently appears on undergraduate reading lists, Andrew Fisher's *William Wallace*, is not really suitable for the purpose and many Scottish history undergraduates have had to have this explained to them, often as part of the process of telling them that their essay or exam answer was unsatisfactory. The volume in question, as any medievalist can confirm, is not a good piece of work and is certainly far from being a reliable portrayal of either Wallace or the society in which he lived: it is merely the least bad of a poor selection. This is the danger of writing of an individual, a location or a period in history – any period

– without endeavouring to acquire a valid understanding of the society involved. For many writers, an important element in their evaluation of Scottish society lies in the nature of the relationship between the 'Anglo-Norman' or 'Feudalist' upper class and the downtrodden 'Scots'. These two classes, separated by language as well as status, are brought together – unwillingly in the case of the nobles – under the leadership of William Wallace, who for the purpose of popular biographies was not, presumably, a member of the 'Anglo-Norman' ruling caste. The problems with this view are legion. First and foremost, no historian worthy of the name would think of Edward I, let alone his Scottish adversaries, as 'Anglo-Norman'. When Edward I came to the throne of England the conquest was already 200 years in the past. Names of French origin dominate English records of the day – they continue to do so in the twenty-first century – but the bearers of those names are not of French nationality.[4] Since the Wallace family had clearly been resident in Scotland for well over 100 years by the time William was born, we can surely accept that they were Scots, but the name Wallace is unquestionably one of 'Anglo-Norman' derivation: should we therefore assume that Wallace was in fact a member of an Anglo-Norman elite that had displaced the native Scots aristocracy? Should we therefore assume – because of his name and the evidently English/French ancestry of one part of his family background – that he was in fact a French-speaking aristocrat? It is difficult to see how John Balliol and Robert Bruce could have been Anglo-Normans but William Wallace a Scot, given that all three shared very similar origins.

Simple anti-factual statements, repeated at regular intervals by enthusiastic writers with little or no understanding of medieval societies, have done a great deal to promote widespread assumptions and beliefs that cannot be substantiated from what is known about medieval societies and individuals. This is the approach favoured by several populist writers who have sought to promote or denigrate particular historical figures at the expense or to the detriment of others. This approach is often used to avoid actually studying the period in question in any degree of detail, and leads to outrageously silly statements like this one:

> There were those magnates, like Patrick, earl of March and the Constable himself, who chose to support Edward out of their own volition, and there were those magnates who were, in fact, more English than Scots anyway. In this category came the elder earl of Carrick, who, despite his marriage to a Celtic heiress, Marjorie of Carrick, was probably born at Writtle near Chelmsford...[5]

It is almost difficult to know where to start. First and foremost, neither the Earl of March nor the constable were in much of a position to offer any resistance to Edward I in the wake of the invasion of 1296; the Earls of Dunbar remained supporters of the Plantagenet party until their defeat in 1314, but since the earldom was located in the very heart of the occupied territories and was therefore surrounded by English garrisons, this can hardly be seen as choosing to support the occupation 'out of their own volition'. Who the magnates were that were 'more English than Scottish' is an excellent question, and one whose answer is unknown to medievalists; the example offered by the writer is one Robert Bruce, father of another Robert Bruce, the one that would eventually become king of Scotland. The Bruces certainly owned property in Essex, and it is quite possible that Robert senior was born at Writtle, though, as far as is known to academic Bruce biographers, there is no secure evidence to suggest that possibility. The writer's understanding of medieval society – and modern society also – may not have been sufficiently well developed for him to be aware that though a cat can be born in a stable, it does not become a horse. Also, Robert Bruce senior was married to Marjorie, Countess of Carrick – he was not, himself, the Earl of Carrick, merely the bearer of the title in right of his wife. The Robert who would eventually become king of Scotland in 1306 was the first Bruce to be Earl of Carrick in his own right. Curiously, few writers have seen any relevance in the fact that Robert I's mother was unquestionably a Gael: the link with his ancestors who had lived in France two centuries before would seem to be considered more significant than the fact that Robert I was the scion of a Celtic dynasty, as well as of a Lowland Scottish one with roots in eleventh-century Normandy.[6]

   The belief, repeated by several writers, that the Scottish nobility spoke Norman French is easily dispensed with. There is no point in Scottish history where French can be identified as the normal language of government; evidence for French speech among the leaders of Scottish society in the late thirteenth and early fourteenth centuries is limited to two examples of dubious value. The first is a French claim that the Scottish king spoke French. It would be very likely indeed that any well-educated gentleman (and kings would most assuredly see themselves as being of 'gentle' birth) would be able to read French, if not speak it; that does not mean that it was either their only language or their language of choice. French was the language of intellectual literature, the international language of the day. It would be ridiculous to assume that all of the English-speaking people of today were *primarily* English-speakers. English is the language of computers and films, of jazz and rock and roll; its primacy as the 'literary' language of the young all over the world can hardly be denied – there are very few educated young Netherlanders, Belgians, Swedes or Germans who do not have a reasonable grasp of the English language, but that does not compromise their nationality, though perhaps it could be construed as a result, in part, of the omnipresence of MTV and CNN. Naturally, it is quite possible that the French observer deduced that King John was a French-speaker because John spoke French to him, since it was easier than attempting to communicate in English.

The other example is derived from Barbour's epic biography of Robert I. When beset by his enemies during his sojourn in the hills after the battle of Methven, Barbour has King Robert read aloud to his followers from a 'romance'.[7] It might be a little rash to simply assume that any romance in the early fourteenth century would most likely be written in French, but it would not be entirely unreasonable, since the vast majority of surviving medieval romances were indeed written in that language. This is a very long way from being evidence that Robert I was even a habitual French-speaker (as opposed to a reader), and we should be in no doubt at all that Robert I would have spoken middle Scots, a form of English, as his first language, as did the rest of the Scottish gentry and baronage. Their ability to communicate with their servants and tenants would have been compromised somewhat if they did not have a common language between them. This has implications for our understanding of those lords with interests in the north and west of Scotland. Although the English language was well established throughout most of southern and eastern Scotland (and had been for centuries, if place name evidence is anything to go by), Gaelic was still the first – and only – language of a very great proportion of Scots throughout the rest of the country. A lord in the west Highlands or the Isles, however 'Norman' or 'French' their surname, would have a very complicated life indeed if they could not speak Gaelic themselves. The basic mechanics of life would require the ability to give orders, if nothing more; however, it was a common practice in both Gaelic- and English-speaking families to 'farm out' their male children to other households, where they would learn the social and practical skills associated with their station in life in a less cosseted situation that they might experience at home – not hugely different in principle to the practice of packing boys off to boarding school. It would seem very unlikely indeed that a youth living in a castle in Argyllshire in the fourteenth century would fail to acquire the language of the community in which he lived. For practical reasons therefore, it would be reasonable to assume that, far from living in a French-speaking sub-community, a modest proportion of Scottish landholders would have needed, for practical purposes, command of both English and Gaelic.

Significantly, Barbour's *Bruce*, which was unquestionably written for a noble audience, was written in Scots little more than fifty years after the events it portrays. Although it is vaguely possible that there had been a vast social change among the Scottish aristocracy in the fourteenth century that had led to the universal adoption of the Scots language in place of French, it would seem very unlikely that such a change should take place without any comment whatsoever at the time, nor that it would fail to have made any recognisable impact on the body of surviving records.

The more we examine the evidence for 'Anglo-Norman' lordship in late-medieval Scotland, the more elusive it becomes. It is certainly the case that Scottish kings encouraged immigration among English land-holding families and that many of the great magnate families (and many more of the minor noble families) of Scotland had antecedents of English and Anglo-Norman origin. Often these origins can be identified in the surname of the family, but evidence of that nature is both unreliable and misleading. Many of these 'migrant' family groups made their appearance in Scotland through the patronage of Scottish kings and magnates, but it should be remembered that many of these 'family groups' actually only consisted of one individual. The high incidence of those names is derived chiefly from the fact that virtually all of the incomers were men. The Scottish ladies they married did not necessarily adopt the surnames of their husbands, but their children almost invariably did. Most of these migrants entered Scottish society at a relatively exalted level; they had the resources to ensure that their children were provided for economically, generally in the form of subdivisions of the family property or acquisition of estates through marriage to heiresses, and founded their own branches of the family with distinct heritable estates, thus spreading the family name. Most importantly, these family names arrived in Scotland in the early twelfth century.

The significance of this is that the majority of the 'Anglo-Norman' families that were prominent in Scotland during Wallace's lifetime had been there for the better part of 200 years, and some of them possibly for rather longer than that, given that 'Norman' mounted soldiers served in the armies of Welsh princes some years before the Norman conquest of England. In the nineteenth century, if not before, many historians and anti-quarians considered the reign of David I to be a sort of 'Norman conquest' of Scotland by the back door. Although this view has long been discredited in academic circles, the proposition still has some currency among popular writers. The purpose of the 'Norman yoke' notions among populist writers is to enhance the reputation of a heroic figure, William Wallace, by showing how constant and patriotic he was, while demonstrating the vacillating, treacherous nature of the nobility. That sort of thing has a wide appeal, but it is not an asset in the study of history, nor is it useful in a consideration of the life and career of William Wallace, who was, after all, a product of the very same 'Anglo-Norman' feudal aristocracy as John Balliol, Robert the Bruce and John Comyn.

The number of men (and they were chiefly men) introduced to Scotland from England and the continent by Scottish kings and magnates to join the Scottish aristocracy was very small indeed – a matter of a few hundred spread over half a century or more – but there is a sense in which they loom much larger in Scottish history that their numbers would suggest. The chief attraction to Scots in importing men of noble status was to acquire the skills of modern warfare and the techniques of modern government. Eleventh-century Scotland may not have been the social and cultural back-water of Europe, but equally it was not in the forefront of contemporary administrative structures. The development of the governance structures of early Capetian France and the spread of those structures across northern and western Europe cannot be examined here, but it is clear that these structures had been widely adopted through southern and eastern Scotland before the death of David I in 1153.[8]

A vital component of these arrangements – the sort that we call feudal, though that was not a term used by medieval writers – was military service attached to land tenure. It is often assumed that these arrangements represented a formalisation of tenure conditions that had not previously existed; however, it is clearly the case that these landholdings were created from existing units that already had formal rental agreements of long standing. Most interestingly, many of these conversions substituted military service for what had previously been cash payments.[9] It could be argued, though very superficially, that the new structures actually represented a backward step in social administration if one were to automatically accept that an economy based on currency is surely more sophisticated than one based on military service. There are two significant flaws to such an argument. Firstly, an economy in which military service plays a part is not the same thing as an economy based on military service: virtually, if not absolutely, every country in the world expects its citizens or subjects to give service in war if called upon to do so, and 'feudal' tenure was merely an expression of the contractual conditions. Moreover, a very large proportion of tenures with a military obligation were also subject to other obligations. Most landholders with contractual military duties attached to their lands – free tenants – were also required to provide their superior with advice, attendance at the hunt and suit of court duties, and a great many were obliged to provide a fixed quantity of that most desirable of commodities: money.

The other great flaw lies in the assumption that military service was, in itself, an unsophisticated arrangement: it actually had benefits for the landlord, the tenant and society as a whole. Because the landlord could remove a military tenant for failure to provide their due service, he could be reasonably confident that the service would be performed as required; because the tenants enjoyed heritable security of tenure, they could be confident that their descendants would have the benefit of the property in the future; and because heavy cavalry service was part of the fabric of Scottish society, the Scots were able to pursue their wars of liberation. Without military tenure there would have been very few Scottish men-at-arms in the thirteenth and fourteenth centuries, and without those men-at-arms there would have been very little prospect of success for the cause of Scottish independence, since man-at-arms service was the mainstay of the day-on-day pursuit of the war and the only viable means of countering the men-at-arms of the English garrisons. Both the literature and the records of the fourteenth century are very clear in that regard. The literature is full of the martial deeds of the political communities and the record material is full of their martial needs: wages, horse valuations and restorations, arms, ransoms, muster rolls and postings.

There were drawbacks to the system, of course. Although the level of knight service for properties was never high in relation to the value of the estate, and although the quantity of service was very seldom, if ever, changed, the cost of the service was not static. It is clear that what was expected of a man-at-arms in the way of horse and equipment quality changed considerably during the later thirteenth century.[10] The landholder might still be only liable for the service of one knight, but the cost of equipping that knight was rather greater than it had been in the past. If the landholder was to perform the service in person, he would need to spend much more than his predecessors; if he chose not to, or was unfitted to so through gender, age or infirmity, the cost of hiring a substitute would be that much more than in the past. In a simple but very effective sense, land tenure for military service was a hedge against inflation, and one that for most landholders at least was acceptable, since the rise in agricultural produce prices in the period that had elapsed since the original charter had been granted – often the better part of two centuries – more than offset the rising price of a suitable mount and arms.

Broadly speaking, land tenure by military service served Scotland well throughout the later thirteenth and the fourteenth century. The significance of great field actions like Falkirk or Bannockburn can be exaggerated all too easily; neither really changed the course of the war, after all. The normal practice of war in Scotland, particularly in the periods 1298–1304, 1312–1328 and from 1333 onward, was largely similar to war in other parts of Europe: it was conducted by surprisingly small numbers of men. The chief striking arm of the forces involved was of men-at-arms, and those men-at-arms were drawn almost exclusively from the ranks of the nobility and, to a lesser extent, the burgesses. Without the active support of a large enough proportion of the noble and commercial classes, neither Balliol, Plantagenet or Bruce kings could hope to acquire and retain power in Scotland.

The military-political class was far from universally constant in their allegiance to Scottish kingship, but equally far from being constant in their allegiance to the Plantagenets. This phenomenon was not limited to the Scottish nobility. Subjects of the kings of England in their capacity as French lords became increasingly fluid in their allegiance throughout the fourteenth and fifteenth centuries. More significantly, in the second and third decades of the fourteenth century, several English lords in the north of England became sufficiently disenchanted with their own kings to choose to seek the lordship of Robert I, approaching him for confirmation of their charters and the like, perhaps for fear that Northumberland, Cumbria and Westmorland might be annexed by the Scots.[11] It would be rash to conclude that such incidents were evidence that certain areas of northern England were diffident about their nationality, or that a Scottish administration in Northumberland and Cumbria would have been considered acceptable to the political communities of those counties, but it would be reasonable to assume that the landholders of northern England might be prepared to accept the imposition of Robert I's rule if he could offer them the stability and protection that Edward II was very evidently failing to provide. We should not think for a moment that Northumberland men seeking the protection of Robert I were in any sense unpatriotic; they were responding to circumstances over which they had no real influence, let alone control.

The issue of the constancy – or otherwise – of the Scottish nobility is one of great importance in any evaluation of the life and career of William Wallace. Both the Balliol and Plantagenet parties were aware that the support of the noble and commercial classes was crucial to their prospects. These were the classes that provided the backbone of civil and military administration. Naturally, both parties strove to enlist the local political community in their respective causes and therefore offered incentives, coercion, persuasion or a mixture of the three to achieve this. Landholders could of course flee to another area if they felt they could not accord with the current source of authority, but they could hardly take their lands with them; if they wanted to stay on their estates – a natural desire at any time, but of huge social and cultural significance 700 years ago – they simply had to accept the government of the day or face forfeiture. The incentives to support whichever party was currently in the ascendant in a particular vicinity were possibly as significant as the disincentives. Alignment with the 'current dispensation' obviously secured title to land, but there were also opportunities within the administration. Jury service and some military service were obligations on most landholders, but the demand for men-at-arms invariably outstripped the supply, so there were generally employment, even career, opportunities with the army – particularly the English army, since wages seem to have been a rarity in Scottish ones. Local stability was vital to the local economy, and landholders might well be prepared to ignore their personal political inclinations for the sake of the continuing commercial viability of their property, as well as the wellbeing of their relatives and tenants. These were crucial elements in the process of deciding political alignment at a given moment. As the incumbent of the chief property of a family network, the lord or lady of the property would have to take some cognisance of the effect that their own political allegiance might have on the other members of the family.

All in all, administrations of all parties seem to have been content to distinguish between different branches of the same family; just because some members of the Ramsay or Douglas families or their allies were in the peace of the Plantagenets did not prevent other members of those families from being in the peace of Robert I or David II, but while an individual might declare for one cause because the bulk of their lands were in areas under the administration of that party, other lands in their possession in areas in the control of the other party would obviously be at risk. If those lands were in the hands of tenants, rather than kept 'in hand' by the landholder, the opposing government might choose to leave the tenant in place so long as they continued to support the party governing that area in order to avoid having to install an alternative landholder; however, it would have been rash to rely on that being the outcome of the defection of one's superior. Any landholder with properties scattered throughout the country (and that would include a hefty proportion of all the magnates) would have to give very careful consideration to the fortunes of others before making a change of allegiance, since their own defection might well lead to the forfeiture of family members and friends: the very people who, in concert, provided greater lords with the military strength that validated their political prominence.

The commercially successful men and women in the urban communities were even more vulnerable to changes of administration than their rural counterparts. Landholders whose properties were declared forfeit for opposing the current administration could expect to have their estates restored as and when their own party achieved its goal, or, failing that, they could hope to reach an accommodation with the successful party. If their estates were laid waste they could hope to borrow money to restock and rebuild on the security of their land; they might be heavily in debt for some time, but the land itself was a secure asset. Families whose status was derived from commercial activity could be utterly destroyed in a matter of hours, even minutes, simply by setting fire to their premises. The family might still retain the land, but restoring a business is dependent on investment and access to the market. A family whose business had already been burnt out once would probably encounter some difficulty in raising the capital for restoration, even if they could be sure of access to the marketplace; if the occupation government had chosen to destroy someone's livelihood as punishment for political activity they were hardly likely to allow that person to retain such market privileges as they had enjoyed in the past, or even to allow them continued access to the market at all.

Curiously, although the burgesses of Scotland were just as prone to transfers of allegiance as the nobility (and everyone else for that matter), they have not suffered the same fate at the hands of historians. No author has written about the treacherous, pro-English tendencies of the burgess class, and, though a very large proportion of that class bore French or English surnames, no author has written about the 'Anglo-Norman' burgesses of Scotland, though a great many have written about the 'Anglo-Norman' nobility. By the close of the thirteenth century any division between the lesser nobility and the more successful families among the burgesses had, in any case, become rather blurred. Noble families married their children into burghal families for the sake of good cash dowries and access to the privileges of burgess participation in commerce, and burghal families married their children into the noble landholding class in search of prestige and influence in the political, cultural and economic life of the vicinity. The pressure on the nobility to provide their children with an adequate standard of living was considerable, but so was the pressure to maintain the integrity of the family estate: an integrity that would be very rapidly compromised by permanent division of the property. A few generations of division and subdivision of the property would result in impoverishment for all, whereas the existence of a family estate empowered the current landholder both economically and politically, giving that individual a capacity to protect and further the interests of the family as a whole.

The status of a family was a vital component in the future not merely of the immediate family members of the current incumbent, but of their cousins, uncles, aunts and so on. This is an important consideration when exploring the relationship between Wallace and the clergy. A number of writers have drawn attention to the support that William Wallace enjoyed from the ecclesiastical community, in contrast to the opposition he faced from the nobility. The distinction between the two is a false one: although it is true that men of very humble origins could make a career in the Church, their numbers were few indeed. Almost all of the beneficed clergy of Scotland, like their counterparts in England or France, were drawn from the ranks of the nobility. There were a number of reasons why this should have been the case. Admission to a monastery or to a parish was largely dependent on the ability of the candidate to find either a sum of money paid to the monastery or to the landholder or institution which had the right of appointment (advowson) to that parish, a right often retained by landholders granting land to the Church, since it was a source, however irregular, of hard cash. It was possible for candidates to borrow money against the future income they would derive from the parish, but the majority of candidates probably gained their positions through a mixture of family connections and a money payment, which itself was likely to be borrowed from a family member. The 'networking' aspect of family connections can be seen in Blind Harry's account of Wallace's adventures before his rise to fame. According to Bower and Blind Harry, Wallace was sheltered by two priests, each of them an uncle. It might seem unlikely that a man should have two uncles in holy orders, but there are a number of qualifying factors to be considered. For one thing, there were very many more priests in relation to the population as a whole in the late Middle Ages than there are today. In addition to perhaps 1,500 parish priests there was an extensive hierarchy of abbots, archdeacons and bishops who, in turn, like other senior members of the noble classes, had chaplains of their own. Additionally, there was the regular clergy of the monasteries, convents and abbeys. Given the relatively limited range of career paths considered suitable for noblemen, it would not be particularly peculiar that two men in one generation of a family should become priests. Further, the terms of relationship used in medieval documents do not completely coincide with current usage. The two 'uncles' concerned need not have been the brothers of his father or mother for him to regard them as such.

The support of the two Wallace priests – and various others – has been seen as an example of a distinction that did not exist in the medieval period: namely, a social and cultural divide separating the noble and clerical establishment. In the view of one writer, the support Wallace derived from the clerical community was based on the fact that:

> Unlike the magnates, most of whom were committed to Edward's cause on account of their extensive English estates, the prelates, by and large, were men of a more independent mind. They were more likely to have risen from the ranks of the Scottish community and were therefore not so susceptible to Anglo-Norman influence.

This statement neatly encapsulates an important aspect of the general perception of Wallace, the nobles and the clergy, and is worth examining critically. The first point to make is that, as we have seen, Scottish clerics were recruited, in the main anyway, from the noble families, and the concept of 'Anglo-Norman' *anything* really has no place in either England or Scotland in the later Middle Ages. Realistically, no Scottish magnates had what we might reasonably call 'extensive' estates in England, or at least certainly not estates sufficient to make the holder a particularly important figure in the local political communities in which their properties lay, let alone give them any stature in the national political community of England. The Bruce family certainly owned estates in Essex, but their wealth, power and influence came from their Scottish properties; they may even had held a barony in that county, but so did several other people. There were undoubtedly people with properties in both countries who endeavoured to protect their inheritances by allegiance to the Plantagenet cause, but they had interests and considerations beyond immediate property rights. It was by no means clear to the Scottish political community that Edward was unquestionably acting outside his rights in 1296. King John had, after all, accepted Scottish kingship on the basis of Edward's suzerainty. Who was to say Edward did not have a right to forfeit his vassal if his vassal failed to give the service due to his acknowledged lord?

It is true that many Scots lords served Edward against the Balliol cause and later against the Bruce cause, but more difficult to demonstrate their willingness to serve the Plantagenet cause when they had a real choice in the matter. It is very tempting for Scottish writers to take a judgmental attitude on this issue, but difficult, apparently, for them to understand that taking a patriotic stance in the face of an occupying army might have serious consequences such as loss of land, livelihood or head, not to mention the loss of any opportunity to protect the interests of the estate, the family, the tenants and the other dependants. Furthermore, lordship was a two-way relationship. The estate holders did not live in isolation from their tenants, and, in the same way that the great lords owed a duty of counsel to the king; minor nobles had an obligation to their superiors. A strong-willed lord with good leadership skills might be able to persuade or cajole his tenants into supporting the political position that he had adopted himself, but any lord would have to give serious thought to his continued allegiance to a cause that his tenants opposed. Lordship was hardly a democratic condition, but it was certainly rather more consensual than is generally realised. Most significantly, if the Scottish nobility were committed to the Plantagenet cause, it was a commitment that went largely unnoticed by English writers, who were clearly of the opinion that, regardless of the overt allegiance of Scottish lords, their hearts and minds were generally 'with their own people'. This is significant in two ways: firstly, because it is shows that there was a perception among the English that the support of Scottish lords for English kings was only skin-deep at the best of times, and that the bonds of lordship and tenant or dependant were of greater significance than oaths given to a foreign king who had been successful in war, but also because it clearly shows the medieval understanding of national identity – that people born and raised in a particular country were likely to have a political inclination that included the defence of that country against foreign interests. English writers, then, were clear that the shared nationality of the Scots was a major factor, perhaps even the most significant factor, in persuading the community to carry on the fight.

Even the most cursory examination of the records of English garrisons and armies in Scotland shows that many Scots did choose to support the Plantagenet party against John I – most famously, of course, Robert Bruce, Earl of Carrick, whose pattern of defection and reconciliation is positively bewildering. Unsurprisingly, the greatest concentration of consistent Plantagenet support lay in the southern regions of the country. Traditionally, this has been ascribed to the cultural and linguistic affinities of the nobility living between the Humber and the Forth, or even the Tay. There were important cultural similarities between the societies of northern England and southern Scotland, but these similarities extended throughout the communities concerned; they were not limited to the aristocracy. A farm worker in Lanarkshire did not lead a markedly different life to a farm worker in Northumberland. The single most important factor in the establishment and maintenance of an English administration in Lothian or Roxburghshire or Dumfriesshire lay in the effectiveness of the military occupation. If the sheriff's orders could be enforced in a particular area, he could oblige the local political community to perform their due military service on pain of forfeiture; this obviously eased the manpower requirement of the administration, but it also helped to keep the local political community out of the ranks of the Balliol (or later Bruce) party. Maintaining the credibility of the occupation was undoubtedly less of a challenge in Lothian, where there was a well-developed network of strongholds and less broken country from which insurgents could operate. Also, a relatively high proportion of the population lived in towns and larger villages – Edinburgh, Haddington, Linlithgow, Winchburgh – and were therefore more vulnerable to the occupation than their compatriots in Wester Ross or Invernesshire, where English government was only achieved very briefly, if at all, and at rare intervals.

It has been suggested that the senior aristocracy of Scotland, the magnates, were more inclined toward the Plantagenet party than the population as a whole; the magnates wanted to retain their positions in Scotland and their estates in England, and were also bound by the common ideals of chivalry to the ruling class in England in a way that separated them from their fellow Scots. Naturally enough, men and women of property and influence certainly *did* want to preserve their prominence in the one and their property in the other. Neither of these issues was necessarily an issue of political allegiance in quite the simplistic way we might imagine. It was perfectly normal for wealthy men and women to invest in properties in other countries, just as they do today. English people owned property in France and vice versa; the two countries were frequently at war, which might interrupt the commercial aspects of ownership (though it might just as easily not) but did not, of itself, bring about the permanent loss of the property.

If the magnates were less than constant in their support of Scottish kingship at all, let alone the kingship of John I or Robert I, the same applied to the rest of Scottish society. The evidence for noble co-operation with the occupation can be seen in the act of homage or in military service in garrisons throughout Scotland, or at least those parts where garrisons were established. We should not assume that the absence of a garrison indicates an inability on the part of the occupation power to place one or maintain one: the administration may have considered that a garrison in a specified location would be unjustifiably expensive or that they had a degree of support in the local community that made a garrison unnecessary, thus saving on manpower which could be better used somewhere else. Obviously, the influence of Scottish magnates in the Plantagenet camp was of great importance; the Earls of Dunbar were vital props to the English occupation in the south-east between 1296 and 1314 and again in 1333–34. The allegiance of the Earls of Dunbar would seem to support the contention that the senior nobility were part of what E.M. Barron saw as an anglophile, southern aristocracy willing to compromise Scottish independence, which was duly saved by the consistent loyalty of the Gaelic/Celtic/Highland community. One might ask where that would leave the MacDougalls and MacDoualls, who were unquestionably Gaelic, Celtic and Highland, and were also, equally unquestionably, consistent supporters of the Plantagenet occupation against Robert I after 1306.

Collaboration is an ugly and inappropriate word for the generality of the relationship between the Scots and the Plantagenet occupations of 1296–1314 and the 1330s and 1340s, but there was, without question, a great deal of practical co-operation, particularly in those areas where the occupation was well supported by castles and secure towns – inevitably, the areas where a larger proportion of the populace depended on commerce and services rather than agriculture for their livelihood. To see that co-operation as collaboration would be akin to charging every police officer, juror, lawyer, judge, local government officer and tax collector who served in France between 1940 and 1944 of being a Nazi sympathiser; there would be a grain of absurd truth to it, but it would be a gross and offensive distortion. The same applies to late-medieval Scotland during the occupations. Without some degree of co-operation with the government there would inevitably be some decay in law and order, with consequences for the commercial environment; furthermore, the issue applies to the whole of the community, not just the noble and the financially successful. We have already seen that a group of Scots of very low status could become aware that the Edwardian occupation might provide an opportunity to improve their lot. Petitioning Edward for the same rights as his husbandmen in England was an astute move. In the wake of victory Edward might well feel inclined to be generous, particularly in regard to a matter which, though important to the petitioners, was of no moment to himself, but it also gave Edward an opportunity to demonstrate quality of lordship in what was, in his view anyway, a fief recently recovered by its liege lord. He could be seen to be taking a real interest in the affairs of his new subjects, a good move in virtually any political arena, and a demonstration of the 'good lordship' that medieval communities needed if they were to prosper.

Acceptance of Plantagenet lordship in Scotland was not, then, a matter of class or status, of linguistic or geographical background, though all of these were probably factors for some or even most people at one time or another. Adherence to one party or another, or even to none at all if one could get away with it, was the product of a much wider and more subtle mix of issues than we might expect. Political issues of any kind can only tell us so much about human motivation. Mankind is not especially noted for consistently rational behaviour at the best of times, and it is very likely that many active participants on either side would have struggled to explain quite why they were serving Balliol rather than Plantagenet interests, save for those whose property lay within an area that was currently secure for this party or that and who were not prepared to abandon their heritage for the sake of maintaining their allegiance to one man, regardless of whether that man represented Scottish sovereignty or English suzerainty.

Wallace's relationship with the aristocracy, or at least with those elements of the aristocracy senior in status to himself (most of them), has generally been seen as a difficult one. Fordoun, Wyntoun, Bower and of course Blind Harry made their readers aware that Wallace was not intimidated by the nobility, and that he was quite prepared to enforce their obedience by the same means as he was prepared to enforce military service from the wider population: the gallows. While this is surely the case, there are a number of issues to be considered. Wallace can be perceived as a leader who rose to prominence, despite the ill will and resistance of his social superiors, as a result of his successes in the field. Through the late spring and summer of 1297 William Wallace was able to assemble a force and conduct operations against the English; it would not be safe to assume that he was alone in doing so, merely that he was the most successful among them, though even that judgement is subject to the possibility that Wallace survived long enough to come to prominence, whereas other men who might have afforded him some competition had already fallen in the struggle.

Wallace was not the sole instigator of resistance, but a man in the forefront of the military aspect of the struggle in central Scotland. Before he and Murray effected the union of their armies at Stirling Bridge, Edward's administration in Scotland had already made him aware that all was not well there, that only one county of Scotland (Berwick) had a complete administration, 'and that only recently', and that the Scots had already appointed sheriffs and baillies in most of the others. Although Wallace was a very active man, he self-evidently could not have procured that situation by his efforts alone. Wallace had obviously made a reputation for himself before Stirling Bridge; he had, after all, gathered an army, but he was not of great political significance. Victory over Cressingham enhanced Wallace's prestige enormously, and it is after that battle that we see more evidence of Wallace the political animal and administrator in his role as

Guardian. The title would, however, have been of little value unless Wallace could depend on the political support of the existing structures of power and influence that had made the reinstatement of a Scottish administration possible. It is difficult to see how that reinstatement, even if it was very scattered, could have occurred without the complicity of a proportion of the senior aristocracy large enough to impose their will or, at the very least, strong enough to discourage immediate local opposition among the rest of the Scots.

It could be argued, and has been suggested or even asserted by some writers, that Wallace enjoyed a good relationship with the ecclesiastical authorities and that that gave him credibility among the great and good. It would seem that this was the case; however, it is most unlikely that the clerical magnates, the bishops, abbots and priors, would have had the level of influence throughout Scotland that would have been necessary to restore government in the name of King John without at least the complicity, if not the active support, of the noble community. Wallace's relationship with the Church before the battle of Stirling Bridge was probably rather less significant than it was afterward. As Guardian, Wallace was a man worth cultivating to ensure that the rights and privileges of the Scottish clerical establishment, not to mention their treasured independence from archbishops, was preserved from English domination. As a leader of a raiding party in early 1296 he may well have attracted the interest of senior Scottish churchmen like Bishop Wishart, but his influence over any aspect of Church matters, beyond the level of driving the odd English priest from his benefice, was probably very slender. It is, in any case, important to remember that the political 'estate' of the clergy may have been nominally separate from that of the nobility, but almost all of the priests, monks and nuns who comprised the Scottish clergy were members of noble families. To a very great extent, the priorities, beliefs and cultural and social practices of one were also the practices of the other. It would be very unlikely indeed that the clergy as a class would adopt a radically different posture from the nobility. Wallace was, however, aware of the value of ecclesisatical support, both moral and financial. His intervention to secure the election of William Lamberton as bishop of St Andrews was not simply a matter of denying the preferred candidate of Edward I, but of encouraging the patriotic party within the Scottish Church.

The popularity of Wallace in the wider community, and in the army in particular, must be seen as an important, even crucial, element in his rise to the Guardianship, but he could not be everywhere at once. To make his rule a reality, he would have needed the co-operation of the administrative, judicial and military practitioners of the community: the nobles and burgesses. To an extent, this can be encompassed in traditional Wallace hagiography: the magnates reject Wallace but the minor gentry, most of

whom would seem to have been either Wallace's cousins or his uncles, if
Blind Harry is to be taken at face value, took him to their hearts. The flaw
in that rationale is, of course, that the minor and major lords did not exist
in either social, cultural, political or financial isolation from one another. In
certain regions, most noticeably Lothian, there were no great lords, but a
great many minor ones who held their property directly from the Crown,
not through an intermediary.[12] In the north and west, where lordships and
earldoms tended to be much larger, there was much more subinfeudation,
and thus a greater degree of dependence of lesser lords on greater ones.
It would be a courageous, not to say foolhardy, action for a minor lord to
give his support to Wallace and the Balliol cause without the approval of
his superior. As we have seen already, English chroniclers were inclined to
think that Scottish magnates were not loyal to King Edward, even when
they were present in his army or otherwise active in his cause. They may
well have been right to do so: when the Earl of Strathearn made captives of
the MacDuff men who had been intent on capturing him, he did not pass
them over to the occupation government. Had the earl been confident of
Edward's victory and Wallace's defeat, he would not have dared to withhold
them from the Plantagenet administration.

If the earl's decision is not an indication of Scottish perception of the
security of the Plantagenet government, the action of the MacDuff men
in attacking the earl certainly is. Evidently the occupation was not strong
enough to overawe opposition, and therefore not able to offer the 'good
lordship', the political and economic stability, on which long-term retention of political power depended. The MacDuff/Strathearn incident also
shows that opposition to Edward's government was not limited to the
actions of Sir William Wallace, nor to the labouring classes and the minor
nobility, nor to the activities of 'Celtic' Scotland. It may have been sporadic,
but it was widespread, both socially and geographically.

If we accept that Wallace was only one of a number of captains of followings in the spring and early summer of 1297, it is crucial to give some
consideration to how he became the leader of a national movement rather
than a minor leader within it. Success is an excellent recruiting officer,
and it would seem that William Wallace was effective in battle. That would
be enough to draw men to him, but whether they would be the men he
required was a different matter. All of Wallace's early engagements seem to
have been carried out by men-at-arms. They may not all have enjoyed the
social status that would normally be associated with man-at-arms service,
but they would seem to have been well armed – in the medieval sense
of 'armoured' and mounted on beasts suitable for the purpose. No doubt

many of the men who sought service (or just adventure) with Wallace were unable to acquire the equipment or the skills to serve as men-at-arms, but self-evidently there were enough of them to provide Wallace with a force able to conduct successful mobile operations on a more or less continuous basis. Such a force need not have been very large to pose a real and continuing threat to the occupation. Most garrisons were very small indeed, and even a band of just thirty or forty men-at-arms would be enough to put them on the defensive. Even if the garrison ran to as many as forty men-at-arms, and few of them did, it would hardly be prudent to commit the entire cavalry element of the garrison to the pursuit of an enemy that might be strong enough to offer battle and win it – a possibility that would be very detrimental to the credibility of the administration, both locally and nationally. Locally it would undermine the power of the sheriff and nationally it would provide good propaganda material for the Balliol cause.

The mobile force that Wallace raised and led in early 1297 probably included men whose status would not normally have led them to man-at-arms service, but who had through whatever means – service in foreign armies, experience of brigandage – become soldiers. Such men were likely few and far between; also, few men would have been willing to commit themselves to absolutely continuous service, so it is reasonable to assume that the majority of the early force was drawn from the noble classes – men with the experience, training, social background and economic muscle to serve as men-at-arms. Given how small the force is likely to have been, a matter of dozens or scores rather than hundreds and thousands, it is quite possible that a fair proportion of them were members of the wider Wallace family, but even if the force was as small as thirty it would be very unlikely that the Wallace family would have been able to fill its ranks. Nor is it likely that all of them would have been 'in capite' tenants – that is to say, men who held their land directly from the king. Some of them, at least, would have been the tenants and dependants of other men; some of them of magnates. Service with Wallace would be very hard to explain to a superior whose allegiance – currently and officially anyway – lay with Edward I.

Situations where inferiors and superiors differed in their political allegiance were naturally fraught with difficulties for both parties. The forfeiture of a tenant who had turned out for the opposition might undermine the prestige of the superior with his other tenants. If the tenant happened to be a family member that would obviously compli-cate the issue further: how difficult would it be to forfeit own your son or daughter? Forfeiture of a particularly popular landholder might not go down too well with the farm tenants or among the local political community. Additionally, the replacement of forfeited tenants with men whose political inclinations seemed to be more reliable might be very counterproductive in the long term, should it become necessary for the superior to defect or accept a change in the administration due to developments either at a local level, such as the fall of a particular stronghold, or at a national level, in the event of a truce being made at an inconvenient juncture for the landholder. Failure to forfeit recalcitrant tenants would not play well with the administration, of course, but then the security of the administration, whether Plantagenet or Balliol, might not be all that secure: it might fall to the opposition, in which case having one or more tenants already in the allegiance of the new administration might provide a means of negotiating an accommodation that would preserve their position in the community and, of course, their tenure. Another important aspect of forfeiture, or rather of granting property, was that the new tenant would have to establish their authority. In peacetime this was probably easy enough to achieve, but forfeitures were very rare in peacetime; in a period of prolonged if intermittent warfare, imposing lordship may well have been a rather more challenging proposition.

The business of protecting and furthering the interests of a family group was, then, a complex and difficult process. The lords who accepted Edward I's kingship in 1296 had very little choice if they were to retain their heritages in the short term. If Edward were to achieve his goal, their properties would be secure in the long term as well, but Edward might not be able to make his rule a reality. In the summer of 1297 it was fast becoming evident that Edward was not going to achieve an easy assimilation of Scotland, and might even be defeated and his administration driven out. In the event of a Scottish victory, even a temporary one, a landholder, even a prominent magnate, might find themselves forfeited by the Balliol kingship if they had become too closely associated with the occupation and were seen as being too hostile to the Balliol cause for a realistic reconciliation – if they were unfortunate enough to be captured, they might even get hanged for treason: Wallace did.

Stirling Bridge gave Wallace a degree of political acceptability, not to mention popular acclaim. It did not turn him into a magnate, but it gave him enough status to be credible as a leader for the Balliol cause. Military success gave him political office, but it was not anticipated initially that Wallace would act as the sole Guardian; he was to share the burden with his companion in arms Sir Andrew Moray. Moray's death some weeks later probably from wounds sustained in the fight, left Wallace to get on with it himself, very probably a situation of his own choosing; had he wanted to share the Guardianship, there would have probably been plenty of willing candidates. It would, perhaps, have been a challenge to find someone who was acceptable to all of the different elements of the Balliol party, but there seems to have been no action on Wallace's part to involve anyone else in wielding executive power.

Clearly, his defeat at Falkirk undermined Wallace's political stature fatally. Even if he had retained the support of the magnates and the clerical establishment, and despite the fact that he still enjoyed a good deal of popularity in what remained of the army, Wallace was definitely yesterday's man, politically and militarily. He had endeavoured to fight a war of manoeuvre and major engagements and had been defeated. The army he had raised had been thoroughly beaten, to such a degree that the Scots would have to adopt a different approach to the war.

The 'revolutionary' and 'guerrilla' tactics attributed to Wallace by historians were in fact totally conventional practice for the thirteenth and fourteenth centuries. Instead of the great forces that had met at Falkirk or Stirling, both the Scots and the English came to rely on the services of men-at-arms. The return to conventional warfare also led to a return to more traditional leadership arrangements. Wallace might have been acceptable as the commander of a large force of all arms invading northern England or confronting Edward I, but in the more closely-knit forces that conducted the campaigns of 1298–1304 social station may have been more significant than in the army of 1296: senior lords with their own followings might not have the same confidence in Wallace that they would have had in a man of greater status and, perhaps, wider experience.

Defeat at Falkirk destroyed Wallace's career in executive politics and destroyed his army, but it did not change the course of the war to any great degree. Edward does not seem to have had any clear view of how best to exploit his victory; his army had been badly damaged in the battle, and there was sickness in the camps, little money to pay the troops and little for them to do if they were kept on station. Edward disbanded his army and returned to England, leaving his administration in Scotland little better off than it had been before the campaign. Wallace had been defeated and driven out of the Guardianship, but little had been recovered in the way of territory and much of that had been lost to the Scots again almost immediately. One of the few tangible benefits had been a brief campaign in Lothian,[13] where a column under Antony Bek, Bishop of Durham had succeeded in recapturing three castles, probably including

Dirleton, and Yester, which had fallen to the Scots in the preceding months, possibly as far back as Wallace's passage through Lothian in November of the previous year.

Edward's victory undermined Wallace and the Balliol cause, but his own withdrawal from Scotland so quickly afterwards can have done nothing for the prestige of his kingship among the Scots. If Edward's lordship was limited to sporadic invasions of Scotland, rather than imposing firm government and stability, there was not a lot to be said for it. It probably did not do a great deal for the morale of the garrisons either. A major expedition, even if did not come to battle with the Balliol forces, would make some impression on the population in the areas that the army passed through, though not perhaps an impression likely to win hearts and minds in the community, but the return of the army to England would inevitably give an impression of weakness as well.

The Balliol party suffered a severe blow at Falkirk, but not one that destroyed either their will or their capacity to continue with the war. It could be argued that the destruction of Wallace as a political force was in fact the most significant outcome from the perspective of both parties. This rather depends on the degree of security Wallace enjoyed in the Guardianship. Wallace governed with what later Scottish writers would call 'raddure'. Not perhaps oppressively, or at least not any more so than the times demanded, but with both vigour and rigour; it would be surprising if he had not managed to offend some of the men around him. His meteoric rise to power may have been sanctioned by an extensive body of opinion among the magnates, but they had not expected that Wallace would reign alone, nor would he have done but for the death of Sir Andrew Murray. The most powerful grouping in the Balliol party was based on the Comyn family, and Andrew Murray was a cousin of sorts to John Comyn, Earl of Buchan.

It would be unsafe to see Murray as a stalking horse for the Comyns, a means of keeping control over, or at least influence in, the Balliol cause. The tradition of service to Crown and country was very strong in the Comyn family; they had, after all, prospered in the service of Scottish kings and would certainly hope and expect to do so again in the event of a Balliol restoration. The leaders of the Comyn family, John, Lord of Badenoch and John, Earl of Buchan were still prisoners of war when Murray's forces seized the north, but it would be unlikely that he could have mustered the necessary support without the knowledge and assent, not to say connivance, of the network of barons, free tenants and officials with Comyn family ties that dominated the political community of north-east Scotland.

The Comyns, and other northern lords as well, could reasonably expect that a man of Murray's station in life would not encourage uncontrollable mob rule: that, if anything, he might be able to impose better order than the English administration. Without the acquiescence, if not support, of the Comyn interest in northern Scotland, Murray's rising might not have got very much further than the attacks on Castle Urquhart and Inverness and, however successful such attacks might be, there would be little chance of exploiting the victory to set up a national administration without a good deal of input from the nobility in general, and, at least in the north-east, the Comyn family in particular. The existence of a Scottish administration in the north, however *ad hoc* and rudimentary, was of huge significance for Balliol activists and sympathisers elsewhere. The reduction of English garrisons proved that the occupation government was not invincible, and the increasingly extensive area under Scottish administration was an indication that the war generally was not going in favour of the English – an encouraging sign for the Scots. Wallace was able to assemble a force of some stature by August 1297, but he would have been very hard pressed to achieve a victory at Stirling Bridge without the army of the north under Murray; he probably would have been obliged to retire in front of what would have been a very much greater force than his own, abandoning the whole of the south of Scotland to the occupation.

The popular view of the Comyns is that expressed by the Scottish writers of the fourteenth century, Barbour and Fordoun. In the tale of how Robert the Bruce saved the nation from the English and from treacherous Scotsmen, the Comyn family stand fair and square with the villains.[14] As relatives, neighbours and associates of the Balliol family from long before the time of the great competition for the Scottish throne, and as remarkably staunch servants of the Balliol cause through seven years of war after 1297, it is hardly surprising that they should have opposed the ambitions of the Bruce family, but they were hardly unpatriotic. Their modern reputation shows the power of propaganda, even 700 years after the event. Fordoun and Bower were both enthusiastic supporters of the Bruce cause, but Barbour was an uncritical fan. He equated the Bruce cause with the Scottish patriotic cause, thus making the political opponents of the Bruces into traitors.

The failure – as presented by contemporaries – of the Comyn men-at-arms to engage at Falkirk may have been the downfall of Wallace; certainly his defeat undermined his political credibility but, at the same time, it is not at all likely that the Comyns left the field in the hopes of bringing about his defeat. These were not stupid men; they must have been aware that their departure would sit very badly with the community. It is infinitely more likely that they deserted from a battle that they could see was already lost. If the Comyns can be legitimately criticised for not being killed in action at Falkirk, the same criticism can be levelled at William Wallace, but in reality both Wallace and the Comyns had a duty to survive the battle, in that they were the recognised representatives of the Scottish political community and the representatives of King John: their feudal responsibilities obliged them to do their best to keep his cause alive in Scotland, not to achieve chivalric but pointless martyrdom on the battlefield.

The William Wallace encountered in historical record is far removed from the Wallace of films or enthusiastic biographers. It may be evident to historians that Wallace was a man of noble lineage, a member of the ruling class (though in a relatively humble degree), but that does rather conflict with the well-established, though erroneous, view of Wallace as a simple commoner drawn into political life by his patriotic fervour. While it is true that the magnate class did dominate political activity and leadership in Scotland – as was the case throughout northern and western Europe – men like Wallace were an integral part of the political community; the distance between the highest and lowest members of that community was one of social and economic degree, but not of class, culture or language. These aspects of his background are not evidence that Wallace was in any sense less 'Scottish' than his neighbours, but seem to present a problem to those writers whose enthusiasm for Wallace the hero clouds their view of Wallace the man. His achievements were very real. Edward I did not make Wallace the target of his ire at random: he did so because Wallace was a threat to his ambition of adding Scotland to his domains. Neither Wallace nor his successors as Guardians actually managed to either restore King John or to completely expel the English, though Blind Harry has his hero accomplish this feat, not once, but three times. They were, however, successful in preventing Edward from annexing Scotland between 1296 and 1304 and, in so doing, made Scots accustomed to the acceptance of administration through Guardians rather than kings, a situation that would arise on the death of King Robert, the captivity of David II and the captivity of James I, then again during the minorities of James II, James III, James V, Mary I and James VI. The various Guardians and regents managed to maintain Scottish independence in the face of a powerful neighbour that may have learned by the middle of the fourteenth century that the physical conquest of Scotland was just too big a project for English arms, but that still had an interest, perceived or real, in keeping the Scots weak. By the time Robert Bruce assumed the kingship, his subjects had already been at war, intermittently, for a decade. For most of that period, the exist-ence of a Scottish political entity was made possible by the efforts of the Guardians of Scotland and by their ability to command military service from the noble and burghal communities. The first Guardianship after the deposition of King John may have collapsed little more than a year after its inauguration, but that year was critical to the fortunes of the Scots. It showed that even without the presence of a king to lead them and to fight for, a strong body of opinion in Scottish society was prepared to take up arms in defence of the political independence of the country, and that that body of opinion extended far beyond the bounds of the customary political class: the landholders, lords and clergy.

Even before he became Guardian Wallace would seem to have been demanding and receiving military service, but after the initial stages of his military career, at the point when his force ceased to be a raiding party of armoured cavalry men (or brigands depending on one's perspective) and started to become a more conventional army, he must have depended on his personal prestige, acquired through successful actions against the occupation, as a recruiting sergeant. Many of the men who joined the army of William Wallace in the early summer of 1297 must have done so of their own volition, as a political act rather than as a path for personal ambition or through the threat of the gallows that Wallace apparently had erected in every town and village. Although he was, by birth and upbringing, a member of that class, Wallace himself was living proof that desperate times could lead to great opportunity. His station within the noble community was low, not to say obscure, and for such a man to gain the respect of a suf-ficiently large portion of society that he could be entrusted with wielding the power of the Crown was remarkable, particularly since the Crown was hardly in a position to confer that authority at all, given that King John was a prisoner in England. Naturally, he faced resentment and prejudice; all successful people do, and those who are successful in politics more than most. Was William Wallace a politician? Of course he was. The entirety of his recorded life – other than Blind Harry's contribution – relates to politi-cal activity by a man of the political community who had, or more likely made, an opportunity to act in a sphere of government normally reserved for more elevated individuals. Most of William's political activity was of the military kind: he was a very violent man, one who enjoyed battle, as was the fashion of his class and time. Fortunately for Scottish historians, he was in the right place at the right time and applied his violent nature to the needs of his prince and his country just when they needed him most.

CHAPTER TEN

Wallace and Fordoun:
'A Doughty and Powerful Man'

Virtually every piece written about William Wallace – newspaper articles, scholarly papers, biographies and general histories of the period – alludes to the unquestioned fact that there is not a great deal of material. This is true; historians have described Wallace as 'shadowy', 'mysterious' and even 'semi-legendary'. There is, however, a rather greater body of material than might be expected. Naturally, William features prominently in the works of the Scottish chroniclers, John of Fordoun, Andrew of Wynton and Abbot Bower. None of these has very much to say about Wallace other than in relation to his rise to power, his defeat at Falkirk and his eventual capture and execution. Historians would of course like there to be rather more material relating to his personal life as well as to his political career, but it would be unrealistic to expect anything more than the material we have. Apart from the fact that Wallace lived and died over 700 years ago and it is therefore likely that a quantity of information has been lost, a man of William Wallace's station in life was not likely to generate very much in the way of documentary evidence, save in the unlikely event of his advancement to a position of consequence. The 'gobbets' – extracts – printed below represent the bulk of such evidence as has survived, both in narrative and record sources. Hopefully the explanatory notes will show the relevance of the extracts, in giving a context both to William Wallace and his adversaries.

As the earliest extant Scottish chronicle covering the Wars of Independence, the chronicle of John of Fordoun is perhaps the most important of the accounts of the war years from a Scottish perspective, despite the brevity of the entries. Like his successors, Wyntoun and Bower, Fordoun was unashamedly patriotic, not to say nationalistic, but not as damning as them in his attitude to the English, despite the fact that the events he described were of relatively recent date at the time of writing. Beyond his prejudice against the English and his belief, shared by Wyntoun and Bower, that the victories of the English were generally brought about through the dishonesty of treacherous Scots or were afflictions from God intended to punish the Scots for pride, Fordoun's work provides a continuous narrative account that is remarkably dependable and sheds a little light on a good many aspects of life and war in the fourteenth century. Fordoun first brings Wallace to the attention of the reader with a fight resulting in the death of the sheriff of Lanark:

RISE AND FIRST START OF WILLIAM WALLACE

The same year, William Wallace lifted up his hand from his den – as it were – and slew the Sheriff of Lanark, a doughty and powerful man, in the town of Lanark. From that time, therefore, there flocked to him all who were in bitterness of spirit and weighed down beneath the burden of bondage under the unbearable domination of English despotism; and he became their leader. He was wonderfully brave and bold, of goodly mien and boundless liberality, and, though among the earls and lords of the Kingdom he was looked upon as low-born, yet his fathers rejoiced in the honour of knighthood. His elder brother also was girded with the knightly belt and inherited a landed estate which was large enough for his station and which he bequeathed as a holding to his descendants. So Wallace overthrew the English on all sides; and gaining strength daily, he, in a short time, by force, and by dint of his prowess brought all the magnates under his sway. Such of the magnates, moreover, as did not thankfully obey his commands, he browbeat them and gave them into custody, until they should utterly submit to his pleasure. And when all had thus been subdued, he manfully betook himself to the storming of the castles and fortified towns in which the English ruled; for he aimed at quickly and thoroughly freeing his country and overthrowing the enemy.

Chapter 98 of Fordoun's Chronicle

Inevitably, all of the chronicle sources give much the same information about Wallace. A good deal of that material is formulaic: Wallace, as a great hero, must needs be heroic, but gentlemanly, decent and an effective leader. No doubt all of the Scottish chroniclers would like to have been able to write that Wallace was completely acceptable to the Scottish political community and enjoyed the unequivocal support of the entire population, but in truth a large body of opinion was not inclined to either Wallace or the Balliol cause, and he had little choice but to enforce his authority with the threat, if not the actuality, of violence. Fordoun is a little more explicit about the nature and status of the Wallace family. He puts them very firmly in the knightly rank of the nobility: William's father and brother both acquired knightly status and had property sufficient to maintain it. This is slightly against the grain of other evidence that indicates the status of lairds rather than knights, but it is important to understand that these were not two clearly defined ranks in society, rather that they constituted that part of the nobility that separated the barons, lords and earls from the commons. Assuming that Fordoun is correct, the Wallace estate was adequate for the support of a knight but as far as the great lords and earls were concerned the Wallaces were 'low-born'. Landholder status was not an automatic guarantee of wealth. Though obviously virtually all of the landholders were rather better off than virtually everybody else, the margins were not necessarily very great between the laird and his tenant, and the laird would almost inevitably have to bear a number of burdens from which tenants were free. Of these, court duty and military service were expensive obligations to discharge: the family of William Wallace, like many others around them, may have enjoyed a social status that was a challenge to maintain on their income.

BATTLE OF STIRLING BRIDGE

In the year 1297 the fame of William Wallace was spread all abroad, and at length reached the King of England; for the loss brought upon his people was crying out. As the King, however, was intent upon many troublesome matters elsewhere, he sent his treasures, named Hugh de Clissingham, with a large force to repress this William's boldness, and to bring the Kingdom of Scotland under his sway. When, therefore, he heard of this man's arrival, the aforesaid William, then busy besieging Dundee castle, straightaway entrusted the care and charge of the castle to the burgesses of that town, on pain of loss of life and limb, and, with his army, marched on, with all haste, towards Strivelin [Stirling] to meet this Hugh. A battle was then fought, on the 11th of September, at the bridge over the Forth. Hugh of Clissingham was killed and all his army put to flight; some were slain with the sword, others taken, others drowned in the waters. But through God, they were all overcome; and the aforesaid William gained a happy victory, with no little praise. Of the nobles, on his side, the noble Andrew Murray alone, the father of Andrew, fell wounded.

Chapter 99 of Fordoun's Chronicle

Information about the battle itself is limited, almost non-existent, in Fordoun's account, the only Scottish casualty of any note being Andrew Murray. As Wallace's partner in command, Murray could hardly be overlooked, and his demise some weeks after the action removed him from the political and military hierarchy of the Scots. Had Murray survived, Wallace would no doubt have had to share his authority with him. In Fordoun's analysis, Murray is very definitely Wallace's junior partner, though this may not have been the view of the men who served under them at Stirling Bridge. It is quite possible that Murray's superior status and the lower incidence of garrisons in northern Scotland allowed Murray to raise a greater force than Wallace, in which case he would probably have had the greater say in their planning. Whether or not his force was the larger would not necessarily be the issue that would settle command influence. Since the hold of the English in northern Scotland had obviously been much less secure than in the south, Murray may have found it rather easier than Wallace to procure the service of men-at-arms.

WILLIAM WALLACE WINTERS IN ENGLAND

In the same year, William Wallace, with his army, wintered in England, from Hallowmass to Christmas; and having burnt up the whole of the land of Allerdale, and carried off some plunder, he and his men went back safe and sound. The same year moreover, on the 20th of August, all the English – regular and beneficed clergy, as well as laymen, were, by this same William, again cast out from the Kingdom of Scotland. And the same year, William of Lamberton was chosen bishop of St Andrews.

Chapter 100 of Fordoun's Chronicle

The election of William Lamberton was a major diplomatic success for the Scots. Edward had a candidate of his own who, if elected, would in theory at least be able to control the extensive income of the diocese that might otherwise go to the support of the Balliol cause. What exactly is implied by the statement that Wallace expelled all the English from Scotland is unclear: there was no point in Wallace's career in the Balliol cause when all the castles and communities of Scotland were in the hands of Plantagenet partisans. It may be that the chronicler is referring to an edict of expulsion issued by the Wallace government, rather than the effective implementation of it. The exclusion of Scottish candidates from benefices – any and all ecclesiastical positions with an attached income, from vicars to bishops – was a policy favoured by Edward I, partly no doubt to give himself a new string of patronage but also to prevent the promotion of Scottish clergymen active in the Balliol cause, men like Bishop Wishart and Bishop Lamberton who could divert a portion of their considerable income to the political cause of their choice. Given the ambitions of the Archbishops of York and Canterbury to bring the Scottish Church under their control, it would hardly be surprising if Scottish clergymen were more likely to support the party that offered better 'lordship' to the Scottish Church as an independent structure responsible directly to the Pope.

THE BATTLE OF FALKIRK

In the year 1298, the aforesaid King of England, taking it ill that he and his should be put to so much loss and driven to such straits by William Wallace, gathered a large army, and, having with him, in his company, some of the noble of Scotland to help him, invaded Scotland. He was met by the aforesaid William, with the magnates of the rest of that kingdom; and a desperate battle was fought near Falkirk on the 22nd of July. William was put to flight, not without serious loss to both the lords and to the common people of the Scottish nation. For, on account of the ill-will, begotten of the spring of envy, which the Comyns had conceived to the said William, they, with all their accomplices, forsook the field and escaped unhurt. On learning their spiteful deed, the aforesaid William, wishing to save himself and his, hastened to flee by another road. But alas! Through the pride and burning envy of both, the noble Estates [*communitas*] of Scotland lay wretchedly overthrown through hill and dale, mountain and plain. Among these, of the nobles, John Stewart and his Brendans; MacDuff, of Fife, and the inhabitants thereof, were utterly cut off. But it is commonly said that Robert of Bruce, – who was afterward King of Scotland; but then fought on the side of the King of

England – was the means of bringing about this victory. For, while then Scots stood invincible in their ranks, and could not be broken by either force or stratagem, this Robert of Bruce went with one line, under Antony of Bek, by a long road round a hill, and attacked the Scots in the rear; and thus these, who stood invincible and impenetrable in front, were craftily overcome in the rear. And it is remarkable that we seldom, if ever, read of the Scots being overcome by the English, unless through the envy of lords, or the treachery and deceit of the natives, taking them over to the other side.

But after the aforesaid victory, which was vouchsafed to the enemy through the treachery of Scots, the aforesaid William Wallace, perceiving, by these and other strong truths, the glaring wickedness of the Comyns and their abettors, chose rather to serve with the crowd, than to be set over them, to their ruin, and the grievous wasting of the people. So, not long after the battle of Falkirk, at the water of the Forth, he, of his own accord, resigned the office and charge which he held, of Guardian.

Chapter 101 of Fordoun's Chronicle

Never one to miss an opportunity to tell his fellow Scots that their misfortunes were self-inflicted, Fordoun manages to simultaneously undermine the achievements of the English. Not only was Edward I accompanied by many Scottish lords and men-at-arms, but the victory was achieved through a mixture of the desertion of Wallace by the Comyns and the tactical acumen of Robert the Bruce. It is certainly the case that some Scots did serve in the English army at Falkirk, but not all of them were lords of any consequence. Thomas Lillok, a minor landholder from Roxburghshire, was provided with a horse from Edward I's stables so that he could serve as a man-at-arms. The horse, but not apparently the rider, was lost in the fighting.

A number of the terms used in this segment call for some explanation. 'Brendans' were people from Bute, an area dominated by Stewart family lordship centred on their great castle at Rothesay. The term 'estates' (*communitas*) was used by Maxwell to describe the local political community: the landholding, clerical and, to a limited degree perhaps, the commercial classes.

Although the withdrawal of the Comyns and their 'accomplices', as Fordoun describes them, certainly took place, it is important to bear in mind the extent and effectiveness of Bruce party propaganda during the century or so after Wallace's death – indeed, it is still effective today. In popular consciousness, the Bruce cause and the cause of Scottish independence are virtually, if not absolutely, one and the same. This was not clear at the time: the Balliol cause was certainly the cause of independence, and the Comyn family supported that cause consistently for years – their opposition to a Bruce kingship was not a product of their desire to be lords of Edward I so much as their determination not to be lords of Robert I. As the chief opposition to Robert the Bruce's kingship after 1306, the Comyns provided a convenient scapegoat for Scottish chroniclers. It would not be surprising if the Comyn party were less than enamoured of Wallace's leadership in 1297–98. The leaders of the Comyn interest, John, Earl of Buchan and John, Lord of Badenoch, surely saw themselves in that role, but it would be unlikely that they would choose to abandon Wallace simply to undermine him: the political risk would have been immense. If Wallace was defeated – as he was – their reputation could be severely damaged, but if he was victorious the damage would be even greater. They would have deserted Wallace in his hour of need, which would undermine their influence in the political community, but, had Wallace succeeded without their help, his own prestige would have been greatly enhanced. Wallace in defeat could be quickly marginalised by the traditional leaders of Scottish society, the great lords, and be replaced with one of their number – one of what Dr Watson splendidly refers to as the 'obligatory' John Comyns, for example – but a victorious Wallace would be very difficult to displace, so long as he maintained his prestige among the people.

It is always possible that after Falkirk men did say that the victory was achieved through the intervention of Robert of Bruce; however, again, Bruce propaganda may be at the bottom of such claims. Attributing victory to Robert contributed to his general reputation as a paladin and undermined the prestige of Edward I, implying that the English were incapable of defeating Wallace without the active intervention of the Scots. So far as Fordoun was concerned, Wallace's resignation was a matter of personal choice; realistically, however, he had no option. His rise to prominence was entirely the product of successful military leadership against the English; defeat at Falkirk made his replacement inevitable.

THE ESTATES OF SCOTLAND MAKE THEIR SUBMISSION TO THE KING OF ENGLAND

The same year [1304], after the whole Estates of Scotland had made their submission to the King of England, John Comyn, then Guardian, and all the other magnates of Scotland, but [except] William Wallace, little by little, one after another, made their submissions to him; and all their castles and towns – except Strivelyn [Stirling] Castle and the warden thereof – were

surrendered unto him. That year the King kept Lent at St Andrews, where
he called together all the great men of the kingdom, and held his parliament;
and he made such decrees as he would, according to the state of the country
– which, as he thought, had been gotten and won for him and his successors
forever – as well as about the dwellers therein.

Chapter 110 of Fordoun's Chronicle

By late 1303 the Balliol cause was in a serious decline. The most important
supporter in the diplomatic war, Philip IV of France, was obliged to abandon his commitment to the inclusion of the Scots in any permanent peace
agreed between France and England; John I had indicated that he was
prepared to accept whatever Philip felt was necessary; and, at last, Edward I
was able to focus his attention – and a very large army – on Scotland. The
Scots had had a good deal of military success since the defeat at Falkirk,
but not enough to secure a political victory, and the Communities of the
Realm, whether in Scottish or English control, were exhausted. With no
king to fight for, the Balliol party had no choice other than to seek terms
from Edward before their military situation deteriorated to a point at
which there was little for Edward to gain by offering terms for an end to
the fighting. The Strathord armistice of February 1304 did not bring an
immediate end to the fighting. The Balliol garrison in Stirling Castle held
out for several weeks, claiming to hold the castle against England, not on
behalf of King John, but on behalf of 'the lion', the heraldic emblem of
Scotland: an early example of simple political nationalism.

On balance, it seems likely that in 1304 Edward still felt that he could
achieve a genuine acceptance of his rule in Scotland. The edicts issued
in his name for the future administration of Scotland hardly constituted
the statesmanlike rationalisation of Scottish laws and procedures claimed
by some anglophile historians, but equally he was not particularly heavy-
handed. Most of the men who had opposed Edward were accepted into
his peace on relatively lenient terms; William Wallace and the garrison of
Stirling Castle were not so fortunate.

STIRLING CASTLE BESIEGED BY
THE KING OF ENGLAND

Just after Easter, in the year 1304, that same King besieged Strivelyn [Stirling]
Castle for three months without a break. For this siege, he commanded all

39 Cambuskenneth Abbey. Little remains of Cambuskenneth today, but in the thirteenth and fourteenth centuries it was a place of some significance and possibly the location for the gathering that acknowledged the Guardianship of Wallace and Murray after the battle of Stirling Bridge.

40 Torphichen Receptory. The headquarters of the Knights of St John of Jerusalem in Scotland and the receiving centre for the income the order derived from its many Scottish properties and annuities.

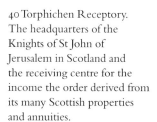

41 Edinburgh Castle from Arthur's Seat. The garrison of Edinburgh capitulated
to the army of Edward I after a bombardment of five days in the spring of 1296.
It remained a crucial part of the English administration until it fell to the Earl of
Moray in March 1314.

42 Dirleton Castle. The castle of
the de Vaux family in East Lothian,
Dirleton was one of the few really
modern fortresses in Scotland at the
time of Edward I's invasion. It was
captured by Balliol forces in 1297
but was recovered for the English
administration by Bishop Antony
Bek the following year.

43 An arming jacket. Chain-mail was very effective against edged weapons, but the impact of the blow would cause severe injury if the mail was not worn in conjunction with a 'jack' or 'gambeson'.

44 A mounted man-at-arms. Contrary to the romantic image of 'Braveheart', Scottish men-at-arms and knights were indistinguishable from their English counterparts.

45 Spearman. Infantry bearing spears and polearms were recruited in large numbers for virtually all European armies.

46 Schiltrom. The word 'schiltrom' did not imply any particular shape of formation, but they were generally rectangular. Falkirk may have been the only occasion when circular schiltroms were used in a large engagement.

47 Polearm. Although swords were widely carried in peacetime as well as wartime, the primary weapon in battle was generally a spear or polearm.

48 A re-enactor plays John I. From the very beginning of John's reign, Edward I sought to undermine John's authority and to provoke him into armed resistance.

49 Hobelar. Light cavalry units were of great value for reconnaissance and foraging duties, but generally dismounted for battle.

50 A trebuchet. A classic medieval siege weapon, trebuchets are surprisingly accurate if carefully maintained. This example is on permanent display at Caerlaverock Castle, Dumfriesshire.

51 Inchcolm Abbey. Located on the island of Inchcolm in the Firth of Forth, Inchcolm was the target of several raids by English forces during the Wars of Independence. It was here that Walter Bower wrote his vast *Scotichronicon* in the mid-fifteenth century.

52 View of Stirling Bridge battlefield from the north. The Scots deployed to the north of the river and attacked the English as they crossed the bridge.

53 View of Stirling Bridge battlefield from the castle. The English army was trapped in the oxbow of the river and much of the fighting took place in the vicinity of the Stirling County rugby grounds, visible to the right of the bridge.

54 View of river Forth from mid-river. The existing Victorian bridge stands slightly downriver from its thirteenth-century predecessor.

the lead of the refectory of St Andrews to be pulled down, and had it taken away for the use of his engines. At last the aforesaid castle was surrendered and delivered unto him on certain conditions, drawn up in writing, and sealed with his seal. But when he had got the castle, the King belied his troth, and broke through the conditions; for William Oliphaunt, the warden thereof, he threw bound into prison in London, and kept him a long time in thrall. The same year, when both great and small in the kingdom of Scotland (except William Wallace alone) had made their submission unto him; when the surrendered castles and fortified towns, which had formerly been broken down and knocked to pieces, had all been rebuilt, and he had appointed wardens of his own therein; and after all and sundry of Scottish birth had tendered him homage, the King, with the prince of Wales, and his whole army, returned to England. He left, however, the chief warden as his lieutenant, to amend and control the lawlessness of all the rest, both Scots and English. He did not show his face in Scotland after this.

Chapter 110 of Fordoun's Chronicle

Quite why the defenders of Stirling should have been excluded from the Strathord agreement is unknown; they may have sought terms that exonerated them from misdeeds committed during the siege, or their declaration that they held the castle 'for the lion' rather than for King John may suggest dissent in the Balliol party. Some Scots seem to have believed that Stirling was excluded from the armistice at Edward's insistence so that his siege engines – specifically, an unusually powerful weapon called the 'war wolf' – could be put through their paces.

Whether this was really the case or whether Edward broke his word to the defenders is not clear, though Sir William Oliphaunt was certainly held as a prisoner of war for some time before he was accepted into the peace of Edward II. Sir William is a classic example of the way in which we tend to assume a common identity between nationalist Scots and the Bruce party. Sir William served the Balliol cause faithfully, but served against the Bruce party after 1306, commanding the defence of Perth on behalf of the Plantagenet occupation in 1312. The reasons for his rejection of Bruce kingship remain a mystery. He may have favoured the Balliols because they were the legitimate claimants; equally, he may have rejected Robert I not because he was a usurper (though he certainly was), but because he was a murderer, and a sacrilegious one at that. These were conditions that Sir William could bring himself to overlook in the fullness of time, apparently, since he was able to make an accommodation with King Robert.

DEATH OF WILLIAM WALLACE

In the year 1305, William Wallace was craftily and treacherously taken by John
of Menteith, who handed him over to the King of England; and he was, in
London, torn limb from limb, and, as a reproach to Scots, his limbs were hung
on towers in sundry places throughout England and Scotland.

Chapter 116 of Fordoun's Chronicle

Again, Fordoun indicates the chief failing of the Scots: their capacity for
betraying one another. This is not entirely fair to John of Menteith and the
other Scots who served Edward I. Between 1296 and 1304 there was a case
to be made for accepting the authority of either side: John I was undoubtedly the legal king of Scotland and had abdicated under duress; on the
other hand, a great number of Scots had given their allegiance to Edward
I in 1296 during the exercise in homage-taking known as the Ragman
Roll. After the Strathord agreement, the remaining Balliol partisans really
had no cause to fight for – the leaders had accepted terms and the war was
over. In those circumstances, the pursuit and defeat of men who still carried
on the fight was the duty of all those men who had accepted Edward I's
occupation administration as the 'government of day', particularly if they
happened to have specific personal military obligations. Sir John captured
William Wallace and has had to bear a good deal of blame for his death,
but it might just as easily have been any one of many other Scottish lords
who were active in the field that summer: the outcome would have been
no different. Once captured, it would have been unreasonable for Wallace
to expect any treatment from Edward I other than a grotesque death. The
execution of Wallace, and the distribution of the grisly segments to various
cities in Scotland and northern England (traditionally Stirling, Berwick,
Perth and Newcastle), gave Edward the opportunity to show his subjects
that revolt would not be tolerated but, perhaps more importantly, that he
was taking firm action and exacting retribution for the damage Wallace
had caused to the king of England and his subjects.

CHAPTER ELEVEN

Wallace and Wyntoun: 'Their Chieftain and Their Leader'

Wyntoun worked from several sources, not all of which have survived, but, like Bower, the most significant of his sources was probably John of Fordoun's chronicle. Like Barbour's *Bruce*, Wyntoun's chronicle is presented in verse; unlike Barbour's *Bruce*, it does not read easily to a twenty-first-century audience. The excerpts below have been 'Anglicised' to allow better access to the information contained within. Unlike Fordoun, Barbour and Bower, Wyntoun has not been the subject of a scholarly examination, though there is a fine Scottish Text Society edition comprising a parallel printing of the two earliest extant copies.

> Here next follows the days
> When rose good William Wallace
> Twelve hundred ninety year and seven
> From Christ was born the King of Heaven
> William Wallace in Clydesdale
> That saw his kin suppressed all
> With English men with great dispute
> Some of their harms he thought to requite
> For [although] he was descended from noble men
> In simple state he was set then
> His father was a manly knight
> His mother was a lady bright

He, conceived and born in wedlock,
His elder brother the heritage [family estate]
Had, and used [kept] all his days.
This same William Wallace
Was attracted to arms and gear
That manly men used then to wear
With a sword both sharp and long
It was his use [way] then to give
Great opposition to English men.
So they made then [decided] on a day
For him to set in hard assay [attack him]
Of his long sword in that intent
First they gave him argument
In til [at] Lanark the English men
Where a multitude [of Englishmen] were gathered then
And tried to seize his sword
[Wallace] 'Hold your hand and speak your word'
[Englishman] 'With your sword you make great boast'

Wyntoun is at pains to ensure that the reader is aware from the outset that Wallace is a man of the nobility, that his father was a knight – and a worthy one – and that his brother inherited the family property. For the late-medieval Scottish reader, this information puts Wallace firmly in a social and economic context that the reader was familiar with. That Wallace should be familiar with arms would come as no surprise to the reader: almost all males of that status would have undergone some degree of military training. By telling the reader that Wallace was 'drawn' to arms and 'gear' (armour), Wyntoun is perhaps informing his readership that Wallace was unusually interested and, by implication, unusually competent in the use of arms. It is not the use of his great sword that brings Wallace into conflict with an Englishman in Lanark, just the carrying of it. First the Englishman endeavours to take Wallace's sword; then insults are offered regarding the parentage of the Englishman:

[Englishman] 'You should not bear so fair a knife [sword]'
[Wallace] 'So said the priest that served your wife.
So long he called that woman fair,
At length his child was made your heir'

And – unsurprisingly, given that Wallace had just insulted the man and his wife, cast doubts of the legitimacy of his son and heir, and disputed the observance of the local parish priest – a fight ensues:

> From that they cast no more words
> But soon they all took out their swords
> In the market [place] of Lanark
> Where English men both stern and stark
> Fought in a great multitude
> Against William Wallace [the] good
> There he gave then dint for dint [blow]
> And no strength could withstand his blow
> As he was in that stour [affray] fighting
> From one [man] he soon struck [off] the right hand

The fight continues until Wallace, though vanquishing his enemies, decides that discretion is that better part of valour and endeavours to escape:

> Then he was a long while
> Fighting in a state of peril
> Until he retired to his lodging
> Defending himself manfully
> But was followed treacherously
> In the town was his leman [lover or betrothed]
> That was a pleasant fair woman

In the finest traditions of chivalrous romance, Wallace's lover, Marion Braidfute, saves him from his pursuers by means of a secret exit and then delays them while Wallace makes his escape to the forests:

> The she made him secretly
> Leave by another way from there
> And with her slight [deception] delayed then
> His foes, while to the wood he ran.
> The sheriff at that time of the land
> The King of England's lieutenant
> Came to Lanark and there he
> Had this woman taken prisoner
> And soon had her put to death

Wallace saw all this from where he was hiding nearby
Therefore he was heavy in heart

Witnessing the death of his partner at the hands of the English naturally did nothing to encourage William Wallace to seek the peace of Edward I. Presumably already an outlaw, since he had been involved in an affray that had led to wounding if not to death, Wallace had little choice but to take to the hills, where he set about raising support from his friends and relations:

And thirty men he got, or more
Then one night he came, with they
That were manly men and stark
In to the town of Lanark
And where he knew the Sheriff
Was accustomed to lodge
In a loft where he lay,
After midnight [and] before day
He strenuously broke in the door
And laid it flat upon the floor
With that, the Sheriff, all aghast
'Who is that?' He spoke out fast
Said William Wallace 'Here am I,
Will the Wallace, that basely
You have set yourself to slay
Now together we must go
That woman's death of yesterday,
I will acquit it if I may
Very quickly after that
The Sheriff he got by the throat
Down that tall stair he trailed [dragged] him down
And slew him there within the town
From when he thus the Sheriff slew
Scottish men close to him drew
That by the English at that time were
Aggrieved and sore oppressed
And this William they made there
Their chieftain and their leader
For he could well take on the task
For he was fair and pleasant,
Manlike, stout and liberal

And wise in government
He spared no Englishmen
To Scots he brought great profit then
The greatest lords of our land,
He made them bow to him.

Wallace then took up the sword, in response to a challenge from an Englishman and then in vengeance for the murder of his partner, but his personality and his success would seem to have made him a focus for men who were in search of a leader. The thirty men who accompanied Wallace on his first operation were joined by men who were already at odds with the occupation. There is no reason to assume that these men were ideologically motivated. In a society where outlawing was a normal part of judicial procedure, there would undoubtedly have been men who had simply fallen foul of criminal law, most, if not all, of whom would very likely have been made outlaws regardless of whether there was a Scottish or English king on the throne.

Naturally, as a popular leader in a romantic history, Wallace's leadership was not simply the product of a strong right arm and a powerful will. The men of his party chose Wallace as their leader because he was a repository of desirable values. He was 'fair' (handsome) and 'pleasant' (charming) and he was manlike, stout and liberal: what could be better in a leader? These are the sort of terms conventionally applied to heroic figures in medieval accounts of gallant noble leaders. If the early followers of Wallace were largely drawn from the lower orders of society, he may have been able to make himself acceptable as leader because he was of a higher status. This does not imply a feckless peasantry desperate to have a 'lord' take control of, and therefore responsibility for, the actions of the group, so much as a recognition that he would be more likely to have at least some of the skills and experience necessary for successful military leadership. The military aspect should not be too heavily stressed, however; in his earliest operations Wallace was hardly distinguishable from a successful leader of bandits. Even if the majority of his adherents were men of noble birth, they were not far removed from the knights and gentry who fell into, or cheerfully adopted, banditry as a way of life in areas of France, England and Scotland at times when central government was ineffectual.

The extent of Wallace's ability to exert leadership in late 1296 and early 1297 was unquestionably less developed that Wyntoun chose to believe. The men he called the 'greatest lords of our land' were hardly queuing up to give service and obedience to William Wallace. There were a number of reasons for them not to do so. Wallace was not a figure of customary political prominence. In the very conservative society of the thirteenth and fourteenth centuries it was certainly possible for a man to rise above his station – even to join the nobility from very obscure origins – but virtually impossible for a man of middling rank to be properly accepted into the ranks of the higher nobility. In normal times the great nobles, the magnates, would expect to take a role in the government of the country and to have a role in the councils of the king. In the minority or absence of a king they would be inclined to expect to have a greater degree of influence than would generally be the case. It would seem unlikely that very many members of the magnate class would have been willing to accept Wallace's command until such time as he had proved himself an able leader, and then only for so long as he could sustain credibility in his administration. In his desire to show the Scots presenting a united front, Wyntoun tells us that:

> Of castles, burghs and fortalices
> The greatest [the magnates] made him service
> The English men out of our land
> He drove them out with stalwart hand.

On the other hand, Wyntoun also tells us that those who would not do Wallace's bidding were put in prison, so his appeal was evidently less than universal. Wallace may have been an attractive and inspirational leader, but he was not above coercing support for the Balliol cause. Wallace certainly enjoyed considerable success from the autumn of 1296 onward, and his ability to gather men would no doubt have had a 'snowballing' effect, enhancing his prestige and his prominence as a focus for resistance to the occupation. His activities did not go unnoticed, however, and Edward I made arrangements to counter Wallace's success:

> So soon the great fame arose
> Of this William of Wallace
> And to King Edward of England
> News of his deeds was carried.
> Because he [Edward] was occupied elsewhere
> He sent Sir Hugh de Carsyngame [Cressingham]
> Who was his treasurer at that time
> To Scotland, with a great force.

Obviously Edward could not afford to let Wallace continue to improve his position, and the commitment of a large body of troops was obviously called for. Wallace was engaged in the siege of the castle at Dundee when he received news of Cressingham's army. Even if the army, led by the treasure, had been of insignificant strength, we can be sure that it would have constituted a 'great force' for the purposes of the narrative. Entrusting the siege to the burgesses – demanding, on pain of death, that they pursue the siege until the castle either surrendered or was captured – William Wallace led his troops south:

> And with his host [army] at great speed
> William Wallace made his way to Stirling
> And at the Bridge of that name over the [river] Forth
> Wallace met with Kersinghame [Cressingham]
> And there they melee'd in a fight
> Where many were cast down dead
> There they struggled very hard
> Until at last Kersynghame [Cressingham]
> Was vanquished with the greater part of his force
> And were killed beside the bridge
> And the remainder of that body
> All turned their backs and fled
> And Scots pursued them fiercely
> Wherever they overtook Englishmen
> They spared none and slew them all.

Wallace's tactical victory was complete in itself as far as Wyntoun was concerned; it was also very much William's victory. Andrew Murray, surely Wallace's equal in terms of popular leadership, his superior in social status and very probably his superior in military experience and command experience generally, is marked chiefly by his death some weeks after the battle – probably through wounds received there. The political and military outcomes of the action were of some moment. Successful command in battle confirmed Wallace's place in the leadership of the Balliol cause, though it is worth bearing in mind that the demise of Murray ensured that all of the prestige from the victory accrued to Wallace. Had Murray survived, he would have shared in that prestige and would probably have provided Wallace with a competitor as well as an ally. Wyntoun is very shy about the process of the battle, though the outline of the action must surely have been well known to him: possibly so well known that he felt a description of the fighting was unnecessary, despite the fact that he was writing for a noble audience – the very class that carried the bulk of military liability. One would think that a blow-by-blow account of the action, preferably a gory one involving Wallace as the nemesis of countless English knights and gentlemen, would be a key part of the work. The brevity of Wyntoun's description may however be a reflection of the nature of the battle and of the participants. Despite Wyntoun's claim that all the great lords gave their obedience to Wallace, there is no indication that Wallace was able to call upon the quantities of man-at-arms' service that such obedience could have provided: the rank and file of Wallace and Murray's forces were, in the main, drawn from the wider community. Although Stirling Bridge was a famous victory over the English there were few 'chivalrous' deeds of arms performed, because there few 'gentlemen' present to perform them and because the action was – for the Scots anyway – conducted on foot. The Scots had not suffered heavy casualties in the battle, but the loss of Murray was a serious blow:

> And few were killed among Scottish men
> But Andrew of Murray was killed then
> Father to Sir Andrew was he
> And held in great esteem

The 'Sir Andrew' in question was a successful leader of Scottish resistance to Edward III in the 1330s. He enjoyed a similar military and patriotic reputation to his father, but a rather longer career. Wallace, as sole leader after Stirling Bridge, faced little internal opposition, and was able to carry the war to the English. His decision not to co-opt another man to replace Murray is a curious one. Although it certainly gave him executive power, it must have been a matter of some concern to the existing structures of power. Wallace and Murray may have been covertly accepted as leaders by those lords whose properties lay outside the occupied territories, or they may have simply assumed office on the grounds that there was no one to oppose them, but either way the dual leadership did represent both the senior and lower orders of noble society: Wallace from the free tenants and minor lords, Murray from the barons and magnates. The death of Murray meant that there was no member of the higher aristocracy directly involved in deciding the policies of the Balliol administration.

> From the day he vanquished Cressingham
> Higher and higher waxed his name

And through the Kingdom as he passed
The Scots joined him, steadfastly
And then, from All Hallow's
To Christmas, he campaigned in England

Invading England had two significant aspects for the Scots. Operations in the enemy's country were preferable as a matter of principle: the damage attendant on war would be incurred by the enemy's people rather than the Scots and Wallace's army could be trained in the enemy's country and fed at the enemy's expense, removing a considerable burden from the shoulders of the recovering Scottish administration. However, the damage to the prestige of Edward I was perhaps seen as more significant. Edward was not comfortably situated in 1297: domestic opposition (due to heavy demands for money and military service, among other things), the growing success of the Scots on the diplomatic front and then a battlefield defeat of some significance did nothing to ease his difficulties. The Scottish situation could only be recovered by a major campaign. The financial and administrative effort required to raise an army, the burden of maintaining such garrisons as remained in Plantagenet hands, considerations of weather and the availability of good grazing, his commitments elsewhere and the lack of interest of many of his barons meant that Edward could not lead an army to Scotland until the late summer of 1298.

Of the battle of Falkirk
That was most irksome to Scots

When Edward with the long legs
Had heard in England afterward
How, in Scotland, William
Wallace had met Carsyngame [Cressingham]
And had him and all his men slain
This Edward did not refrain
In Scotland, with a great army
Gathered, he came as a man of war.
On St Mary Magdalene's day
At Falkirk they all assembled
There William Wallace took on hand
With many great lords of Scotland
To meet with the King in fight
There many were struck to death

> King Edward of England then
> Had many Scottish gentlemen
> That through dispute or from envy
> Supported him maliciously

Here Wyntoun has touched on a problem that haunted medieval kings and is still an issue for medieval historians. Wallace, according to Wyntoun, was joined by many Scottish lords, but many 'gentlemen' of Scotland were in the peace of Edward I. As we have seen, the ethical questions of allegiance were thorny ones. Allegiance might be given under duress, but was it still binding? In any case, the practical aspects of survival and retention of one's heritage under the occupation government would have ensured some degree of Plantagenet support from the political community in those areas which were still under Plantagenet control prior to Edward's 1298 campaign. It would be reasonable to assume that some of the members of the political community who had been wavering, or even on the brink of declaring for Wallace, or rather for the Balliol cause, would be discouraged from doing so by the arrival, or perhaps just the threat, of a large army on the doorstep. Regardless of personal sentiment and regardless of how it had been achieved, the bulk of the political community had, at one time or another, acknowledged Edward I as their liege lord. Strictly speaking they could be forfeited and hanged for rebellion if they failed to give him their service and loyalty. The sheer size of Wallace's following probably would have prevented a mass forfeiture by Edward, however successful he might be in battle, but Edward was a vindictive man and might easily single out individuals as examples to others or perhaps to give himself what is now known as 'closure' on the matter.

> And the Comyns in those days
> Did not love William Wallace
> But with the loyal Scottish men
> That in the field were fighting then
> Together stood in serried ranks
> Striking before them manfully
> So that none might defeat them
> However Robert Bruce, with a ruse
> – He served there with King Edward
> But was made our King afterward –
> And with Sir Antony Bek, a wily man,
> Who of Durham was bishop then,
> Found a path around a hill

Along which they picked their way
Behind backs [of the Scots] they passed
Then they came on and laid on fast
So they made the discomfiture [defeat]
The Scots were defeated in that manner
There John Stewart, [fighting] on foot,
And with him the Brandans of Bute
And the gentlemen of Fife
With MacDuff there, lost their life
Through dispute and great envy
The Comyns in their entirety
Left the field as they saw fit

For Wyntoun, the crucial issue in the defeat of the Scots is a flanking manoeuvre inaugurated by Robert Bruce. This neatly shows that Robert was a tacti-
cally aware leader and the English would not have been able to gain victory
without him. This segment demonstrates the success of Bruce propaganda.
By the time Wyntoun wrote his chronicle, the Bruce cause and the cause
of Scottish independence had become more or less synonymous in people's
minds; this was not the case at the close of the thirteenth century, when
for many the Bruce claim was no more than simple baronial opportunism
and aggrandisement on the part of a family that had abandoned King John
for King Edward, then defected to the Balliol party for the duration of the
revolt of the nobles in 1297, at which point he entered the peace of Edward
I once more – all in less than eighteen months. In a further success for Bruce
propaganda, Wyntoun portrays the Comyn family in the worst possible light.
Merely by stating that the Comyns did not love William Wallace, Wyntoun
invited the reader or audience to despise the Comyns for failing to support
the national hero, and strengthened his case by claiming that, moved by envy
of Wallace's position, they abandoned the field to the enemy. Since almost
all of the Scottish army had been deployed on foot, there was probably very
little contribution that the tiny mounted force provided by the Comyns and
other Scottish men-at-arms could have made in face of Edward's overwhelm-
ing superiority in heavy cavalry. It is clear that many Scottish men-at-arms
served in the infantry at Falkirk. MacDuff and the 'gentlemen' of Fife were
most certainly of noble status and would have been trained to fight from
the saddle: their service on foot was surely a tactical choice on the part of
Wallace, perhaps to provide a 'stiffening' of well-armoured men and/or to give
a political encouragement to the troops – a sign that their leaders would not
be able to gallop off in the event of defeat, but would stand to the fight like

everyone else. What Wyntoun signally fails to do is to offer any justification for the actions of Robert Bruce in the service of Edward I.

The battle was lost, and with it, the Guardianship of Wallace. His rise had been the product of military leadership, not of inherited political and social status: one major battlefield defeat was enough to completely undermine his authority among the noble classes. At least he was realist enough to accept the situation:

> Beside the water of the Forth he
> Resigned the office of warden [Guardian]
> And refused any further office in Scotland,
> Leaving such cares to whoever would take them
> For he preferred to live simply
> And not to live in such adversity
> And he wished that the loyal commons of Scotland
> Had not died under his command
> Of his good deeds and manliness
> Great tales are made I have heard
> But not so many I think
> As he actually performed
> One who would record all his deeds and achievements
> Would make a great and worthy book
> But to write them all here
> I have neither the wit or the leisure.

Wallace then, as a great hero should, accepts his fate as a defeated commander and gives up the position of Guardian, regretting only his failure to defeat the English and the deaths of so many Scots at the battle of Falkirk. His political persuasion had not suffered from his defeat and Wallace remained active in the Balliol cause. In late 1299–1300 he was in France with Bishop Lamberton, perhaps consulting with Duns Scotus, the eminent Scottish academic who taught there and whose theories of consensually accepted kingship under God's direction may have had some influence on the Scottish constitutional developments later articulated in the Declaration of the Clergy, the Declaration of Arbroath and The Quaesto.

The Scots had a good deal of success on the diplomatic front until 1302, when Philip IV's army was beaten by Flemish infantry at Courtrai. Suddenly desperate for peace with Edward I, Philip abandoned his previous insistence that the Scots had to be included in any peace settlement. Philip strengthened his resolve – or perhaps assuaged his conscience – by procuring an acceptance from King John for whatever measures he felt necessary to procure a quick peace. Wallace returned to the fight, leading forces against the English, but no longer acting as the commander of the main effort of the Scots. King John's decision to accept Philip's actions without reservation rather pulled the rug from under the Scots: if King John was no longer interested in the cause of his own restoration, who exactly were the Scots fighting for? Edward was now in a position to focus his efforts on Scotland and set about reducing Scottish resistance through a combination of military pressure and political concessions. By the terms of the Strathord armistice, the Balliol party laid down its arms and paid fines or accepted terms of banishment as the price of admission to the peace of Edward I. Not all the Scots could hope to take advantage of the armistice arrangements: William Wallace was specifically excluded and no one was to accept his submission on any terms other than unconditional surrender. Wallace continued the fight, but his capture was inevitable so long as he remained in Scotland:

> The time that William Wallace was taken
> And sent to England soon thereafter
> One thousand three hundred and five years
> After the birth of our Lord dear
> Sir John de Menteith in those days
> Captured, at Glasgow, William Wallace
> And sent him into England soon
> Where he was quartered and undone
> By great spite and felony
> There he bore that martyrdom

Since Edward had refused to entertain any suggestion of terms for Wallace other than to put himself utterly in Edward's mercy, the consequence of capture was execution. Quartering was a process reserved, largely at least, for criminal behaviour with a political dimension. Naturally, the writer sees Wallace's death as a result of malice and spite on the part of the English, but it is difficult to see how else Edward could have reacted if he was ever going to achieve the conquest of Scotland. Given Wallace's relatively low status within the political community it is also difficult to see what terms Edward could have accepted for Wallace's surrender, or why he should be willing to give terms at all. Great lords and earls could reasonably be expected to take part in the major political events of the day. As men with customary political supporters, they represented, however tenuously, an aspect of public opinion; as local potentates they could lead and influence that opinion. When it came to making terms for the cessation of a war, magnates and senior barons had something to offer – local influence. A man of more obscure status – like Wallace – might have some standing in the community, but could not mobilise an extensive network of dependants and tenants. The majority of men and women of that status who found themselves on the 'wrong' side at the end of hostilities could expect to be accepted into the peace of the winning side for little or no penalty, either under the terms of the armistice agreement or simply because their status was not of sufficient consequence to attract individualised attention from the opposition. Wallace was far too famous to be ignored and was far too committed to the Balliol party to be persuaded to join the Plantagenet cause, but in any case he had nothing to offer Edward. By the time of his capture, Wallace was the leader of a small force of fugitive men-at-arms whose defection to the Plantagenet party would have been meaningless.

CHAPTER TWELVE

Wallace and Bower:
'A Man Successful in Everything'

The chronicler Bower was the abbot of Inchcolm, an island abbey in the Firth of Forth. Unashamedly nationalistic, Bower describes his own work thus:

Christ! He is not a Scot that is not pleased by this book.

Like Fordoun and Wyntoun, Bower drew on sources that no longer exist, including, perhaps, the verse and narrative accounts that Sir Thomas Grey claimed to have studied in Edinburgh and Stirling castles while he was a prisoner of war of the Scots in middle of the fourteenth century. Professor Watt suggests that Bower's work relating to Wallace was never completed, and that Bower may have been the first person to commit some of Wallace's deeds – real or apocryphal – to paper. Bower first introduces us to Wallace in 1297, when, although the Scots had been routed in the summer of 1296, resistance to the Edwardian occupation was already developing to the extent that the Plantagenet administration was in danger of being eclipsed by the Scots.

In [1297] the famous William Wallace, the hammer of the English, the son of the noble knight [Sir Malcolm Wallace of Elderslie] raised his head. He was a tall man with the body of a giant, cheerful in appearance with agreeable features, broad-shouldered and big-boned, with belly in proportion and lengthy flanks, pleasing in appearance, but with a wild look, broad in the hips, with strong arms and legs, a most spirited fighting man, with all his limbs very strong and firm. Moreover the Most High had distinguished him and his changing features with a certain good humour, had so blessed his words and deeds with a heavenly gift, that by his appearance alone he won over to himself the grace and favour of all loyal Scots. And this was not surprising, for he was most liberal in his gifts, very fair in his judgements, most compassionate in comforting the sad, a most skilful counsellor, very patient when suffering, a distinguished speaker, who above all hunted down falsehood and deceit, and detested treachery: for this reason the Lord was with him, and with His help he was a man successful in everything: with veneration for the church and respect for the clergy, he helped the poor and widows, and worked for the restoration of wards and orphans, bringing relief to the oppressed. He lay in wait for thieves and robbers, inflicting vigorous justice upon them without any reward. Because God was greatly pleased with works of justice of this kind; He in consequence guided all his activities.

Bower does not really have anything more to say by way of introduction to Wallace than Wyntoun or Fordoun. He just adds more of the same conventional platitudes that sympathetic chroniclers were inclined to apply to their favoured monarchs: to a degree there is a difference, inasmuch as William Wallace was not a king, but essentially a popular and (until July 1298) successful military leader. Bower's description of Wallace's physical appearance is considerably longer than that of Fordoun or Wyntoun, but is no more informative; he merely tells us that Wallace was 'big and strong' several times in different words.

As a cleric Bower no doubt felt that it would be a good idea to associate a great hero with a reverence for the Catholic Church, which, in Bower's time, was starting to have to address the challenge posed by Lollard sentiments, by telling us that Wallace was always respectful to the clergy, Bower could neatly bring heroic patriotism and doctrinal conservatism together. Previous writers state that Wallace was of noble status, from a family that was perhaps more lairdly than knightly. Bower sees Wallace as a knight from the very outset of his career:

> When Wallace was a young knight, he killed the sheriff of Lanark an Englishman who was dextrous and powerful in the use of arms, in the town of Lanark. From that time therefore, there gathered to his side, like a swarm of bees, all those who were bitter in their outlook and oppressed by the burden of servitude under the intolerable rule of English domination… His older brother, Andrew, was a belted knight who held a patrimony of lands in keeping with his status.

Andrew, then, according to Bower, was the inheritor of the family property on the death of Sir Malcolm, and it would seem less than likely that the Wallace family property was extensive enough to provide two knights with the income to support their status. It would be very unlikely that William would be made a knight without a very particular cause if he did not have a heritage adequate for his needs. In the winter of 1296 and the spring of 1297, when, presumably, Wallace was first assembling a body of men, it would be hard to identify who exactly would have felt they had the authority to make anyone a knight. In theory, any knight could make another, and in practice many people were knighted by great lords rather than by kings, particularly during a royal minority, for obvious reasons. However, although knighting was largely the business of the great and good, and though there is evidence to suggest that Wallace was knighted by one of the Scottish earls in 1297 or 1298, it is not impossible that he was knighted by some obscure Scottish lord in late 1296 or early 1297, possibly in an attempt to give Wallace some degree of political and social credibility by raising his military status. Bower is certainly very clear about the intolerable nature of the English occupation; what he is less clear about is the nature of the occupation – he does not elaborate on the aspects of the occupation which made it oppressive enough to be worth resisting. Not everyone was moved to do so, but Wallace was prepared to ensure that they did:

> When William had been appointed guardian of the realm, and was destroying the English on all sides and daily gaining ground, he brought all the magnates under his control within a short while, whether through force or through his prowess. And if any of the magnates did not gladly obey his orders, Wallace apprehended him, persuaded him and held him in custody until he submitted entirely to his will. And so, once everyone had been brought under his command, he applied himself in a manly fashion to attacking the castles and fortified towns where the English were in control, skilfully intent on the liberation of his homeland and the overthrow of his enemies.

On the one hand, Bower tells us that Wallace brought all the magnates of Scotland into the Balliol camp through his leadership and prowess in battle, which is simply untrue: a great many Scots were in the peace of Edward I throughout the late 1290s. On the other, he tells us how Wallace dealt with magnatial opposition: a sure indication that his campaign was neither immediately successful nor universally popular. Had it been so, there would have been little need to coerce support, and the imprisonment of magnates certainly smacks of coercion. This is the second occasion that Bower mentions fortified towns and castles in connection with Wallace.

This is something of a curiosity, since, though there were many castles in thirteenth-century Scotland, there would seem to have been very few walled towns. The very low incidence of war in Scotland over the preceding hundred years or more had not encouraged the development of fortification other than Berwick, Perth and possibly Inverness. Of these, Berwick was almost certainly the best protected, but even there the town defences were not very well developed.

Wallace's interest in acquiring the support – freely given or otherwise – of the lords and lairds was essentially the same as that of Edward I. Without the local influence that the political community could exert, it would be very difficult indeed to maintain any sort of regular administration at all, and without the man-at-arms service that only the political community could provide in any useful quantity it would be more or less impossible either to defeat the enemy or to maintain the security of the country, but the mainstay of his power, especially in the early stages of his career, was his ability to motivate the wider community. If there was to be a large Scottish field army it would have to be recruited and trained:

> And as regards the whole multitude of his followers he decreed, on pain of death, that once the lesser men among the middling people (or in practice those who were less robust) had been assembled in front of him, one man was to be chosen out of every group of five men to be always in charge of the other four and to be called a quaternion; his commands were to be obeyed by the others in all matters, and whoever did not obey was to be killed.

The term 'middling people' occurs from time to time in several medieval sources, both in chronicle and record. Barbour and Bower use it on a number of occasions, and various people were empowered by Edward I and by Edward II to admit 'middling sorts' of men to Plantagenet peace. Evidently the term was well enough understood in fourteenth-century England and Scotland to require no explanation. Like almost any term that has an element of class identification, 'middling' defies precise definition, and probably always did. It would be reasonable to include the more prosperous tenant farmers, burgesses and town-dwellers who were financially successful, but not burgesses and minor clerics among the 'middling' people, but in financial terms the lesser landowners – lairds and even the less prosperous knights and barons – were little removed from that level of wealth, if at all. That does not mean that lairds, knights and barons would accept that they were of 'middling' status themselves, but the exclusion of knights in some of the documents granting the power to accept allegiance perhaps suggests a 'blanket' provision to ensure that the Crown had the opportunity to assess the situations of the more prominent members of society before deciding on any preconditions for their rehabilitation in the Plantagenet dispensation.

As well as the 'middling folk' Bower has Wallace turn his attention to those who were 'less robust'. It is difficult to know what Bower expected the reader to take from this. He goes on to describe what appears to be a physical 'pecking order' to define command:

> In a similar manner also on moving up to the men who were more robust and effective, there was always to be a tenth man (called a decurion) over each nine, and a twentieth over each nineteen, and so moving up to each thousand (called a chilliarch) and beyond to the top.

It might be the case that Bower is drawing attention to a division within Wallace's army based on equipment and ability – that where he refers to the 'less robust' he does not mean the halt and the lame, for whom presumably Wallace would have had little application, but to more and less well-equipped men. A division along those lines would give Wallace some degree of flexibility; he would be able to direct the efforts of his most effective troops according to the tactical situation. As he made his way across the country he could use the lighter troops to overawe minor opposition and retain the better-armed element of the army for commitment against any serious threats. Traditionally, it has been assumed that the command structure described by Bower consisted of units of four men under a fifth, two such units under a 'decurion' and two of the resulting units under a – presumably – senior decurion. Such a structure would be have a very high incidence of junior leaders: out of twenty men, no less than five would have a command responsibility, and, if Bower is to be believed, the sanction of the death penalty to enforce their authority. An alternative possibility is that Bower conflated two distinct forms of organisation – that units of five men were the basis of the less well-equipped formations and units of ten men the basis of the better armed ones. Regardless of his approach to army organisation, or, for that matter, his approach to recruitment, Wallace definitely raised an army to fight against the English, and Edward I could hardly afford to ignore that:

> The fame of William Wallace therefore, which was spread around everywhere, at length reached the ears of the King of England with news of the harm done to his men. Intent as he was on many kinds of difficult business

elsewhere, he sent his treasurer, Hugh de Cressingham with a large force to
curb the audacity of William personally and subdue the kingdom of Scotland
to his rule. On hearing therefore of the arrival of such a man with an armed
force, the said William, whom was then occupied with the siege of the castle
of Dundee, he at once committed responsibility for the conduct of the siege
to the burgesses of that same town under pain of loss of life and limb, and
advanced with great haste with his army towards Stirling to meet with this
same Hugh. And in the fierce battle that took place at Stirling Bridge in
September 1297 the same Hugh de Cressingham was killed and all his army
was put to flight. Some had their throats cut with swords, others were taken
prisoner, others were drowned; and when, with God's help, they had all been
overcome, the said William secured a blessed victory with no mean renown.
On his side, amongst the number of the nobles of Scotland, only Andrew de
Moray (father of the noble Andrew) was wounded and died.

Bower tells us very little about Stirling Bridge, possibly because there was
not really a great deal to say for the benefit of a noble audience or readership. While a Scottish victory was undoubtedly a 'good thing' – and
sanctioned by the Almighty – the battle of Stirling Bridge did not provide
the traditional arena for great deeds of arms. More pertinently, there may
not have been a great deal for chroniclers to write about. The nature of
the action is fairly straightforward: the Scots advance on an English army
as it is in the process of crossing a bridge. The English are unable to bring
their force to bear efficiently and are clearly beaten. Other than tales of
individual moments of heroism, there was probably very little to be made
in the way of useful observations about deployment and manoeuvre. The
role of Andrew Murray, however, is diminished in Bower's account of the
action when compared to the account of Fordoun. He is not credited with
bringing a force to the battle, nor with any having any command status in
the army. Even his knighthood is ignored, though Bower was careful to tell
the reader that Wallace was already a knight at the inception of the resistance
to the Plantagenet government, though no other source suggests this. The
only plausible reason for Bower to marginalise Moray would be to enhance
the prestige of Wallace. The martial status of Moray's son, also Andrew and
a successful Scottish commander in the 1330s, is of more significance to
Bower than the career of Moray himself. Bower goes on to quote lines from
a verse account of Wallace's deeds, but does not tell us the source:

> For this reason the Scots adopted a stout heart at the instigation
> Of William Wallace, who taught them to fight,

So that those whom the English held as living captives
Might be made renewed Scots within their homeland
So that they might, besides, help King John to reign
In his own kingdom .because if they wanted to serve
An alien King they could lose their rights.
Hence in the year one thousand three hundred less
Three times one the Scots are said to have vanquished
The savage English, whom they put into mourning for death
As the bridge bears witness, where the great battle is recorded
Which lies beyond Stirling on the river Forth.
The third before the ides of September was the dare of this grace
Offered as a celestial gift to the faithful Scots.

Bower and his source were in no doubt of the true source of victory: it was ordained by God for the benefit of his faithful Scots. Similarly, Bower and his source agree that William Wallace was the mainstay of the Balliol cause in 1296–97, raising and training men for King John. Stirling Bridge was, to the Scots, a good deal of the country – despite Bower's patriotic claims earlier in his work – and it remained in English hands. Wallace had entrusted the siege of Dundee Castle to the burgesses of the town during his absence at Stirling, an indication that the Balliol cause did enjoy some degree of popular support outside the traditional political community. This is not to suggest that the burgesses were not part of the regional political community themselves, but it is important to bear in mind that only a very small percentage of the men and women who lived in a burgh enjoyed the status of burgess. Although the burgesses would undoubtedly wield a good deal of influence in the town they were still only a very small minority who had to conduct their lives in a close community. If they failed to reflect the general tenor of political feeling in the burgh populace as a whole, they might find themselves in a rather hostile environment. If, for example, the burgesses had taken on responsibility for the conduct of the siege against the will of the community as a whole, they could be in a very difficult position with their neighbours, employees and customers, should the town be penalised for collaboration with Wallace in the event of the English recovering the burgh. Equally, the participation of the burgesses in the siege is not proof that, as a body, they felt strongly either about Scottish independence or William Wallace. If the bulk of the townspeople were enthusiastic about Wallace and King John, the burgesses would have very little choice but to join in the struggle. Further, Wallace was unquestionably capable of extorting military service, and the burgesses could provide him with modest numbers of men-at-arms, not because of their landed status, but because their financial status would make it very difficult for them not to equip themselves accordingly. It is impossible to convey the significance of status in medieval societies, but we might reasonably assume that those on the fringes of noble status would be likely to take care to maintain their identity separate from the 'lower orders', and serving as a man-at-arms would be good for one's personal prestige.

Wallace's prestige was, unsurprisingly, greatly enhanced by his victory at Stirling Bridge, but battlefield success needed to be supported by the successful recovery of towns and territory, so Wallace made his way back to Dundee to continue the siege of the castle there:

> On his arrival there the English keepers, terrified by the turn of fortune at the victory at Stirling, persuaded themselves to surrender the castle uncondi-tionally with a vast haul of weapons and treasure. When this became known, fear and trembling overcame the enemy. Of the other castles which the English had wrenched from the hands of our people, some the Guardian cast down himself, some he entrusted to the steady keeping of Scots, not a few he left empty.
>
> And so as the season of autumn approached there was a threat of major dearth and shortage of food in the kingdom, since there was a shortage of grain resulting from inclement weather. On this account, once the crops had been brought into the yards and barns, the Guardian ordered the summons of all and sundry Scots who were capable of defending their homeland to invade the country of their enemies, and find their sustenance there, and to spend the wintry part of the year there so as to spare their own food supplies that had been gathered in their yards, as we have said. Therefore he had, from every sheriffdom and shire, barony and lordship, town and village and country estate he had special lists drawn up of every man between sixteen and sixty who was fit for warfare. So that no man could be absent unnoticed from a stated time and place without his knowledge, he laid it down as a fundamental law that not only in every barony, but in every sizeable township a gallows was to be erected on which were to be hanged all those inventing excuses to avoid army service without valid cause when summoned. And this was done.

Wallace was clearly determined to develop an army worthy of the name in late 1297. He had one victory under his belt, but must have been aware that Stirling Bridge was a most unusual form of action and was in no sense indicative of the normal combat relationship between an English army and a Scottish one. At the close of thirteenth century the English, under Edward I, had progressed militarily by leaps and bounds in comparison to their northern neighbours, for whom war was a new phenomenon in 1296, since there had not been general war in Scotland for a century. If Wallace's army was going to have any prospect of victory against a properly structured and led English army at some future date, he would have to take drastic steps to ensure the recruitment, retention and competent training of that army. Wallace could probably hope to receive a fairly steady intake from men in search of adventure – men whose fortunes had already been destroyed by the war, outlaws and outcasts in search of a free meal and easy pickings – but these groups would never provide him with the scale of force required to meet the English in battle.

The obligation of all men to serve in the defence of their country was hardly revolutionary: Scots had served in war on many occasions in the distant past and a force had been raised for the 1296 campaign, though it never saw action. The system imposed by Wallace in the autumn of 1297 may or may not have been a radically different one to the traditional method of raising men for war, but service itself was not, strictly speaking, a new burden on the community, more the revival of an obligation that had not been required for some time. This does not mean that the people were wholeheartedly committed to waging war: if the service had been readily and willingly offered, there would have been no need to construct gallows in every barony and sizeable township. The logistical challenge of maintaining a large army in Scotland – an army of several thousands – would have been considerable at any point in the medieval period, but in a time of food shortages would be virtually impossible without causing serious hardship in those areas where the army was billeted. The obvious solution was to take the army into England, where they could be pro-visioned at the expense of someone else's communities. The other great attraction of operating south of the border was that it would afford some opportunities for training and gaining some degree of combat experience. It was unlikely that the English would be able to raise an army large enough to threaten the Scots before they retired to Scotland, so any action that did occur was likely to be on a small scale, in which case the Scots could hope to accrue experience without taking a major risk. Bower throws an incidental sidelight on an aspect of social administration here. He tells us that lists of eligible men were made in every sheriffdom, shire, barony, lord-ship, town, village and country estate. These divisions were not hierarchical in any sense. A barony might be part of a lordship or earldom, but might not; a town might belong to the king or a magnate or a bishop; it might

lie within the boundaries of an earldom but not be a part of it in any
political sense – hence each type of land tenure status had to be addressed
separately. If Wallace's writ had specified enlistment from the men of all the
sheriffdoms of Scotland, many would have avoided service (or would have
tried to anyway) on the principle that they were not men of this or that
sheriffdom, but of this or that barony or burgh. Wallace was not prepared
to tolerate failure to serve and took swift action against draft evaders:

> He himself, when organising an expedition with an enormous army and
> finding that some burgesses of Aberdeen had not come, appointed, as we
> have seen, quaternions, pentarchs, decurions, centurions and chilliarchs to
> command those put under them in this way, and intended to make a quick
> journey into England before the feast of All Saints; he then turned his horse
> with all haste and with a very small body of men punished those from
> Aberdeen and its environs that had stayed away from the army without valid
> excuses. He returned to the army more quickly than you would believe,
> and crushed underfoot and laid waste the whole of Northumberland up to
> Newcastle, spending the winter from All saints until the Purification of Our
> Lady, or at least, as some books record, staying there with the army until
> Christmas. After burning the whole region of Allerdale he returned home
> safe and sound with his Scots enriched by the spoils.

The burgesses of Aberdeen and their rural neighbours, it would seem, were
not in a hurry to join the fight and needed to have the urgency of the situation impressed on them – no doubt by means of a few hangings. Bower
evidently faced a problem familiar to medieval historians: his sources did
not always agree with one another. In this instance, we might conclude
that Bower was not entirely convinced by the source – or sources – that
he generally trusted, to the extent that he felt obliged as a historian to
record an alternative construction of the events.

Edward of course could not ignore Wallace's invasion of England, though
he seems to have had no doubts about the validity of his own invasion of
Scotland the previous year:

> Hearing this, King Edward, ablaze with anger and unable to contain himself
> in his sorrow, abandoned the war that he had planned against the King of
> France, a move which gave great comfort to the French. For in the judge-
> ment of some, if the Scots had not drawn him from France through their
> efforts in battle, the greater part of the lineage of France would have been
> in danger. So, turning away from France, King Edward made his way to his

own domains, where, observing the slaughter and destruction inflicted on him and his subjects by the Scots, he wrote a threatening letter to William the Guardian of Scotland, declaring, among other matters, if the King had remained in his Kingdom in person Wallace would not have dared to attempt such deeds; but if he dared to invade England again, he would at once realise that the avenging hands of the King himself were seeking retribution on him and his men for their presumption. In short, when William Wallace heard of the impudence and threatening boasts of the King, he sent a message back to him to say that he would visit his kingdom again before the celebration of Easter.

When therefore, the armies of both kingdoms were gathered on either side near Stainmore it looked like there would be a battle. Then on the Scottish side the squires and courageous young men of the army asked the Guardian's permission to make a trial of the English in front of the line of battle in order to gild their own spurs. So as not to allow this to happen anywhere at all, he commanded them all by the voice of a herald to maintain their position previously given to them and to advance with their accustomed seriousness and also with the deliberation expected of them.

Again, Bower tells us something of Wallace's army in an indirect manner. The request from the 'squires' and 'courageous young men' of the army that Wallace should allow them to pursue personal fame and glory by engaging in knightly skirmishes in front of both armies shows that Wallace's force did not consist solely of men from the labouring and commercial classes, but that it had an element of men-at-arms willing, even eager, to test themselves against the enemy in a traditional chivalric manner. More than that, Wallace's response to the request shows a grasp of the practical realities of battle and indicates that the role of the men-at-arms in Wallace's army was to carry out their orders, not to engage in romantic combats with English gentlemen. Telling the men-at-arms that he expected them to behave with their 'accustomed seriousness' and with 'deliberation' may have been an appeal to their military vanity – the implication that a force is particularly well disciplined and effective invariably goes down well with the members of that force, even if with nobody else. In fact the Scots had probably not seen enough action at this point for any portion of the army to have developed an 'accustomed seriousness' or 'deliberation' in battle; all the same, it is clear that the social classes which traditionally had the greatest burden of military obligation – the lords, knights, lairds and burgesses that could afford the necessary arms and horse and the time to train with both – were an integral part of Wallace's army, that they were considered an important element in that army, that Wallace had every intention of making use of them in their proper role and that he understood the weaknesses of the cavalry army (primarily, the tendency to get involved in irrelevant fights, and the weakness of control once the force has been committed to battle). Keeping his troops in good order seems to have stood Wallace in good stead at Stainmore:

> On the other side, the King of England, resounding with his innumerable multitude and his pretentious clamour of trumpets claimed that he would destroy the Scottish army as though this was not difficult. When, however, the King saw the Scots advancing sensibly with harmonious and resolute step not half a mile distant from a clash, on the advice of his staff officers he turned round his men and gave way to the ill-luck of the hour. Seeing this, the Scots wanted, as one man, to pursue the fleeing King. But the Guardian forbade this on pain of death, saying that in the course of other struggles between the Kingdoms it was the prepared plan for a splendid victory to wait until the arrogant King of England, with his army and his fearsome commanders turned tail before the commons and patriots of Scotland on land which he claimed as his own before a sword had been drawn on the other side. Once this speech from his eloquent speech had been heard by the entire Scottish army, dismounting and throwing themselves to the ground they glorified God and St Andrew and the holy confessor Cuthbert whose memorable passage from this world was being celebrated that day, because through the energy and care of such a leader the valour and power of their enemies withered away, and both the Scots and Scotland won the distinction of a famous victory with everlasting renown. But the English say that their King was not present there in person, but that someone else resembling him gleamed in his suit of armour.

In addition to being a widely-experienced commander himself, Edward had the services of several men with long and successful military careers behind him. On this occasion, it would seem they decided that discretion was the better part of valour and that the Scots were not in a condition or position that offered any good opportunities for the English; however, Edward might well have decided to retire in order to encourage the Scots to advance upon him in the hope that an opportunity would arise, failing which he could continue to retire if threatened. Although Wallace would have had a force continually in service for some weeks by this point, they would still have been rather green, and attempting to manoeuvre in front of a competent enemy with strong and daring leadership would have been a very risky undertaking. It seems much more likely that in fact no confrontation occurred at Stainmore, and that Bower has wittingly or otherwise conflated two separate Scottish campaigns in northern England: one under William Wallace in 1297 and another in the reign of Robert I, possibly in 1322. At this juncture Bower returns to the subject of Stirling Bridge, no doubt to reinforce the prowess of Wallace as a commander by showing that he knew when to force battle and when not to. According to Bower's source, the battle at Stainmore did not take place because the English, having arranged to fight there, refused battle:

> Then the same man named Wallace gathers the Scots
> He gathers them like grains because he is called 'Valais' in French
> He pursues the English in order to continue the war
> And to renew the freedom of Scotland by war
> The was the destruction of the English of such a kind and magnitude
> As the northern regions have never experienced the like
> The whole of Northumberland perished as far as Newcastle
> Thus toward Stainmore the Scots achieve their aims
> In the aforesaid year of the Lord once more the English return
> Ready to fight for Berwick I tell you
> On the feast of Cuthbert in the spring, steadfast
> The Scots looked on, they thought they were to fight on the battlefield
> As the English had promised, but they did not keep
> To what they had promised but at once took flight
> When the Scots saw this, they departed sorrowfully
> England bears backwards the disgrace of their King's shield
> The Scottish assembly, praising the latest gifts
> Give thanks in their need, even if the gifts were not complete.
> Every house rises and exults with praise
> The King flies, hence England groans sorrowfully.

As Guardian, Wallace was obliged to see to the civil needs of the country as well as the military situation. Bower describes Wallace's administration of government and justice, and outlines some of the difficulties Wallace faced from his own side:

> So while Scotland, through the wisdom of the Guardian, was making a remarkable and successful recovery, since every man remained safely on his own property and cultivated the land in the usual way and very often triumphed over his enemies, the magnates and powerful men of the kingdom, intoxicated by a stream of envy, seditiously entered a plot against the

Guardian under the guise of virginal innocence but with their tales tied together. Hence some who had been restored to their castles and properties by him after they had been completely excluded by the same English, muttered with proud hearts and rancorous minds, saying to one another ' We do not want this man to reign over us'. But the ordinary folk and populace, along with some of the nobles whose attitude was more sound and more in line with the public interest, praised the Lord on account of the fact that they themselves, saved from the attacks of rivals by the help of such a champion, were able to have the comfort of their own homes. What stubborn folly of fools! Wallace did not force himself into rulership, but by the choice of the Estates he was raised up to be ruler after the previously-nominated Guardians had been removed. And when you, Scotland, had been headless and unable to defend yourself, Wallace had appeared as a mighty arm for you and a salvation in time of trouble. Why is covetous envy so much in control in Scotland? How sad that it is natural for Scots to detest not only the happiness of other people, but also the happiness of their own countrymen, and this in respect of inferiors, lest they should be made equal to themselves, and in respect of their superiors because they are not equal to them and to their peers because they are equal to them.

Clearly Bower was unimpressed by his fellow countrymen: possibly an occupational hazard for historians. Bower was at pains to make the reader aware that the Scots were generally their own worst enemy – that having been 'cursed' with a larger, richer, more populous and aggressive neighbour (though it should be stressed that conflict was not actually the normal condition of relations between Scotland and England until Edward I chose to make it so) the Scots repeatedly demonstrated their sinful nature by betrayal and selfishness. Because, from Bower's perspective, the English were an unusually wicked nation, it was unthinkable that a good, just and loving God could allow them to prosper other than as a means of punishing the Scots for their own wickedness. The reaction of some of the Scottish nobles to Wallace's Guardianship was typical of such tendencies. If we can be sure that Wallace faced internal opposition, we cannot be sure that that opposition was necessarily unreasonable or unpatriotic. There must certainly have been some resentment of Wallace's leadership among the magnates and the barons; some of them must have felt that their traditional leadership roles were under threat. Equally, there would very probably have been some resentment of Wallace's rise to power among people of a similar background: they might be accustomed to taking orders from their social superiors, but not from their equals.

Bower is rather generous in his justification for Wallace's authority. It would seem that there really was no generally accepted Scottish Guardian for some months after the deposition of King John. Wallace's Guardianship was unquestionably an outcome of the battle of Stirling Bridge, not a choice made by a parliament or council, though it is likely that his position was endorsed by a significant portion of the magnates and the men who had been, or continued to be, officers of the Crown. Without some degree of acceptance, however covert and informal, it would have been a huge task to install a government in the name of King John.

Bower may be referring to a council of magnates, who, according to some English chronicle sources, ruled the country on behalf of King John from an indeterminate point before the invasion of 1296; however, the very existence of this council is open to question – it may have been an invention of Bruce propaganda, designed to undermine the Balliol dynasty. Wallace would seem not to have formally adopted the position of Guardian until after the battle of Stirling Bridge, and to have done so with the support of the army, not of a formal political forum. There again, with the army behind him it would have been rash indeed for men in the Balliol camp to oppose Wallace's promotion.

In the year 1298 the said king of England, grieving at the losses inflicted on him and his people by William Wallace in numerous ways gathered a large army and entered the country of Scotland with hostile intent, having certain of the nobles of Scotland to help him. Meeting him, the said William, with the rest of the magnates of the said kingdom engaged in an arduous battle near Falkirk in July on the feast of St Mary Magdalene, not without severe loss among both the leading men and the men of middling rank of the Scottish nation, and was put to flight. For on account of the malicious outlook they had adopted, arising from the stream of jealousy which the Comyns directed to the said William, they abandoned the field and escaped with their accomplices uninjured. When their malice became known, the aforesaid William, desiring to save his men and himself, hurried to flee by another road.

Robert Bruce, pursuing them from the other side, when a steep and impossibly deep valley came into view, is said to have called out to William, asking him who it was that drove him to such arrogance as to seek so rashly to fight in opposition to the widely-acknowledged power of the King of England and of the more powerful people of Scotland. It is said that William replied to him like this, 'Robert, Robert, it is your inactivity and womanish cowardice that spur me to the liberation of the native land that is legally yours. And indeed it is an effeminate man even now, ready as he is to advance from bed to battle, from the shadow to the sunlight, with a pampered body, freely taking up the weight of battle for the liberation of his own country, the burden of the breastplate – it is he who has made me so presumptuous, even foolish, and has compelled me to attempt or undertake these tasks.' With these words, William himself took to a speedy flight, and together with his men sought safety.

This exchange between Bruce and Wallace may be nothing more than pure invention on the part of Bower or his sources. If Wallace was committed to the legitimist descent of Scottish kingship – and he surely was – why did he not declare for Bruce if he believed that the Bruce claim was sound? The short answer is that the Bruce claim was not sound and that Wallace did not declare for the Bruce party because he was utterly committed to the Balliol cause. The roots of this passage probably lie in Bruce propaganda: there was no doubt that Robert had been in the peace of Edward I, more than once in fact. Because he, or his sources, felt it made a good, round, moral tale and sound propaganda to boot, Bower – or his sources – chose to make Wallace the inspiration of Bruce's regal ambitions, though Bruce probably did not need much inspiring:

> On account of all this, Robert himself was like one awakening from a deep sleep; the power of Wallace's words so entered his heart that he no longer had any thought of favouring the English.

The imperatives of successful propaganda show themselves again here. Robert defected to the English again around 1301, almost certainly in reaction to the successes of the Balliol party at that time, particularly on the diplomatic front. The Balliol cause might suit Robert as an alternative to the Plantagenet cause, as long as there was no real prospect of John being restored.

> When William Wallace and his men had slipped away from the battle, sadly as a result of the arrogance and blazing jealousy of both kingdoms, the noble community of Scotland lay miserably prostrate across mountains and hills, valleys and plains. Among the nobles the most valiant knight John Steward with his men and MacDuff of Fife with his men from that place were utterly destroyed. It is commonly said that Robert de Bruce, who later was King of Scotland but at that time supported the King of England provided the opportunity for this victory through his own vigour. For when the Scots stood fast in their ranks and could not be defeated by force or craft, the same

Robert, making a long detour around a mountainside with a force under Antony de Bek, took the Scots in the rear from the opposite side; and thus the Scots, who at the earlier stage stood unbroken and unconquered, in the later stage were overcome. And it should be noted that we rarely if ever read that the Scots were overcome by the English except as a result of their leaders or guile or deceit on the part of commoners going over to the other side.

Here Bower is a little more developed than other accounts. He has Robert de Bruce, the future king of Scotland, exchanging words with Wallace across a ravine while Wallace endeavours to escape the battle, but before the arrival of the English attack in the Scottish rear, implying that Wallace left the field immediately on hearing of the desertion of the Comyns. It would seem, by Bower's account anyway, that Wallace had identified the battle as lost at some point before Bishop Bek's column made their presence felt and acted accordingly; there would have been no advantage in throwing his life away in a fight that had already been lost:

After the said victory, which had been granted to their enemies by the treachery of the Scots, the same William understood through these and other realistic considerations the clear wickedness of the said Comyns and their supporters, and choosing rather to be of lowly position among the common folk than to be in command when that involved their ruin and heavy loss to the people, he voluntarily gave up his office not long after the battle of Falkirk beside the river Forth.

Since his rise to the Guardianship was achieved through his success in war rather than on account of inherited political status, it was virtually inevitable that the loss of a major battle would be enough to destabilise Wallace. In practice, he probably had no choice at all about resigning the Guardianship. The place of the Comyn family in the accounts of Bower and (though perhaps to a lesser degree) Wyntoun and Fordoun is subject to Bruce propaganda. It is quite possible that the Comyns had very sound military reasons for leaving the battlefield when they did: the realisation that the fight was already lost and that there was no value in death on the battlefield. The fact that they did so does not seem to have been held against them as an example of unpatriotic behaviour at the time; John Comyn was appointed to serve as Guardian in Wallace's place and would lead a force of Scottish men-at-arms to victory at Roslin in 1302.

Defeat at Falkirk and resignation of the Guardianship did not bring Wallace's career to an end, but his political leadership was finished. Bower has little to say about Wallace's activities thereafter until the Balliol party came to terms with Edward I in 1304.

> In the same year [1304], after the whole community of Scotland had sub-mitted to the King, John Comyn, then the Guardian, and all the magnates of Scotland apart from William Wallace and his adherents, one by one in succession submitted to him, handing over all their castles and town except from Stirling castle and its keeper. The noble William was afraid of the treachery of his countrymen. Some of them envied him for his uprightness and others were seduced by the promises of the English, and others with tortuous machinations and infinite care prepared traps for him, hoping thereby for the favour of the King of England. In addition persuasive argu-ments were offered to him by his immediate close friends that he, like the others, should obey the King of the English, that they might thus obtain peace.

The desire for peace is not a topic that attracts too much attention from Scottish chroniclers, other than in declarations that only the aggression of the English prevented the Scots from living peaceably and disturbing none, but it must surely have been an issue for the men who served on either side. Some small portion were professional soldiers pursuing a career, but for the majority of those who served as men-at-arms, let alone in the infantry, military service was an unavoidable obligation: if a person wanted to retain their property – not to mention their life – they would have to discharge any military service obligations attached to that property. Given the choice of enjoying their estates in peace or continuing a struggle against the English on behalf of a king who had been deposed nearly a decade before and who was apparently not interested in reclaiming his own kingdom, it would be surprising if some, perhaps most, of Wallace's supporters did not consider surrender. After eight years of war, broken only by a few short truces, there must have been many who had just had enough.

> Besides, others were sent by the King himself to persuade him to do this, promising on the King's behalf earldoms and wide possessions in England or in Scotland to be chosen by himself and held by his heirs for ever. He despised these approaches, and speaking for the liberty of his people like a second Mattathias he is reported to have answered 'Scotland, desolate as you are, you believe too much in false words and are too unwary of woes

to come! If you think like me, you would not readily put your neck under a foreign yoke. When I was growing up' he said, 'I learned from a priest who was my uncle to set this one proverb above all worldly possessions, and I have carried it in my heart.

I tell you truthfully, freedom is the finest of things;
Never live under a servile yoke my son.

And that is why I tell you that even if all Scots obey the King of England so that each one abandons his liberty, I, and my companions that wish to serve with me in this matter shall stand up for the liberty of this kingdom. And, may God favour us! We others shall obey no one but the King [of Scots] or his lieutenant'.

It is extremely unlikely that Edward I sent any kind of offer of terms to Wallace. The entire point of excluding Wallace from the terms of any general settlement was to try to force him to put himself entirely at Edward's will, admitting liability for raising rebellion against his legal king. As far as Wallace was concerned, Edward had never been his king; therefore he could not be guilty of insurrection against the Crown. Historians, particularly Scottish ones, have rather assumed that Wallace was right to refuse to put himself at Edward's mercy because Edward would have had him executed immediately, if for no other reason than to demonstrate to the population as a whole, and to the lesser nobility in particular, the dangers of encroaching on the status of the great lords – the people considered to have a natural place in political leadership. However, if Edward was committed to executing Wallace there would have been no point in inviting him to sue for clemency. Moreover, had Wallace surrendered and appealed for mercy and then been turned down, his execution might have reflected badly on Edward's reputation. He might not have been a magnanimous and generous man, but he probably would have preferred to be thought of as a liberal and knightly man. Finally, Edward was a man who recognised talent: it is not impossible that he might have found a place for Wallace in his operations in France or Flanders. Given Wallace's obvious popularity, it might have proved better for Edward had he followed the principles of Lyndon Baines Johnson in regard to tents and urination. Wallace being executed – and barbarously at that – in London was a grisly motivator for Scots; if Edward had been able to 'turn' Wallace to the Plantagenet party he would probably not have proved to be a great asset in himself, but his change of allegiance might well have seriously undermined the credibility

of the Scottish cause. By the time of Wallace's capture the Balliol cause
had effectively come to an end; it is difficult to see what Wallace hoped
to achieve by continuing the fight: what was he fighting for? What did
he hope to achieve? Most importantly, if kingship was a vital component
of national identity and governance, who did Wallace envisage as the successor to King John if John himself rejected Scottish kingship? Would his
right extend to his son Edward (who made strenuous efforts to secure
the Scottish throne for himself in the 1330s–1350s) or would it pass to
the Bruces?

Once he had rejected the possibility of throwing himself on Edward's
mercy, of course Wallace had no real choice about fighting, since his enemies were hunting him down; however, his rejection was still a political
decision. Surrender may not have been an attractive option, but it was still
an option. By refusing it, Wallace was, consciously or otherwise, moving
toward a more subtle political stance than just support for the Balliol party,
and, assuming that Bower's account of the exchange between Bruce and
Wallace on the day of the battle of Falkirk is an invention, Wallace never
expressed any sympathy for the Bruce party. If he was not a Bruce adherent
and if the Balliol cause had been abandoned by its theoretical leader, John,
then perhaps it was the case that by 1305, if not before, Wallace was active
not in the Balliol cause but in the cause of Scottish independence from
England, regardless of who became king. If so, it would be unsafe to assume
that libertarian sentiment of a sort was an entirely new phenomenon
in Scottish cultural and political life. Wallace's uncle, Bower tells us, had
instilled a contempt for subjection in his nephew, telling him that liberty
was a greater blessing than any store of earthly treasures, but it is not clear
what exactly 'freedom' or 'liberty' meant in a thirteenth-century noble
context. Wallace's uncle, a priest, was like the rest of his family a member
of the lesser aristocracy – the men and women who in a later period
might be described as the 'parish gentry'. People of that station enjoyed
a rather better lifestyle than the vast majority of the populace, but they
were subject to various sources of authority: the king, his officers, and any
feudal superior from whom they held land, not to mention being subject
to the influence of local potentates – earls, great lords, bishops and abbots.
From whom, then, was Wallace to protect his liberty? Bower probably
expected his reader to assume that Wallace's uncle was demonstrating the
traditional fear of the Scots that they might be conquered and assimilated
into England; however, in Wallace's youth there was no tradition of war in
Scotland at all, let alone a fear that the English would invade and enslave
the Scots. There had of course been violent clashes between England and

Scotland in the past; Scottish kings had been obliged to surrender specified castles to English garrison for short periods and William I had even been an prisoner of war. But all these things were three generations in the past when Wallace was a boy and had not, in any case, led to a general hatred between the nations: that was the achievement of Edward I.

In 1305 the noble William Wallace, suspecting no evil was deceitfully and treacherously captured by Sir John de Menteith at Glasgow. He was handed over to the King of England and dismembered at London, and his limbs were hung up on towers in different parts of England and Scotland to dishonour the Scots. By this that tyrant sought to destroy the fame of William Wallace forever, since in the eyes of the foolish his life seemed to have been ended with such a dishonourable death. But such a death does not count against him, for it has been written;

The sudden death of a just man after a good life
Does not lessen his merits if he dies thus.

CHAPTER THIRTEEN

Wallace and Blind Harry: 'One Man of Great Renown'

W ritten nearly 100 years after the events it relates, Blind Harry's (or Henry's) epic verse narrative was largely, according to the author, drawn from an earlier verse biography of Wallace written in Latin by one Blair, allegedly Wallace's chaplain. The unreliability of Blind Harry's work is not in dispute: many of the tales that Blind Harry recounts with Wallace as the hero had already appeared in John Barbour's biography of Robert I, written in the later fourteenth century. Plagiarism was not seen as an abiding sin among later medieval writers; indeed, it was seen as evidence of scholarship and research. It is traditional, not to say rational, to treat chronicle accounts of any kind – verse or prose, Latin, Scots, English and French – as highly suspect; however, evidence relating to the life of William Wallace is somewhat thin on the ground, so evidence of any nature must be given some consideration. It is not, in any case, reasonable to reject chronicle evidence out of hand. Barbour's *Bruce* contains some very obvious errors and a number of significant omissions, but it also provides us with a good deal of material that is not supplied by other writers. The fact that a piece of data is recorded in *The Bruce* but not elsewhere does not, of itself, compromise the data. No serious study of the battle of Bannockburn would reject the Scottish cavalry attack on the English archers, but the incident is not mentioned by any other contemporary or near-contemporary commentator.

Blind Harry is the only writer to give us much of a picture of Wallace's background and early life. There has been considerable doubt expressed as to whether or not Blair's Latin verse biography of Wallace ever actually existed, the implication being that Blind Harry invented his own source to give some degree of credibility to the deeds of other heroic figures that he ascribed to Wallace or to stories that he had just plain invented himself. This may have been the case; there is no proof of the existence of the Blair manuscript other than the references to it in *The Wallace*; however, it would seem unlikely that Harry would have been able to 'get away with' such an ambitious deceit. Evidently the original manuscript was written in Latin, and though the ability to read Latin was one of the hallmarks of the educated person in the Middle Ages, it is reasonable to assume that the majority of the literate population preferred their leisure reading to be in their own language. In any case, works of this nature were not intended as personal reading only. Their episodic nature and the racy and exciting style (by medieval standards) indicate that they were also intended to be performance pieces. However nicely the Blair manuscript read, the fact remained that since it was in Latin it was far from accessible. However beautifully the lines were recited, they would still have been unintelligible to the vast majority of the literate strata of Scottish society, let alone the vast bulk of the populace. It might not be unreasonable to see *The Wallace* as an attempt to make the deeds – the 'gestes' – of Scotland's greatest patriotic hero available to the people. Of course, 'the people' is a rather difficult term in this setting. Only a very small part of the population had either the opportunity or skills to derive much benefit from the translation of a heroic narrative from Latin into Scots.

Whatever appeared in the Blair manuscript, Blind Harry happily added other stories from the oral traditions current in the fifteenth century. Even if all of the material taken from Blair was absolutely accurate, the Blind Harry manuscript would still be less than reliable. The material that Harry acquired from other sources cannot be reliably sifted from that of Blair; also, Harry was not above ascribing the feats of other heroes to his own, not to mention a probable, if not obvious, propensity for making up the odd piece of information himself. The validity of Blind Harry's account is, to the say the least, limited; however, it was not really intended to be a factual record of the life of Sir William Wallace of Elderslie, but a fabulous – in both senses of the word – entertainment for hall or reading-room. The relationship between *The Wallace* and *Braveheart* is wider than just the expression of the written word as motion picture. They are both 'fantasy' portrayals derived from the acts of William Wallace; neither is an attempt to explain the events and processes of the Wars of Independence.

The following extracts from Blind Harry's epic have been transcribed into modern English for the benefit of readers without a background in late-medieval Scots. Blind Harry's verse is not as easily comprehensible as that of Barbour, nor is it as satisfactory an artwork, so it is not so rewarding a read.

Whatever historical value there may be in *The Wallace* as a record document is limited to the earlier books, largely because they constitute virtually all of the information that relates to William Wallace's life and career before May 1297. This does not mean that the material has any validity whatsoever, but it is all there is and cannot simply be ignored. The trail of dead Englishmen and Scottish 'collaborators' who, if Blind Harry is to be taken at face value, must have lain in the wake of William Wallace would soon have brought his career to a close; his enemies would have been able to locate him by following the bodies. All the same, Wallace's rise to the Guardianship was, without doubt, made possible through his martial success against the English. Given his relatively junior status in the ranks of the nobility, his acquisition of a following of men-at-arms was almost certainly achieved through his individual prowess in combat. The skill and valour with which William repeatedly overcomes outrageous odds quickly becomes tedious as well as incredible; an extensive examination of the Blind Harry text is not the most rewarding of experiences and the extracts chosen for this volume are all taken from the first two books. Hopefully the 'Anglicisations' made to them will make the material more accessible for the average reader. The best presentation of the earliest surviving text is the Canongate edition edited by Dr Anne McKim and there are a number of modern prints of the 1722 'modernisation' of the entire poem by William Hamilton of Gilbertfield. To date, no thorough examination of the Blind Harry text has appeared in print to compare to Professor Duncan's edition of *The Bruce* – a surprising fact, given the significance of the poem in Scottish political history. *The Wallace* was among the very first books to be printed in Scotland (*c.*1507) and remained a popular work until the nineteenth century.

BOOK ONE OF THE WALLACE

Our ancestors, of whom we read
And bear in mind their worthy deeds
We ignore through idleness
And turn to different business.
To honour enemies is our intent;
Who we have met with in bygone times.
Our old foes come of Saxon blood
That never yet meant well for Scotland

Harry opens his work with a statement that encapsulates the general attitude of the Scots to the English at the time of writing. That antipathy had been the currency of Scots-English intercourse for well over 100 years by the time Harry embarked on *The Wallace*. Traditionally, scholars have tended to see the Wars of Independence as the issue that upset the previously rather good relationship between the two countries, exemplified by the reigns of Alexander II and Alexander III in Scotland and the reign of Henry III in England. If there had been no tradition whatsoever of Scots-English rivalry it would surely have been very difficult for Wallace – and the other leaders of resistance whose names have not been recorded – to raise forces against the occupation, unless the Edwardian government was particularly heavy-handed. The first serious confrontation of the wars was Edward's siege and storming of Berwick, during which the inhabitants of the town taunted their attackers by alluding to the fact that all Englishmen had tails – a popular tradition in anti-English sentiment throughout the Middle Ages. The reference to Saxon blood is a propaganda device and nothing more. The Wallace family, in common with their compatriots throughout southern, central and eastern Scotland, shared a good deal of their ancestry with their counterparts in England. Harry continues in a similar vein, drawing attention to the traditional English priority in Scotland: conquest.

> It is very well known, on every side
> How they have endeavoured in pride
> To hold Scotland in subjection forever

For Harry, the fight is not merely a struggle for political independence; the success of the Scots is clear proof that God favours their cause. From the perspective of Harry and his contemporaries, this was not a completely irrational conclusion. England was unquestionably a far larger, wealthier and militarily stronger nation than Scotland, but despite several very serious defeats the Scots had been able to secure and maintain that independence through force of arms. By the time Harry wrote *The Wallace* there had been almost continual war between Scotland and England for more than 150 years. During that period the English had achieved several very convincing victories on the battlefield – Falkirk, Halidon Hill, Neville's Cross and Humbledon – as well as being able to install administrations in southern Scotland, not once, but twice, but they had still been defeated eventually by a smaller nation with major internal divisions. Robert I had defeated the English in the early fourteenth century despite having to fight two distinct, though interconnected, civil wars, against the MacDougalls in the west and against the Comyns in the north-east. King Robert's successor, David II, had been a boy of six or seven when he became king; his authority was threatened by the invasions of Edward III and Edward's support for Edward Balliol – who did after all have a clear legitimist claim to the Scottish throne and therefore enjoyed a degree of sympathy from traditionalist and conservative elements in the Scottish political community – but he still managed to enforce his kingship, despite being defeated in battle, captured and held a prisoner in England for many years. Within (or nearly so at least) Harry's own lifetime another Scottish king, James I, had spent his entire youth and early manhood as a 'guest' of Henry IV of England and the Scots had suffered a devastating defeat at Humbledon, but English kings from Edward I to Henry V had been consistently unable to bring Scotland under their dominion. As a patriotic Scot and a Christian, Harry could hardly look at the history of his country without seeing the benevolent hand of God, but his priority is of course to record the career of William Wallace, commencing with the immediate background of the Wallace family in Lanarkshire.

> We read of one man of great renown
> Of worthi blood that rules in this region
> And henceforth I will relate
> Of William Wallace of whom you have heard

Harry could be confident that his readership, whether the lone reader in the library or an audience of boisterous gentry in a hall, would indeed have heard of William Wallace. Harry gives Wallace a context of class and lineage that would be perfectly familiar to that audience. They may have been mistaken in the belief that the Scots and the English were of different 'blood', but they did believe it, and would have wanted to believe that they shared their 'roots' as well as their status with the noble Wallace: a status that Harry reiterates frequently by, among other things, showing Wallace's descent from men of rank:

> Sir Ranald Crawford, sheriff of Ayr
> Had a daughter fair
> And young Sir Ranald, sheriff of that town;
> His fair sister, of good fame and renown
> Was married to Malcolm Wallace
> That held Elderslie heritably
> Auchinbothy and various other places.
> He was the grandson of another Wallace…

The connection of the Wallace family to that of the rather more prominent Crawfords would have been of great significance to a medieval audience, not because they were aware of Sir Ranald Crawford, but because they were familiar with knightly and shrieval status. A marriage between the two families would be very unlikely unless the Wallace family enjoyed a degree of noble prestige, but the point is pressed further in the next few lines. Malcolm Wallace is described as holding 'in heritage' the estate of Elderslie and certain other properties. Land might be held under a variety of arrangements – commercial lets, favourable lets, token rents, leases for a year, for several years, for life: all these can be found within the accounts of one estate in one year – but the most prestigious form of landholding was tenure direct from the king for military service on the basis of a charter granting ownership of the property to the recipient and to his heirs. 'Heritage' landholding demonstrated the long-term status of the family line as well as the immediate status of the current incumbent of the chief property. Blind Harry, quite correctly, placed his hero in the social context of the minor aristocracy of medieval Scotland:

> Malcolm had, by this bright lady,
> Sir Malcolm, a full knight,
> And William also, who, as chronicles record,
> Was the rescuer of Scotland
> When it was lost through treason and falsehood
> Overcome by foes, he freed it through [God's] grace
> When Alexander our worthy King had lost
> By misadventure, his life, near Kinghorn.

William Wallace would have needed little introduction to the readership, but the need for his intervention is made clear by the nature of the initial defeat of the Scots in 1296. Since Harry, like John of Fordoun, Andrew Wyntoun and Walter Bower before him, was convinced that God favoured the Scots in their defence against the English, it was clear that something caused the various heavy defeats the Scots had suffered in the past. In the finest traditions of Scottish chroniclers, Harry hits on the obvious scapegoat: Scots who betrayed their fellow countrymen. Harry proceeds to relate a highly coloured version of the events of 1291–92 that constituted the competition for Scottish kingship between (primarily) John Balliol and Robert Bruce, which was arranged with the help of Edward I, before returning to his hero.

To Wallace again I will now briefly return.

Scotland was lost when he was but a child

And overcome through our enemies' wiles

His father, Malcolm fled into the Lennox

His eldest son joined him there

His mother fled with him from Elderslie,

Passing through Gowrie and resting at Kilspndie.

His father the knight sent him

To his uncle, who in a well-intentioned manner

Lived well in Gowrie,

An aged man who received them kindly.

Harry's dating of events is far from reliable: when Edward I invaded Scotland in 1296 William Wallace was a grown man, if an obscure one. Given the nature of Edward's invasion, it is difficult to see what prompted Sir Malcolm to flee Lanarkshire for the Lennox unless he was among the men who we can identify coming to Edward's peace in through 1296–97. The absence of his name from the various documents relating to acceptance into English peace, or from lists of men and women forfeited from or restored to their properties in the aftermath of Dunbar and Edward's progress to Elgin, does not mean that Malcolm was not one of their number, merely that evidence of his acceptance, surrender, defection or capture has not survived. By the autumn of 1296 the greater part of the political community of Scotland must have believed that the Edwardian occupation was likely to be in place for some time, if not permanently; those who wished to retain their family estates under the government of Edward I would have had to accept his lordship. At least one writer has chosen to see the early adventures of William Wallace as presented by Blind Harry against the background of the English occupation of 1291–92. It is likely, even probable, that there was something in the way of friction between the garrisons that Edward installed in certain Scottish castles during the 'Competition', but not enough to have troubled the administrators of the time, it would seem. The possession of these castles had been a condition stipulated by Edward as part of his terms for taking responsibility for conducting the process of deciding on the kingship. This was not an unreasonable position to take, within the framework of medieval international relations: Edward would, in theory, be responsible for ensuring that the successful contender received possession of his assets promptly, once the outcome had been decided, and therefore could be expected to want to have control over what happened in those assets. The forces Edward committed to the Scottish castles in 1291–92 were very small indeed and it is more likely that they were regarded, and acted, as a support to the existing arrangements for the maintenance of law and order, not a replacement for them. James MacKay suggests that the castles remained in Edward's hands throughout the reign of King John, which is clearly not the case, but the officers appointed by Edward, who seem to have acted in tandem with the existing sheriffs, certainly had a fine opportunity to learn about conditions in Scotland: experience that might stand them in good stead in the event of a war. The knowledge that could be acquired extended well beyond questions of the strengths and weaknesses of the king of Scotland's castles and those of his great lords. Most, if not all, of the free tenants who owed military service to the king were obliged to serve time at a specified castle or pay a fee in lieu of service, but they also owed forty days' field service every year. Failure to enforce an obligation meant it fell into desuetude, and it is therefore likely that sheriffs were empowered to ensure that all the men in their sheriffdom who owed service as men-at-arms were equipped to a suitable standard – something that could only be achieved by reasonably regular inspections of man and mount. Professional curiosity, if nothing else, would surely motivate English soldiers serving in Scotland to take a look at their Scottish counterparts:

> They sent Wallace to school at Dundee
> Where he showed himself a worthy student
> Thus he continued until his prime
> When he did many great feats of arms
> When saxon blood came into this realm
> Working the will of Edward that false King
> Many great wrongs they committed in this region;
> Destroyed our lords and broke their buildings down
> Both wives and widows, they took them at their will
> Nuns and maidens, whom they liked to spoil
> They played the part of king Herod in Scotland
> When they came across young children
> The most valuable bishoprics they
> Took into the hands of their archbishops
> They would not spare churches, not even for the Pope,
> But gripped everything by the violence of war
> They gave Glasgow, as is well known
> To the diocese of Durham
> Only small benefices escaped them
> And for those gains they killed very worthy clerics
> Hanged barons and caused great damage.

Harry's description of the 'perfidious' English follows in a well-developed Scottish literary tradition. Not only had the English invaded and conquered, but they had oppressed people of all ranks and genders. No doubt there were many dreadful incidents under the Plantagenets, but Harry's priority is the sympathy of the audience, not historical validity. His claim that the greater bishoprics of Scotland were granted to the archbishops of England – York and Canterbury – is simply untrue. Not content with that, Harry mentions in passing a savage English atrocity at Ayr, where, he tells us, it is 'well-known' that eighteen score (360) were killed. Since this particular incident would seem to have passed unnoticed by all other writers, we might reasonably conclude that it, too, was an invention of Blind Harry: a propaganda item of that magnitude would hardly have been ignored by Fordoun or Bower. For Harry, Wallace is the complete man; a virtuoso on the battlefield, a man of gentle birth and a scholar as well.

> William Wallace, before he became a man of war
> Thought it a great pity that Scotland endured such harm
> It caused great sadness in his mind
> For he was wise, worthy, brave and kind.
> He still lived in Gowrie with this man [his uncle]
> As he grew, and as his knowledge increased
> He was greatly saddened at heart
> He saw the English multiplying greatly
> And often lamented to himself
> At his many of his kin that had been killed.
> Though he was seemly, stark and bold
> He was only eighteen years old
> He bore arms, either a good sword or knife
> For often he made good use of them in a fight.

Wallace, as a hero ought, took exception to the presence of the invaders and brooded over the predicament of his country and the loss of several of his relatives, though Harry's reticence about the names of these relatives perhaps suggests the needs of literature rather than of history. Naturally, as a hero, Wallace was inevitably bold and good-looking, but it would be very unlikely that he should only have been eighteen years old at the beginning of his career. A man of his background, that of a very minor noble indeed, would have found it hard enough to persuade men to accept his leadership; a boy would have found it even more of a challenge. Political leadership at an early age was not, however, unheard of in the medieval period. In 1334–35 Robert the Stewart and Andrew Moray were able to establish themselves as the leaders of the Bruce party though both were very young men: the Stewart would have been about eighteen at the time. But both the Stewart and Murray were men of considerable importance among the Scottish magnates; their status as great lords offset their youth. There seems to be no doubt that Wallace was a young man when he became Guardian, but not so young as all that.

> One day he was sent to Dundee
> He knew little of the cruelties of life
> The constable, a vicious man of war
> did great harm to the Scots.
> He was called Selbye, he was spiteful and violent
> He had a son nearly twenty years old
> Who used to go into the town almost every day
> With there or four other men for entertainment
> A total shrew, wicked by intention
> He saw Wallace and approached him.
> He [Wallace] was large and impressive, well-dressed
> In a garment of fine green cloth.
> He called to him, 'You! Scot! Wait there.
> What devil dresses you in such excellent clothes?
> An Irish cloak would be more suitable for you,
> A Scottish knife at your belt
> Raw hide brogues for your feet.
> Give me your knife. Why do you dress so well?'
> He made to take his [Wallace's] knife from him,
> But Wallace seized him by the collar
> He drew out his knife
> But for all he was surrounded by his friends
> They could not help him
> [Wallace] gave him a mortal wound.
> The squire fell, he was no more.
> His men chased Wallace, angry and surprised.

Harry's account of this incident shows Wallace in the guise of the perfect victim and the occupation forces as oppressive and arrogant. Throughout history there has been a tendency for the members of imposed governments to be heavy-handed in their dealings with the communities they rule. There is no reason to assume that the Plantagenet occupation was unusually severe, but occupation forces are seldom popular and any attack upon them is likely to find support. It is of course perfectly possible that the fracas at Dundee took the course that Harry describes. A powerful-looking, well-dressed Scot, particularly one unfamiliar to the men of the local garrison, might well attract an unfavourable interest. It is important to remember that medieval towns were very small indeed, mere villages by modern standards, so a new face in town was unlikely to pass unnoticed. The importance of the passage is its clear message that Wallace was unquestionably the victim of malicious aggression; he was engaged on his own private business, disturbing no one, when he was insulted and assaulted by a member of the garrison of Dundee Castle. As far as Harry was concerned, Wallace did no more than protect himself from an attempted robbery. After a few days of lying low he decided to leave Dundee for a more congenial environment – one where he would not be the object of a murder investigation. Naturally, given that he had just left a dead man behind him, the garrison troops were conducting a search for the culprit, so Wallace adopted a disguise:

> Then Wallace would no longer sojourn there
> His mother dressed herself in pilgrim's garments,
> He disguised himself, and shortly left with her
> A short sword hidden beneath his clothes.
> He had many enemies in that area.
> Both on foot [Wallace and his mother] they took nothing with them
> If any asked, they said they were going to St Margaret
> Whoever venerated her found great friendship
> From southerners because she was English.
> They took the ferry near Lindores
> The passed through the Ochils very quickly
> They rested at Dunfermline that night.

Saint Margaret, queen of Malcolm III, had indeed come to Scotland from England, though she was Hungarian by birth. She was instrumental in the reform of the Church in Scotland in the later eleventh century and was beatified for her zeal. Her grave and shrine at Dunfermline was a popular destination for pilgrims. Saint Margaret's popularity among the English, and perhaps the fact that she was, by the way of late-medieval thinking, a 'non-mythological' saint, might well have stood Wallace and his mother in good stead as they passed through the country. From Dunfermline they made their way to Linlithgow, joining the party of the wife of the captain of Linlithgow garrison, who was herself returning from a pilgrimage – presumably, like the Wallace party, to Dunfermline. Although Linlithgow was a centre of local administration before 1296 there would not seem to have been anything more ambitious than a royal manor there: the great fortress or 'pele' that functioned as a major centre for the military administration's operations against the Balliol party in 1301–04 and the Bruces in 1306–1313 had yet to be constructed in 1296–97. If the Dundee incident was rooted in reality at all – and it may have been a total fabrication on the part of Blind Harry or one of his sources – it would have to have occurred before Wallace achieved fame (or notoriety, depending on your point of view) in the summer of 1297 and could hardly have occurred before Edward I's invasion in the spring and summer of 1296. Harry's claim that Wallace made the journey from Dundee to Dunfermline 'wondrous' fast is something of an understatement. The two towns are separated by a good thirty miles as the crow flies. Even on the longest of summer days a thirty-mile hike is quite an undertaking; medieval roads were not good, to say the least, and the party had to negotiate the Ochil hills – scarcely a major mountain range, but a challenge to travellers on foot. From Linlithgow, the Wallace party made their way to Dunipace:

His uncle lived there, a man of great wealth.
This noble priest, also named Wallace,
Put them at ease and was a very kind man.
He welcomed them, and gave them to understand
That the whole region was in a ferment
He treated them well and said 'My dear son,
Your mother and yourself will stay here with me
Until matters improve.
Wallace answered, 'We shall go to the west,
Our kinfolk have been murdered and I resent it,
Also, many other people in that region
If God gives me leave I shall take vengeance.
The priest sighed, and said 'My son so free,
I do not know how redress can be achieved
What can be said? At this time
He [Wallace] would not stay with him, despite his generosity.
His mother and he [Wallace] went to Elderslie.
The next day she sent for her brother.
He lived in Corsby and was the sheriff of Ayr.

Her late father had lived there for a long time.
Her husband was killed at Loudon Hill.
Her eldest son, who was extremely strong, but even so
They cut his tendons in that melee.
He fought on his knees, yet killed many Englishmen
Until they attacked him with more than enough fighters
Who bore him down with spears from all sides.
There they slew a good knight of great renown.

Again, Blind Harry is at pains to make the reader aware that Wallace was a member of the noble class, even if at a very low level. The references to the family of his mother serve to reinforce his status. Had Wallace's father married a person with markedly lower status than his own, Wallace might not have been quite so easily identifiable to a late-medieval Scottish audience. The theoretical and sentimental aspects of the chivalrous life were still of great cultural and literary life in the middle of the fifteenth century, when Blind Harry wrote *The Wallace*. In order to ensure the maximum identification between the hero and the reader, Harry makes use of all of the points of connection between the two. Naturally, an audience that saw itself as part of a traditional and ancient military elite whose privileged position was earned by service in the field and endorsed by God was likely to be entertained by tales of dashing bravery and narrow escapes.

By the time Harry put pen to paper, war between England and Scotland was a long-standing tradition. Scots even went to other countries to fight against the English when there was not enough fighting to go round locally, but this had not always been the case. Although there may have been some tradition of minor animosity (see above) between Scots and English (and even that is open to question), there had certainly been no tradition of war before the invasion of Edward I in 1296. Harry's assumption that all Scots would be fiercely hostile to the English was probably perfectly valid in the mid-1400s, but not in the mid-1290s. This would have little significance for either Harry or his audience; their interest lay in entertainment rather than history. His audience mostly consisted of noble landholders: people who were familiar with the sort of life Wallace lived before his rise to fame. Harry's brief digression to mention the deaths of Wallace's father and brother in battle is a further means of promoting identification. Most Scottish nobles in the fifteenth century would have had forebears who had been killed in action against the English and would undoubtedly be able to attest to the fact that their sires had died nobly, overwhelmed by great numbers and surrounded by their dead foes. Many of them would also have had forebears who had been killed fighting *for* the English; in the period between the armistice of Strathord in 1304 and the inauguration of Robert Bruce as king in 1306 there was no 'official' Scottish patriotic movement of any kind. Those men who, like Wallace, continued the fight after Strathord did so without the benefit of any sort of political status that might safeguard life and limb in the event of capture. They were effectively 'unofficial' combatants; in modern times they probably would not have been protected by the various protocols that apply to prisoners of war. Similarly, men who supported Robert I in the early days of his kingship ran the risk of being executed for treason. In the period between Strathord and the point where Robert I could reasonably claim to be *de facto* king of Scotland and the head of a legitimate and effective structure of lordship and government, even the most patriotic of Scots would have had good cause to accept the rule of the Plantagenet administration and to support it – through the discharge of military service obligations if necessary – against threats to the stability of the community. Wallace was most assuredly a threat to that stability.

> To return to the tale; at Elderslie
> Sir Ranald soon came to his noble sister
> Welcomed them home and asked their intentions.
> She begged him to go to Lord Percy,
> She was so tired of war that she could travel no further
> And wished to purchase amnesty that she might rest in peace
> Sir Ranald had the Percy's protection
> To conduct negotiations for a remission.

The 'protection' issued to Sir Ranald would have been a document indemnifying him from any accusations of consorting with the enemy. As a senior officer in the Plantagenet administration, Percy might well have had the authority to admit people to the peace of Edward I, though probably not persons of very high status, for whom the king was likely to seek particularly binding assurances of future loyalty. The purchase of an amnesty for political misdemeanours or for criminal activity was not uncommon in medieval societies. A cash settlement was regarded as an 'end' – *fine* – to the matter in question: hence the modern term a 'fine'.

Sir Ranald procured a remission for Wallace's mother but was well aware that William would not rest easy under the occupation even if he managed to avoid arrest for the killing he had already done, so he made arrangements for him to travel to the estate of yet another relative:

Sir Ranald knew well a quieter place
Where William might avoid the disorder,
With his uncle Wallace of Riccarton.
That good knight of renown was called Sir Richard
That whole area was his heritage
But he was blind – from his courage
against English men, who do us [the Scots] great harm
In his youth he was a worthy man of war –
Through an unfortunate wound.
But he was wise, and his advice sound
Wallace was sent to him in February,
In April he left,
But did such good service as he could in that area.
After a while he wanted pleasure,
And on the twenty-third of April
He went to the Irvine water to fish,
That was what took his fancy.

Once again, the scene is set with William minding his own business –
fishing – when he is confronted by the power of the occupation. Wallace is
approached by Lord Percy, captain of Ayr Castle, accompanied by five score
(100) men clad in 'garande' (appropriate, proper) green. The significance
of uniform colours among Percy's retinue may be nothing more than a
dramatic device on the part of Blind Harry; however, the Earl of Lincoln's
troops appear to have been clad in green in the late 1290s or early 1300s.
It is not generally believed that the practice of providing retainers with
uniform or 'livery' jackets occurred before the fifteenth century; however,
Barbour does describe the men who assembled at Berwick in the retinue
of William de Soulis in 1320 as a force of over 300 'esquires' dressed in
'livery'. The 'esquires' in question would have been men whose status
would have obliged then to serve as men-at-arms and whose background
would have trained them to do so: William Wallace was a man of similar
status himself. It is possible that Barbour's use of the term livery does not
imply uniform garments, but rather that all of the men were bearing their
own heraldic devices on their shields: that is to say, they were 'gentlemen'
rather than men-at-arms. The distinction would have been a subtle one,
though probably perfectly clear to those concerned. A man might become
a man-at-arms as a career choice if he could acquire the necessary arms,
mount a horse and most importantly, display the skills required for the
job; that would not make him a 'gentleman' or 'noble' in the eyes of men

who served for periods specified in their charters as part of their general social obligation and in exchange for heritable land tenure rather than for wages. Some men with significant heritage lands did in fact serve for wages in Scottish garrisons, though in the main that would seem to have been a career for younger sons rather than 'in capite' landholders.

The men of Lord Percy's retinue would have been drawn almost exclusively from the minor nobility: the class of men and women sometimes described as the 'parish gentry'. Many of them will have served for wages or on the understanding that they would eventually be granted fiefs in Scotland or elsewhere; all of them would have expected to make some sort of career progress through service in Percy's retinue.

In Harry's account they are both arrogant and incompetent. They demand Wallace's catch of fish but are unable to force him to part with it, an incident that leaves five of their number dead. Again Wallace has been the victim of the unreasonable behaviour of the English and is once again obliged to abandon home and hearth.

> When Wallace had done this noble deed
> He took a horse and the arms that they had dropped
> And gave up the craft of fishing,
> And went to his uncle to tell him of his predicament
> And he nearly went mad with despair
> And said 'Son, these things grieve me sorely
> And you will probably come to harm over this
> 'Uncle, he said, 'I will stay no longer
> If I can ride this English horse.'
> Then, with only a boy to serve him
> He would not take his uncle's sons.
> That good knight said 'Dear cousin, I beg you,
> When you want good men, ask them of me.'
> He gave him gold and silver,
> Wallace bowed, and quietly took his leave.

BOOK TWO OF THE WALLACE

Wallace made his way to 'Auchincruff' after the incident of the fishing trip, to take advantage of another relative of the Wallace name. The wide geographical spread of the Wallaces in the Blind Harry account is perhaps exaggerated, but familial connections were an important aspect of medieval political life. Men and women of the noble classes (at least) were generally much more aware of their relations than we are today. Very few of us are aware of our second or third cousins; many, if not most, of us would have some difficulty it explaining the terms accurately. For men and women of Wallace's station and class the wider network of relations was a crucial aspect of political leadership and responsibility: probably more so in the unsettled environment of the late thirteenth and early fourteenth centuries. For 200 years Scotland had enjoyed a degree of political stability rare among European nations; there had been wars with England and Norway and a good deal of internal strife, but in the main there had been peace and growth. The Wars of Independence, unsurprisingly, brought political instability that perhaps made the 'permanent' bonds to relations seem more stable than bonds of political alignment. Great lords and kings had a rather more complicated agenda than the lesser nobility that comprised the bulk of the political community and might be obliged to adhere to, or reject, a family member through the *realpolitik* of their office – the relationship between David II and Edward III, for example – but in difficult times people do tend to become more reliant on their families. The network of Wallace families that Harry describes is doubtless exaggerated – the Wallaces were not a major family – but it surely existed and it would be most curious if it had not been an important element in supporting William in the first months of his political career.

> He travelled to Auchincruff without delay
> But only rested there a short time
> A Wallace lived there, who welcomed him warmly.
> Who thought little of the English.
> Both meat and drink he had there
> When he went to Laglyn Wood
> This gentleman often received him
> And provided him with supplies.
> One day he decided to visit Ayr
> With only a boy for company.
> He left his horse beside a wood
> And made his way to the market cross on foot.
> The (lord) Percy was in the castle of Ayr
> With a great number of Englishmen.

The presence or otherwise of Lord Percy as garrison commander at Ayr Castle is not the significant issue here. The best of heroes should have a habitual adversary; since Edward I spent little time in Scotland himself, it would be difficult to sustain a series of incidents in which Wallace would repeatedly defeat him and still maintain any dramatic credibility. Wallace's credentials as a fearless man are rehearsed again: Wallace heads toward danger with 'only a boy' for company. Naturally he is once again the victim of English aggression and – again naturally – is completely triumphant and leaves another scatter of English corpses in his wake before making good his escape, despite a pursuit by men on horse and foot.

William was not the only member of the Wallace family to fall foul of the occupation. No sooner does Harry have William escape from Ayr than he has him return there, bored with life on the estate of the squire of Auchincruff. In the marketplace of the town William witnesses an altercation between the steward of Lord Percy's household and the servant of Sir Ranald Crawford, Sheriff of Ayr and uncle of William.

> When he had bought his goods
> Lord Percy's stewart sought him out
> And said 'You, Scot. To whom do you carry this?'
> 'To the sheriff' he said ' by heaven's King.
> This is for my lord, you find your own'
> Wallace happened to be nearby
> He called 'Good friend I beg you
> Leave the sheriff's servant alone
> The steward was a hot-tempered man
> And thought Wallace challenged him rudely
> 'Go away Scot, the devil speed your leaving
> If you are as evil as you lead me to believe'
> He carried a hunting staff in his hand
> And with it he struck William hard.
> He did not hesitate on account of the staff
> But seized him by the collar,
> Struck him a fatal blow with a knife
> And put a stop to his stewarding.
> Men of arms approached Wallace there
> Four score were well armed and ready
> For defending the town against the Scots on market day
> But Wallace boldly drew a sword of war,
> Drove it into the hauberk of the first

And stabbed him to death through the torso,
And several others before he left that place.
Another he struck with an awkward blow
Above the knee and broke the bone in two.
The third he struck through his pisan of mail (collaret)
The neck severed, his armour of no avail.
Thus Wallace; as fierce as a lion.
Those Englishmen that were equipped for battle
To defend the street with long, strong spears
They cannot approach him for fear of his sword blows.
Wallace was well armed
But they came for him with sharp spears
And surrounded him [...]

Not even Wallace can withstand the attack of eighty opponents and he is eventually overpowered and taken prisoner. Like so much of Harry's account, this is not a tale that surfaces anywhere else, but that should not be taken as evidence that Wallace was never a prisoner. Whether he was or not, it may have been the case that Scots in the fifteenth century either believed that Wallace had been captured or simply accepted that this episode constituted a good dramatic passage and nothing more; after all, dashing escape from perilous circumstance is one of the traditional feats of heroes.

Some explanation of the relationship between the sheriff of Ayr and the captain of Ayr Castle is required here. The sheriffdom was a crucial part of the social structure both in Scotland and England. The sheriff had responsibilities that ranged from upholding the law in the king's court to the collection of taxation and customs, the maintenance of good order and the administration of military service, even to the extent of leadership on the battlefield. The commander of a castle held for the king (in this instance Edward I) was more usually referred to as the 'constable'. Often sheriff and constable would in fact be the same person. This had been a normal practice under Alexander I and Alexander II and probably for some considerable time before that. Edward I, Edward II and Edward III all appointed Scots as sheriffs and constables, giving some support to the view that the Plantagenet administrations in Scotland had the potential to establish themselves securely. While it is certainly true that the Scots were not united in their support for the Balliol party in the 1290s, let alone the Bruce party in the reigns of Robert I or David II, the fact remains that entrusting local power to Scottish magnates was always something of a risk for English occupation governments.

The potential for defection was very high. No case illustrates this better than that of Patrick, Earl of Dunbar. In 1333, in the wake of the battle of Halidon Hill, he defected to the Plantagenet cause. He probably had little choice in the matter since he had a large and victorious English army in his doorstep, and Edward III's protégé, Edward Balliol, had a legitimate claim on Scottish kingship which he might be able to make a reality with the support of English troops and money. Throughout 1333–34 Edward III and Edward Balliol expended a great deal of time and effort on defeating the Bruce cause; various Scottish chroniclers – Fordoun for example – are quite clear about the dire straits of the Bruce party, telling us that King David's kingdom was reduced to only four castles. There are a number of issues to be considered here. One is the shortage of viable castles: Robert I had slighted several Scottish castles; no doubt some had been destroyed through action; probably some had been abandoned by their owners and fallen into decay. More importantly, possession of castles was a poor indicator of administrative success in terms of either security or effectiveness. Several sheriffdoms had no royal castle for the English to occupy and many Scottish baronial castles would have been too modest to be worth the investment of a sizeable garrison even if they were in sympathetic hands, nor could the security of private castles be taken for granted. When the Earl of Dunbar returned to Scottish allegiance, the castle of Dunbar was immediately transformed from an instrument of government in the Plantagenet and Balliol interest into a centre of resistance to that government. Dunbar's defection, just at the juncture that historians have tended to see as the lowest point in the fortunes of the Bruce party, suggests that the position did not seem hopeless to the astute and well-informed Earl Patrick.

Blind Harry's epic continues in similarly violent and patriotic vein for a further ten books of rather laboured and tedious verse. It cannot be said to be a rewarding read, though it is perhaps a useful insight into the military and patriotic values of Harry's audience in the fifteenth century. Their relationship with the English differed from that of their forefathers in the early fourteenth century. By the mid 1330s it had become apparent that the English had lost their war and that the conquest of Scotland was too great a project for the kings of England; Harry's audience had no fear that their country would be conquered. Although they were well aware that they could be beaten on the battlefield (and both they and their ancestors frequently had been), they were also aware that the Wars of Independence were in the past and that a crucial element of success had been a man of obscure, though noble, status: Sir William Wallace.

CHAPTER FOURTEEN

In the Eyes of the Enemy: Wallace in English Records

Inevitably, the appearances of William Wallace in English records are related to his military and political activities, either directly – reports of his activities against the Plantagenet government – or indirectly, such as the reports of spies in the Balliol party. The extracts printed below have been culled from a number of sources, chiefly Bain's *Calendar of Documents Relating to Scotland* (and the supplementary volume collated by Simpson and Galbraith), the Reverend Stevenson's *Documents Illustrative of the History of Scotland* and the website of De Re Militari, the specialist medieval military studies society. A great deal of material from English state documents has been published and is therefore 'available' in the widest sense of the word, but not easily accessible to those who do not have the benefits of a good library. English records are very much more extensive than Scottish ones or, for that matter, those of France or the Low Countries: partly a product of more intensive government, partly of sheer good fortune. Understandably, Scottish Crown records between 1296 and the middle of the fourteenth century are rather sparse. In addition to the difficulty of maintaining records at all, let alone storing them for the benefit of historians, which would itself be a challenge for a state at war, English administrations collected Scottish records for the use of their officers, some of which, but not all, were returned at the conclusion of the 'Perpetual Peace' of Edinburgh-Northampton in 1328.

It is possible that the first mention of William Wallace in written record is from the records of the army of the English army of 1296. It is by no means certain that the William Wallace referred to in the case was in fact 'the' William Wallace; however, Wallace was not a particularly common name. It would be rash to assume that all the Wallaces of thirteenth- or fourteenth-century Scotland were related, but reasonable to assume that the majority (at least) of men and women bearing the name Wallace, and of knightly or lairdly status, would be likely to be related in some degree. Sharing a name was not the same thing as sharing a political conviction and it is all too easy to see medieval political life in terms of family-based interest groups. The Wallace family, like most, if not all, others of their rank, were divided in their allegiances at different times, and it is important to remember that that was a common situation during the Wars of Independence. Most families of any stature had members in the Balliol camp, the Bruce camp or the Plantagenet camp at different times, either because they felt that at a particular juncture the Plantagenets or the Bruces offered the better prospect as the source of authority or because they had no choice – because at that moment the party in power in their locality could not be challenged. It is conceivable that none of the individuals named Wallace who appear in English or Scottish records were related to William Wallace at all, with the obvious exceptions of his father and brothers. It is certainly possible, even perhaps likely, that the William Wallace of the Plea Rolls was not William Wallace the Guardian, but it is likely that, if they were not one and the same, they were very probably related in a degree that medieval society would consider 'near'.

CALENDAR OF DOCUMENTS RELATING TO SCOTLAND

This extract is from the gaol delivery (the presentation of accused persons for summary trial by the army court) made at Perth on 8 August 1296:

> Matthew of York, accused by Christian of St John of robbery, that on Thursday next before St Botolph's day, he came to her house at Perth in company of a thief one William le Waleys, and there took by force her goods and chattels, viz. beer, to the value of 3 shillings, replies that he is a clerk and not bound to answer. The jury find the charge proved and he is adjudged to penitence.

Matthew tried to persuade the court that as a clerk (that is, a member of the clergy) he was not obliged to stand trial before a secular court of this nature, an argument that the court evidently dismissed. The crime was rather more serious than it might seem to us: three shillings worth of beer

was a considerable quantity in an age when a 2d per diem was considered
a decent, though not remarkable, labouring wage and £10 per annum
constituted a perfectly respectable professional salary.

> Letter from Sir Hugh de Cressingham to the King relating his activities at
> Berwick and elsewhere, the submission of the Scots to Percy and Clifford at
> Irvine and that William Wallace still holds out in Selkirk Forest.
>
> *CDS vol. ii no. 916, 23 July 1297*

Wallace had evidently become a leader of some stature by July 1297. Since
Cressingham could refer to him by name and tell Edward that Wallace
'still' held out in the forest he had obviously been active in the preceding
months, given the slow rate of communications between Edward and his
officers. The submission of the Scottish nobles, chiefly Bruce and Stewart
adherents, at Irvine was good news for Edward – a useful victory at no
great cost – but the time taken to dissuade the nobles at Irvine inevitably
afforded Wallace greater opportunity to assemble and train troops and to
establish his will across a greater area.

The mills of government, then as now, could grind exceedingly slow.
In 1305 a jury of barons sat to decide on various debts claimed by John
Sampson for losses incurred during his service as commander of Stirling
Castle, which he was obliged to surrender to the Scots in 1299. The claims
allowed by the jury give some insight into the nature and quantity of
equipment that a castle commander might need to have, and to the potential loss that could be incurred by defeat.

> He [John Sampson] lost in Stirling castle when he surrendered it by the King's
> order, to Gilbert Malherbe a Scottishman, horses, armour, robes and other
> [items] to the value of £61 13s 10d.:- viz. A bay horse which cost him £13
> 7s 8d was eaten for default of other food; also a 'ferrant' horse which cost
> him eight pounds and a mare that he bought from Gilbert de Braconer for
> one mark were eaten; a 'bausan' horse which cost him forty shillings and was
> ridden by Sir William Danant towards the King for news of the castle and
> the country, was lost at Lund, and a 'Liard' [horse] costing him four marks
> was lost on a St Bartholomew's day when William le Waleys came to take
> away their supplies. He also lost when leaving the castle two aketons that
> cost him more than forty shillings; two gambesons, more than four pounds,
> with 'cotes armes', one 'jupel feytis', more than twenty shillings, a hauberk
> and a habergeon, price fifteen 'soldz', a 'pisane' and 'cape de hust' cost him
> ten shillings, 'jambers quisez which cost more than eight shillings, a chapel

de feer [fer: iron], price twenty shillings, a chapel de nerfs price forty pence, gauntlets [gants de fer: gloves of iron] costing him five shillings, a pair of plates cost him more than a mark, a pair of treppes [a set of cloth and leather horse armour], price two marks, three swords, a misericord and two anlaces with ivory handles price ten shillings, two sumpter and two hackney saddles, costing him more than twenty-four soldz, two sacks 'a draps dequir, with 'houces' and appurtenaces, price, sixteen soldz, a gentleman's bed and all appurtenances, price fifty-three shillings and 4d, two robes 'un falding, price thirty shillings, two 'naps' two 'touailles', price six shillings and eight pence, 'lyngedraps' cut and uncut, price half a mark, 'livres, forcers, besas, lanoir, batin, barriz, mazre pots darreine', and 'mult de hustilements come appent a gentil home' to the value of twenty six shilling and eight pence and more, two buckles of gold, price ten shillings, eleven gold rings, price twenty-two shillings, two 'correys de dasy' mount ed with silver, price ten shillings, three silk purses, price three shillings, ten silver spoons, price twelve shillings a tent price thirty-three and fourpence and ten shillings in silver when leaving the castle.

CDS vol. ii no. 1949, 1305

The barons' report lists several more items, including twelve shillings for messengers sent to the king and the princely sum of nine pence paid to spies. The list of arms and armour obviously greatly exceeds the needs of any one man, as does the number of horses claimed as lost by the petitioner. However, any man-at-arms would have to have rather more than the equipment he stood up in when serving in a garrison: men whose equipment or horses fell short of the minimum standards might lose a portion of their pay for as long as their kit or mount was 'insufficiand'. It would seem that John Sampson was obliged to provide men of his garrison with a horse in order to keep them mounted and thereby effective members of the men-at-arms element of the garrison. It was normal practice in Edwardian armies to offer *restauro* – compensation – for one of the horses brought on campaign by men-at-arms. The horses would be valued by senior officers and/or civil administration officials (though it is important to bear in mind that there was a great deal of overlap between military and civil administrations in Edwardian Scotland) and, from that point on, the owner would be indemnified for the loss of that horse, but not for the others he would require for the adequate discharge of his duties. In this instance John Sampson was probably obliged by operational necessity to provide Sir William Dannant with a mount, and the other animals were eaten – surely proof positive of operational need, not to say dire necessity. A garrison that ate its horses was a garrison that had given up hope of restoring its authority without the intervention of a relief column. The degree to which Wallace and Moray's operations in 1297 took Edward by surprise is indicated by the size of the garrisons he installed at the start of the occupation; the extent of the problem the Balliol party posed for Edward is shown by the steady increase in the planned size of those garrisons over the next few years. Although men were recruited for all arms of service for the garrisons – archers, crossbowmen, hobelars and men-at-arms – it was the latter department that bore the brunt of the fighting, the infantry element of a garrison being largely responsible for the security of castles or towns from which the men-at-arms could conduct offensive operations, prevent Scottish encroachments, maintain law and order and generally impose King Edward's government throughout the sheriffdom. In February 1300 the Edinburgh garrison came to a total of 347 men, representing a major commitment of money and stores for the occupation government. Only thirty-nine of these men were men-art-arms, a relatively small force for the wide variety of tasks to be fulfilled, but not out of line with the complements of the garrisons of other major fortresses at the time, nor when compared with the garrisons maintained in Stirling and Edinburgh castles by Edward III in 1335–37, when he still perhaps thought he could retain Lothian, Roxburghshire and Berwickshire permanently. After 1337 the garrison complements shrank steadily. This was possibly a reflection of the difficulty of recruiting Scots, but more probably the garrisons were no longer expected to take a major role in the community, but just to retain Edinburgh, Roxburgh and Berwick castles, thereby keeping the Scots occupied without the expense of mounting major campaigns in a regular basis.

> Sir John de Kyngestone the constable [of Edinburgh Castle] has five esquires, seven chargers, thirteen hackneys
> Sir Walter de Sutton has [a] socius
> Sir Ebulo de Montibus has one esquire, two chargers, three hackneys
> Sir Gerard de Fresnay has two esquires, two chargers, two hackneys
> Sir Thomas de Morham has two esquires, three chargers, four hackneys
> Sir Herbert de Morham has two esquires, three chargers, four hackneys
> Sir Henry de Cantelou has two esquires, three chargers, four hackneys
> Sir … de Lees has two esquires, three chargers, four hackneys
> Sir John de Luda has one esquire, one charger, two hackneys
> Peter de Lubat and eleven others have twelve chargers, thirteen hackneys
> … De Vliers and one other are without chargers
>
> *CDS vol. ii no. 1132*

Twenty-three other men-at-arms are listed as having the requisite chargers, but the original document is in poor condition. Although the conclusion of the return puts the garrison man-at-arms strength at sixty-seven, it only accounts for sixty-two. For the (alleged) sixty-seven there were, however, only sixty-three chargers, of which three were deemed to be 'insufficient'.

The balance of the fighting strength of the garrison consisted of eighteen crossbowmen and fourteen archers 'of the new garrison' and twenty archers of the 'old', presumably a consequence or rotating the detachments allocated to the garrison.

Self-evidently, the infantry element of the garrison was intended primarily, if not exclusively, for the defence of the castle. Their numbers would be far too small to constitute a useful contribution to the defence of a town, let alone to allow them to mount operations in search of the enemy. Field service was, as a general rule, the province of the cavalry. The primary role of the garrison was to protect the administration's area of influence: enforcing the rule of the Plantagenet government, maintaining law and order, preventing the Scots from establishing their rule in the occupied territories. The only two possible approaches were to either install troops all over Scotland in large numbers or to maintain powerful mobile formations in key installations. The first would have been prohibitively expensive, and even if Edward had been able to find the finance there would have been great difficulties in raising such a large force and even greater problems in maintaining its strength over any length of time. The only realistic proposition was to enlist men-at-arms to provide the rapid strikes which might discomfit the Scots. There were two advantages to the latter, particularly in regard to financing the structure. If the Scottish political community could be brought to accept Plantagenet lordship, those of them with military liabilities attached to landholding would have to discharge their obligations or face forfeiture, though in fact, those who accepted Edwardian lordship would have every reason to serve in the garrisons since they would, in their view at least, be doing their duty as citizens in trying to suppress disorder.

Service attached to land did not attract either pay or the replacement value of a charger lost on active service. The risk to the man and the horse were seen as part of the *quid pro quo* that went with landholding. Although the service of these men must have been recorded in order to ensure that all the service was discharged, it would seem that such records were maintained by sheriffs and magnates who had responsibilities for army call-outs. It is possible therefore that the Edinburgh garrison of 1300 comprised many more men-at-arms than are enumerated in the muster roll. The political community of Lothian consisted of some hundreds of families with military liabilities; however, there are two points to be borne in mind. Service attached to land was for a specified period, generally believed to be forty days. To ensure the service of one man-at-arms on every day of the year there would need to be nine men liable to replace him: one every forty days for 360 days – the balance of five days would equate to one-eighth of the service of a tenth man. Additionally, not all of the men and women responsible for providing cavalry service were obliged to give forty days. Many charters specify the service of half or quarter of a knight, so the business of actually making use of cavalry service effectively was probably something of an administrative challenge. The value of such service might be open to question: men who fight unwillingly seldom do so very effectively and the security implications of enlisting men from the community would not have been reassuring for castle commanders; on the other hand, making men give service might help to develop a 'habit' of allegiance. Allegiance itself was an issue, though, when it came to extracting military service. In 1300 the Plantagenet administration was not in particularly good shape: the greater part of Scotland was either in Balliol control or at least outside Plantagenet control. Although the occupation government was rather more secure in the south-east and south-west than elsewhere, they were not in a position to prevent men from Lothian, Roxburghshire and Dumfriesshire from adhering to the Balliol cause. Enlisting local military service was not simply a challenge of administration: the capacity of the administration to successfully demand service was limited by the extent of Edwardian rule – a diminishing area, despite brief recoveries in the periods when Edward could commit a field force.

Edward's administration may or may not have been successful in extracting the man-at-arms service of Scottish communities, but he could certainly enlist men for wages. Two of the knights in the garrison of 1300, Sir Herbert Morham and Sir Thomas Morham, were Scots. It would seem likely that their 'esquires' were also Scots. In this context 'esquire' should not be construed as a servant or a man aspiring to knighthood employed to help the knight in and out of his armour, but a man-at-arms. Broadly speaking, men-at-arms were men of noble birth, though the term 'noble' extended to a very wide range of incomes and gradations of social status that would be difficult, not to say impossible, to define even for members of that society, let alone for social historians of modern times. Each of the knights in the garrison was accompanied by one or more esquires or, in the case of Sir Walter de Sutton, a *socius*. There must presumably have been some distinction between an esquire and a *socius* since there are several examples of both terms in a single document. The term could be translated as 'comrade' or 'associate', but there is an implication of leadership as well. Knights received greater pay than other men-at-arms due to their greater social status, but we should not ignore the possibility that it also reflected the greater likelihood of a knight being called upon to take command of a detachment, or even perhaps more or less permanent sub-units within the formation.

The layout of the muster roll is obviously of some significance. The listing of unnamed squires – and one *socius* – in sub-groups with named knights may be no more than an indication of the prominence of the knights; however, it may be the practical expression of service owed for land. The esquires would not need to be named, since they would be rotating from duty in divisions of forty days, depending on the level of their obligation.

The role of the garrisons, obviously, was to counter Scottish resistance, maintain a visible manifestation of English power in the community and to provide the sort of support for the administration that could be termed 'aid to the civil power': in short, to secure Edward's authority throughout the occupied territories. Although it was part of their function to discourage Scottish inroads, the garrison forces were not expected to carry the war to the enemy other than in local operations. The Scots might not be able to confront an invading army in a conventional open field engagement, but in 1300 the Balliol cause was far from defeated.

1300 was not a good year for the English occupation in Scotland. The Balliol party, despite their severe defeat at Falkirk in 1298, continued to make steady if unspectacular progress. Orders from Edward in relation to a truce in the autumn of 1300 give a clear impression of the extent of his administration in Scotland: only three locations north of the Forth are mentioned – Dundee, Perth and Banff. Dundee and Perth were burghs of some importance, but at this point were more in the nature of isolated strongholds than centres of administration. Broadly speaking, the Scots retained control of Scotland north of the Forth and a good deal south of the Forth, but were unable to confront the English effectively in the south-east and south-west on a regular basis. The English, on the other hand, seem to have been unable to make progress against the Scots, save for the periods in which a large army could be committed.

The warden of Scotland [the head of Edward I's occupation government] to ride by the castles to see if the truce is kept; to have with him one hundred men-at-arms and three hundred foot. All the rest of the forces in the King's pay to be disbanded, except that the castles be in sure guard. Item ['further' or 'also'], that all the men-at-arms and foot in the counties of Northumberland, Cumberland, Westmoreland, Lancaster and York obey the warden in all points.

The order of the Scots war:- Sir John de Segrave to provide Roxburgh, Edinburgh, Linlithgow, Stirling Kirkentolowe [Kirkintilloch] with men and victuals, and see that the castellans of these places attack the enemy with all force, and make no truce, under pain of forfeiture to the King. Item, Sir Robert Clifford in like manner to provide Caerlaverock, Dumfries, Dalswinton and Thybres [Tibbers]. Item, the earl of Hereford to provide Lochmaben similarly and the King will help him in part. Item, Sir John de St John for Buittle in same manner. Item, Sir Henry de Beaumont for Jedburgh in the same manner. Item, to earl Patrick for Dunbar in the same manner. Item, to Sir John de Waux for Dirleton in the same manner. Item, To Sir Aymer de Valence for Sellechirche [Selkirk] and Bothwell in same manner. As to the town[s] of St John [Perth], Dundee, Ayr, Banff, they must keep themselves by truce as best they can till Pentecost next. The Scottish people outside of castles, dwelling at the King's faith, who have not given truce to the enemy, or done other easement or relaxation to them, to hold a good front to the enemy.

CDS vol. ii no. 1163

It would seem curious that, having agreed a truce with the Scots, Edward should immediately send instructions to his commanders in Scotland that they should not take truces, but should 'attack the enemy with all force'; however, the instruction refers to the immediate situation. The truce was agreed on 30 October, but presumably it was 'in the offing' for sometime before that. As peace, or even a truce, becomes closer there is a perfectly understandable tendency for soldiers to become less eager to engage the enemy and their officers less inclined to make an issue of it. Edward would be concerned that if his garrisons relaxed in the last days before the truce became effective the Scots might be able to seize objectives that they would be able to retain and reinforce during the truce; however, if his garrisons were active right up to the cessation of hostilities they might be able to recover assets from the Scots. The remaining installations of the occupation government north of the Forth may not have been covered by the provision of the truce. Edward gave them licence – indeed, instructed them – to make individual truces with the Scots as they saw fit 'until Pentecost next', which was the duration of the truce.

King Philip of France to his lieges at the Roman Court. Commands them to request the pope's favour for his beloved Wiliam le Walais of Scotland, knight, in the matters which he wishes to forward with his holiness.

CDS vol. ii no. 1184

After the battle of Falkirk, although Wallace had lost or resigned the post of Guardian, he continued to be active in the Balliol cause both militarily and politically. In 1299 or 1300 King Philip of France instructed his representatives at the curia to encourage the Pope to look favourably on a Scottish envoy, William Wallace. Wallace had been knighted by this point, though by whom is unknown.

The King by his letters patent grants to [his] dear servant Edward de Keith, all goods and chatells of whatever kind he may gain from Monsire Guilliam le Galeys the King's enemy, to his own profit and pleasure. Provided, however, that if said Edward by chance under colour of this gift takes anything from other people at the King's peace, he shall duly answer to those from whom such is taken.

CDS vol. ii no. 1424

Wallace's activities did not go unremarked by the Plantagenet government. Some time before 1303 his property was granted to Edward de Keith, an East Lothian man. Keith is described in the document as Edward's 'cher vadlet', implying that Edward de Keith was not yet a knight, but was serving or had previously served as a man-at-arms in Edward's army. Keith was granted Wallace's goods, but Edward was clear about the extent of the licence granted. Keith was to make full reparation for any material confiscated from others: an indication that Edward was well aware that heavy-handed and indiscriminate behaviour on the part of the administration, whether it was manned by Scots or English, would be counterproductive and diminish the credibility of his government among those who might otherwise accept his rule, or even actively support it.

In the wake of the defeat of his army at Courtrai in 1302, Philip IV had been obliged to come to terms with Edward I. Philip had been holding out for the inclusion of the Scots in any settlement of his war with England, but was forced to abandon them in the search for a rapid end to hostilities. The negotiations at Strathord were based on the Scots ending hostilities in return for lenient terms for admission to Edward's peace. It would seem that from the outset Edward had no intention of accepting the surrender of William Wallace and certain other leading figures in the Balliol party within the framework of a general peace agreement, but preferred to require specific terms for the men he saw as the source or inspiration of resistance.

> The King's directions as to castles and conditions as to receiving the bishop of Glasgow, William le Waleys, Sir David de Graham, Sir Alexander de Lindseye and Sir John Comyn.
>
> *CDS vol. ii no. 1444*

Wallace was evidently still regarded as a person of some consequence by King Edward. This document could be construed as an indication that Edward was still prepared to offer terms for the surrender of William Wallace: he was evidently prepared to offer terms to his colleagues, Graham, Lindsay and Comyn. However, the document does not offer identical conditions to each of the men: the surrender of Wallace was probably only acceptable if it was to be unconditional.

> It is granted to all who surrender with Sir John Comyn by beginning of the sixteenth the present February, that they shall save life and limb, imprisonment and disinheritance only.
>
> *CDS vol. ii no. 1447*

Sir John had been able to procure reasonable terms for the Balliol party, under the circumstances. John Balliol's decision to allow the king of France complete discretion in relation to Scottish diplomatic matters had effectively removed him from any realistic prospect of restoration. If he was unwilling to be restored to the kingship, there was little point in Scots fighting against the Plantagenet occupation. Edward could have made a case that virtually all of the Balliol party activists had accepted his kingship at some point and were therefore guilty of flagrant disregard of their oath to their sovereign lord, in which case the 'guilty' parties could have been sentenced to death and disinherited. The fact that they were not has been seen by some historians as evidence of a magnanimous and statesmanlike approach on the part of Edward. There is some merit to that case: Edward was trying to achieve acceptance of his rule and that would be arranged more easily if he had the support of the Scottish political community. Two important considerations that have not been addressed by those historians were the need for Edward to reach a settlement quickly and the military condition of the Scots. Edward was prepared to commit large armies for service in Scotland, but the cost was very heavy; there were continual problems with recruitment and once an army was in the field the desertion rates were very heavy indeed. There was no lack of will on Edward's part, but the difficulties of raising and maintaining troops for the Scottish were very real. Additionally, he could bring an army to Scotland in search of the enemy, but he could not easily force them to accept battle, in which case a lot of money was being spent on wages for soldiers who had very little to do: in itself a recipe for poor relations with the local communities on which they were billeted.

The Scots might not be willing to offer a general engagement, but equally they could not be ignored. The existence of a 'rebel' army was in itself an affront to Edward's prestige and so long as the Scots maintained a force there was always the possibility that a portion of the English army might be defeated when detached from the main force. Even a relatively modest clash can have a debilitating effect on an army that cannot bring its superiority to bear on a weaker opponent. Without the prospect of a major fight, the English armies in Scotland could do little more than traverse the country. This was to some extent a positive activity, in that it demonstrated the power of the king, but could easily be counterproductive if the army caused a lot of damage.

The Scots had their own reasons for seeking an armistice in 1304. First and foremost, it was now very difficult for the Balliol party to maintain that they were fighting for the rights of their king, the conventional understanding of national political sovereignty in the Middle Ages. Without a king to restore the position of men like Comyn and Lindseye, Wallace was very insecure. The bishop of Glasgow might be saved from the scaffold by his ecclesiastical status, but any of them might well hang for treason if captured. At the close of 1303 the Balliol party was still effective militarily. Their sharpest defeat was five years in the past and they had secured a notable victory over the English just a year before. The Balliol cause was not yet defeated in February 1304, but it was unlikely to prosper, and the leaders, certainly the secular ones, must have been concerned for their futures. Better by far to negotiate with Edward while they were still a force to be reckoned with and when Edward himself had other matters to attend to.

> The King to Sir Alexander de Abernethy. [The king] is greatly pleased to hear that he keeps watch at the fords of the Forth. On no account is he to leave his post or receive William le Walays and his men to peace unless they surrender unconditionally.
>
> *CDS vol. ii no. 1463, 3 March 1304*

Clearly Wallace had not been prepared to accept the terms agreed between the Balliol and Plantagenet parties at Strathord. Understandably perhaps,

Scottish historians and romancers have been inclined to see the refusal of
Edward to give terms to Wallace as evidence of a vicious persecution of an
honest patriot. To a degree, this is probably the case – Wallace was unde-
niably a patriot. However, there is another perspective to be considered.
If the leadership of the Balliol party was the legitimate representation of
the Scottish nation's kingship and government, by continuing the struggle Wallace was, in a sense, acting against his own leadership and, strictly
speaking, against the will of the man Wallace saw as king of Scotland: John
Balliol. It would not be fanciful to suggest that there would have been an
element of fourteenth-century Scottish public opinion that saw Wallace
as a compulsive troublemaker.

  Edward may well have taken a vindictive attitude to William Wallace;
the mockery that constituted Wallace's trial hardly suggests a fair and
honourable approach to the conduct of justice. However, Edward
could not have extended terms to Wallace subsequent to the Strathord
armistice without undermining his own authority. Also, it should be
noted that the instruction refers not only to William Wallace (no longer
referred to as 'monsire' – knight) but to William Wallace and his men:
a suggestion perhaps that Wallace had become *de facto* leader of an
element in the Balliol camp that rejected the settlement. As long as
Wallace remained active with a band of armed men, the Plantagenet
government would have to seek him out as much as they would any
other party of brigands.

> The King to William de Hameltone, his chancellor. Signifies that he has
> appointed John de Segrave, Pierre Mallore, Rauf de Sanvyz, John de
> Banquelle and John le Blund his mayor of London, or any three [of them],
> his justices to deliver his gaol of the Tower of London of William de Waleys
> according to the law and custom of his realm and demands letters in their
> favour under the great seal.
>
> *CDS vol. ii no. 1685, 18 August 1305*

Medieval spellings are notoriously irregular and the name of William
Wallace is no exception. Walays, Walais and Waleys are among the more
common variants; however, the definite article constituent of his name
is remarkably constant. Occasionally it does not figure at all – a simple
William Wallace – but the most common construction is William *le*
Wallace: there is no doubt that 'le' Walays/Walais/Waleys was the more
general usage. Although there can be no certainty that any of the other
men of a similar status bearing the name Wallace were related to William

Wallace of Elderslie, it is quite probable that some proportion of them were. Adam le Wallace of Ayrshire, John le Wallace of Over Eyton, Berwickshire, John, son of Thomas le Wallace of Fife and Nicholas le Wallace of Ayrshire all appended their seals to the Ragman Roll in 1296. In 1292, during the succession dispute, one William le Waleys sought and received permission to abandon a court case against his son John, relating to possession of a tenement in Ulvesby. It is reasonable to assume that this was not the William Wallace who would eventually become the Guardian of Scotland, but it is more likely than not that they were related in some degree.

Inquisition made at Perth on Wednesday next after the decollation of Saint John the Baptist, in the King's thirty-third year, before Malise, earl of Strathearn, lieutenant of the Warden north of the Forth and Malcolm de Inverpefray, knight, deputy of John de Sandale chamberlain and William de Bevercotes, chancellor of Scotland on certain articles touching the person of Michael de Miggel, by Gilbert de Hay, David de Graham, John de Cambroun, Constantin de Lochor, Edmund de Ramsay, Roger de Mekfen, Patrick de Oggelvyle, knights, Eustace de Rothref, Henry de Feelaye, Malcolm de Kinross, Gregory de Fordale, Thomas de Lethfy, Bernared de Cokerel, William de Balendolaucht, Patrick son of Schirolis, Bethan de Doul, Kennachy his brother, Colin de Mentaghe, Henry de Trody, Adam de Cardene, John Walthop, Henry de Buchfodyr, Maurice son of Malcolm, Adam de Pethilloch, William de Montalt; who say on oath, in Michael's presence, that he had been lately taken prisoner forcibly against his will by William le Waleys; that he escaped once from William for two leagues, but was followed and brought back by some armed accomplices of William's, who was firmly resolved to kill him for his flight; that he escaped another time from said William for three leagues or more and was brought back a prisoner by force with the greatest violence and hardly avoided death at William's hands, had not some accomplices of William entreated for him; whereon he was told if he tried to get away a third time he should lose his life. Thus it appears he remained with William through fear of death and not of his own free will.

The earl, Sir Malcolm and some of the others append their seals.

[Endorsed] The chamberlain is commanded to give him his goods and chattels of the King's special grace.

CDS vol. ii no. 1689

The support of the jurors would seem to make it plain that Michael had indeed been the victim of Wallace, in the sense that he had been obliged to fight for the Balliol cause against his will. This might seem an unlikely proposition; a man might surely escape his captors in the confusion of battle or slip away unnoticed in the night. As to the first possibility, the chances of managing a defection during an action would be very slim indeed; for a brief period one might well be in danger from either side. The general practice of combat in southern Scotland throughout the Wars of Independence was one of brief clashes between quite small parties of men-at-arms. A deserter or defector would have to be very confident that their horse was more than a match for any others in the party if they hoped to make a clean getaway.

It is always possible that Michael benefited from a degree of collusion among the jurors, or that the jurors were keen to be seen as putting the past behind them. Michael was not a new recruit (or forced conscript, as the case might be) to the Balliol cause in 1305; he had been active before 1299, when he was a prisoner of war in Nottingham Castle. There he was retained for exchange under a cartel for Sir James de Lindseye, who by 1304 would be a leading figure in the Balliol party, but who in 1299 was a prisoner *of* the Balliol party. It would seem reasonable to suppose that Michael had been a voluntary adherent to the Balliol cause in 1297–99. If he had not wanted to rejoin the fight for John I's restoration he could have defected to the Plantagenet party, instead of returning to Scotland after an exchange of prisoners.

Andrew Fisher has suggested that the absence of cases similar to Michael's is an indication that his was a rare example; however, it is not clear that the appointment of a jury for this purpose was a rarity simply because there are no other known examples, nor that Michael's case was uncommon even if there were no other similar inquisitions made. The 'Miggel' situation might even have been regarded as a test case to decide whether such incidents could be dealt with by local juries drawn from the normal suitors of the sheriff court, in which case there would be no other examples since there are no Scottish sheriff court records for the period. Mr Fisher goes on to say that 'the nobles of course, had made their own peace with Edward and were collaborating with the English'. This is hardly a fair assessment of the situation. The peace of 1304 was accepted by the majority of the political community, both for themselves and for their tenants. It was not the product of popular democratic decision-making, but it would be absurd to look for that in a medieval context; it is a perfectly valid example of conventional, even legitimist, medieval political practice. Scottish kingship had been vested in John Balliol and both he and his lieutenants had accepted that the Balliol cause could no longer be sustained. Having accepted Edward's kingship, and having been accepted into his peace, the Scottish nobility and the community as a whole were naturally expected to take part in the establishment of law and order. The pursuit of William Wallace and his adherents was an inevitable consequence of his refusal to surrender unconditionally. Had the Strathord agreement extended automatically to all of the nobility, William Wallace would of course have been included in their number.

> The King ordered the body of Ralph de Halibourton to be delivered to Sir John de Moubray of Scotland, knight, to be taken to Scotland to help those seeking to capture William Waleys. Sir John and others giving security to re-enter Ralph at the parliament in London in three weeks after Easter day [18 April 1305] after seeing what he could do.
>
> *CDS vol. ii no. 1808*

The Strathord agreement gave Edward the opportunity to release prisoners of war, which was useful in two ways. It saved money on prisoner allowances and the necessary security arrangements to prevent them absconding, and it allowed Edward to bring men from the Balliol party into his service, not least for the purpose of settling affairs in Scotland. The 1304 agreement effectively made an outlaw of William Wallace and such men as chose to carry on with the fight; the Balliol party had made its peace with King Edward, so any man who entered that peace was obliged to uphold the king's government, giving Edward and his lieutenants an opportunity to assess the reliability and competence of their new adherents.

> William de Ros, brother of the late Sir Robert de Ros of Werk, shews the King that when his brother joined the Scots, he refused, and saved the castle of Werk-upon Twede [Tweed] to the King, who promised him a reward. When the Earl of Warenne and Sir Hugh de Cressingham led the King's forces to Stirling to put down William Waleys and his band of evil-doers, the petitioner, after the constable of Stirling castle and great part of his garrison had been slain at the bridge, threw himself into the castle with Sir William le fiz Waryn and Sir Marmaduke Twenge by the said Earl's order, but had to surrender it for want of victuals, whereon William Waleys spared his life from being Sir Robert's brother; but as he

would not renounce his allegiance, sent him to Dumbarton castle, where
he lay in irons and hunger till its surrender to the King after the battle
of Falkirk. He prays a grant of the 'petyt maner' of Belestre in the King's
hand by his mother's death.

CDS vol. iv no. 1835

The Wars of Independence are difficult to categorise precisely. The 'First
War of Independence' is generally perceived as coming to an end with
the victory of the Scots under Robert I at the battle of Bannockburn
– though in fact King Robert's war continued, with several truces (some
agreed with the English, some imposed in exchange for money from the
communities of northern England) until the 'Perpetual Peace' of 1328.
There had, however, been a peace agreement accepted and ratified by the
representatives of the Scottish (Balliol) and English (Plantagenet) causes
in 1304. People whose positions had been affected by the course of events
between 1304 and 1328 might have good cause to seek 'justice' from the
king of their choice if they had suffered from their allegiance or had been
denied the conditions allowed to others in comparable circumstances. As
late as June 1367, the provisions of the Strathord armistice and the name
of William Wallace were still cropping up in English Crown documents as
people sought to recover rights and property lost in the fighting.

At the opening of hostilities in 1296, Sir Robert de Ros of Wark in
Northumberland chose to join the Scots in their war with Edward, apparently because he was in love with a Scottish woman of patriotic vein. His
brother William served Edward loyally and was captured when Stirling
Castle was surrendered to the Scots after the battle of Stirling Bridge. Sir
Robert's actions may have brought the family into disrepute; William found
it necessary to remind the king of a promise of reward and of the quality of
his service generally, not to mention his sufferings as a prisoner of war in
Dumbarton Castle. The manor that William hoped to acquire would seem
to have been the property of his mother until her death, when it was taken
into the king's hands – no doubt because the principle heir was Sir Robert
who had, presumably, been forfeited for his treason and rebellion.

Exemplification of letters patent by the late King [Edward II], granted at
Clipston 6th November 1312, on her frequent petition, in favour of Margaret
daughter and heir of Robert de Roos of Wark-on-Tweed, pardoning her
as she was in her minority when her father joined the Scots in plundering
Werk in Northumberland, and afterwards joining William Waleys, and thus
entitled to the conditions granted by Edward I to John Comyn of Badenagh

and other Scotsmen in arms against him, and their heirs if then minors, and cancelling of her father's forfeiture. The exemplification granted at the request of Gerard Salveyn cousin and heir of the said Margaret.

CDS vol. iv no. 133

At the time of the original letters patent, the Scottish administration of Edward II was in a decline and had been for some time, but was still a formidable structure. There was every reason to believe that it would still triumph against the Bruce party, which, although it had enjoyed steady success for several years, was still a long way from achieving the general military ascendancy that it would enjoy between 1314 and 1332. The future of the Bruce dynasty itself was not assured. The executions of most of King Robert's brothers and the fact that his queen was still a captive in England meant that his only clear heir was his remaining brother, Edward, and there was a very real chance that either of them might be killed in action, leaving no serious candidate for Scottish kingship and no effective source of authority apart from the Plantagenet government. People whose futures should have been protected by the 1304 agreement were, naturally enough, wise to ensure that the obligations of the government were clearly understood. What exactly Gerard Salveyn hoped to procure by having the rights of his cousin confirmed is not clear, but a recognition of an obligation that the Crown could not properly discharge might lead to some form of compensation, even if only a token gesture in recognition of responsibilities undertaken in the past.

The vast number of records generated by the Wars of Independence is largely the product of English government departments and officials: very little has survived at all in the way of Scottish administrative records from the Guardianship years of 1296–1304. The earliest document to give a lucid picture of the state of affairs in Scotland in the summer of 1297 is a letter from Sir Hugh de Cressingham to Edward I. Sir Hugh had consulted with the king's officers in Northumberland and they had decided to mount an operation against the Scots. He mustered his army, amounting to 300 men-at-arms on 'covered' horses and 10,000 infantry at Roxburgh, and was on the point of marching on the enemy when he was joined by Sir Robert Clifford and Sir Henry Percy, fresh from their negotiations with the 'noble revolt' leaders at Irvine.

And we should have made an expedition on the said Thursday had it not been for the arrival of Sir Henry Percy and Sir Robert Clifford, who arrived on the Wednesday evening in the said town, and made known to those of your people that were there, that they had received into your peace all the enemies this side of the Scottish sea [the Firth of Forth]; and they were answered that even though peace had been made on this side, nevertheless it were well to make an incursion upon the enemies on the other side of the sea of Scotland, if they saw it was necessary; or that an attack should be made on William Wallace, who lay there with a large company (and still does) in the forest of Selkirk, like one who holds himself against your peace. Whereupon it was decided that no expedition should be made until the earl's arrival; and thus matters have gone to sleep, and each of us went away to his own residence.

The practice of enlisting troops in Ireland for service in Scotland was a common one during the Wars of Independence. The greater number of these were infantry deployed to the west of Scotland, but Irish hobelars and men-at-arms served in Plantagenet armies and garrisons throughout Scotland, as did contingents of foot. Naturally the army needed to be supplied with provisions: even a very prosperous area could not support the food requirements of an army of thousands for very long, even if it were plundered to an extreme degree, the sort of behaviour that would do nothing to encourage the people of Scotland to accept Edward's kingship. After all, if he could not protect them from his own troops, how could anyone expect that he would protect them against the troops of the Balliol party? Lordship was perceived as a relationship of mutual benefit – the superior in search of acceptance of their authority, the inferior in search of stability and protection.

That the justiciar and treasurer... of Ireland array 300 hobelars and ensure that sufficient aid is provided to cover the victualling and other costs of these men in coming to the King, staying in Scotland and returning. They are to send all the victuals they can to Skineboroness, to be there by 24 June, and are to require and bind merchants to bring victuals, sending the names of such merchants to the wardrobe.

Calendar of Patent Rolls 1292–1301, no. 488, December 1299

That writs be sent to the sheriffs of Somerset, Dorset, Devon, Cornwall and Gloucester and to the bailiff of Haverford and justice of Chester, ordering them to require merchants to bring victuals to Carlisle. Similar writs are to be sent to the earl of Cornwall. The King wishes that these writs instruct the addressees to purvey livestock (and other victuals), and similar commands are to be sent to those making the purveyance for Berwick.

That there be great purveyance of victuals in the counties between the mouth of the Thames and Berwick and that they be brought to the ports in these counties, to be sent to Berwick for sustenance of the army all the following winter. The officials of these parts are to induce and bind merchants to bring victuals for sale to where the King will be all the time he stays in Scotland, [returning] the names of such merchants to the wardrobe and [promising] them that they will be well paid and kept from harm.

That the justices of both benches and the barons of exchequer be at parliament on the second [Sunday] in Lent, when the bishop of Chester will tell them the arrangements for their adjournment to York.

That all the sheriffs of England and certain men of the counties warn all who have £40 of land or more to be prepared to come with horses and arms to Carlisle.

That the horsemen and footmen chosen to go to Berwick, who returned after receiving the King's wages, should be imprisoned during his will.

Calendar of Close Rolls 1296–1302, no. 382

The following extract deals with the policy of the English negotiators in relation to the position of the Scots in 1299:

Item, in the peace treaties and truces made by the cardinal bishops of Albano and Palestrina, papal ambassadors, or in any of the three treaties made between the Kings of France and England, no mention was ever made of the King or kingdom of Scotland. However, the King of France specifically named the counts of Hanonens' [Hainault] and Luteburgens' [Luxemburg], the dauphin of Vienne, and Godefrey de Brabancia as his allies in the first of these truces, and said in general that he had other allies from Flanders, Gascony and elsewhere of whose names he was at that time ignorant. Moreover, a year or more before any of these truces, the former King of Scots freely admitted his many crimes against the King of England, handed over his kingdom, swore on the gospels to be faithful and not to harm the King of England in any way, and placed himself at the King's disposal. The Scots nobles took a similar oath and many of them went with the King of England to fight in Flanders, receiving his wages like other of his liegemen, at the time that the said truce was made. Therefore the ambassadors state that the former King of Scots, his kingdom and subjects, can in no way be included in any negotiations; they explained to the pope that they had nothing to say to the French ambassadors concerning this and that, if the French were to mention it, they should not be heard.

A good first line of defence of any occupying power anxious to retain the territory that it has acquired is to deny the legitimacy of the opposition. Throughout the 1970s and 1980s, British governments refused to admit to any dealings with the paramilitary organisations on the grounds that they would furnish their enemy with a degree of credibility simply by recognising them as political entities rather than as essentially criminal organisations. In 1299 the English ambassadors were eager to ignore the Balliol party entirely, whereas the French were very keen to make the inclusion of the Scots a condition of having talks at all.

The normal practice for raising troops in thirteenth-century England was by instructions issued under the Great Seal. For reasons that are not clear, possibly as a means of avoiding political resistance from his magnates, the king had endeavoured to raise troops on the basis of writs issued under the exchequer seal – a measure that did not appeal to the barons of the treasury, who suggested a return to the earlier system. The manpower demands made in writs for army service bore little real relationship to the actual numbers that were enlisted. Like much medieval legislation it is more an expression of the desired outcome than a genuine expectation. This has not always been clear to historians, and is one of the factors that leads to the acceptance of self-evidently unrealistic estimates of the numbers involved in war. Broadly speaking, garrison muster rolls can be taken as a relatively precise record of the number of men receiving wages and also the role of those men. The number of men serving in a field army on the march was probably not very clear to the commander of the force, let alone to an official or chronicler far removed from the scene. The difficulty of raising anything like 15,000 or 20,000 men from the north of England for service in Scotland, and the even greater difficulty of preventing large-scale desertions once they had been recruited was a recurring problem for Edward and for his successors. To some extent the problem was offset by enlisting troops from Wales and Ireland. No doubt Edward's allusion to the great labours of the Welsh in previous years was also an indication that in the spring of 1300 his authority in Wales was not so secure that he could afford to draw troops to another theatre of war.

The recruitment problem was not just a matter of numbers; there are many instances of local administrators selecting their quotas from the ranks of the halt, the lame and the socially undesirable. The offer of liberty to convicted felons in exchange for military service was by no means uncommon and, from the point of view of the communities, was an understandable practice. From the king's perspective it was less than helpful, obviously: hence the stipulation for 'suitable' footmen.

> The King accordingly orders them, with the chancellor, to make and send writs under the great seal to the counties beyond Trent for the choosing of between 15,000 and 20,000 suitable footmen, who are to be at Carlisle by the third or fourth day after St John next, as he ordered them before. He does not wish them to summon footmen from Wales, who have been excused for the great labour they have done before in his service. The treasurer and the bishop of Durham recently sent Mr Richard Dabingdon to distribute the King's victuals at Carlisle to John de St John, Robert de Clifford and the others who are there at the King's wages from Easter until Trinity next; the King thanks the treasurer for this and orders him to send all the aid and counsel he can so that these men may stay until the King comes there. He approves of the arrangement made between the treasurer and John de Creppingg, John de Byroun and the sheriff of York, that they would prepare the whole country and be at Richmond within 3 days when summoned, and [also of the arrangement] as to the bishop of Durham's men. Orders the treasurer to send aid to the march whenever he hears that it is required, and to ensure that the castles of Lochmaben and Dumfries are better stored with victuals and other supplies, because John de St John has informed the King that they are poorly supplied. The King has heard that the covenant of Robert le fiz Roger expires at Pentecost and has asked him to remain until St John; he orders the treasurer to recompense Robert suitably for this stay and to ensure that the garrisons of the march are maintained in strength until the King comes to Carlisle.

Desertion was a continual threat to the integrity of medieval armies. The order that the named men should be arrested 'whether in franchise of not' is an instruction to override the normal practices of civil law. Numerous areas of both England and Scotland were, for most civil and criminal purposes, outside the jurisdiction of the court of the king's sheriff. Many, though not all, baronial tenures included a heritable legal jurisdiction, but there were several other individuals, generally senior prelates and magnates with court 'franchises'. Each baron, earl, lord, bishop or abbot with a court was responsible for maintaining law and order within the bounds of their franchise and had the benefit of pocketing the proceeds of justice. The purpose of the instruction was to prevent men arranging to have their case heard in the court of someone from whom they could rely on for or, more importantly, procure a favourable outcome.

Privy Seal writ from Edward I to John de Drokenesford, Keeper of the Wardrobe
Sends under his seal the names of foot-soldiers of Yorkshire who have departed from the King's service without leave, wickedly and treacherously deceiving him, whereby he and his host have suffered great harm and inconvenience. Orders that John and the bishop of Chester [Walter de Langton, treasurer] ordain that these men, whether in franchise or not, be taken and safely held in prison and in distraint, and not delivered up without the King's special command; also that their lands, tenements and goods in that county, whether in franchise or not, be seized and kept in the King's hand without delay, and that the King be answered to for the issues of these lands until he ordains otherwise. Because the King has heard that sheriffs and bailiffs sometimes counsel, abet and maintain things whereby he is ill served, he orders John in no wise to trust them in the execution of this, but to assign it to certain trusty men who will diligently apply their attention to perform the King's commands in all points, in such a way that the men remaining in the King's host in Scotland may take example from the punishment of these men who have served him so ill.

15 July 1300

The social structures of medieval societies make it inevitable that the bulk of the surviving data refers to the activities of the noble, administrative and commercial classes. Their prominence in civil and military life and, to some extent, the fact that war was generally carried on by men drawn from the nobility and the burgesses serving as men-at-arms has been instrumental in developing a widely-held belief that the infantry was not an important element in the wars of the chivalric age. Since such a large proportion of the mass-enlistment field armies – the kind raised to carry out or resist major invasions and to offer battle – was comprised of footmen it has to be asked: 'what were they there for?' Edward I was evidently convinced that the infantry had a function in war since he was very anxious to procure the services of another 10,000 in addition to those already in the field. The quality of the recruits was still of some concern to the king, since he specifically asked for the strongest and the fittest. Had his local administrators been conscientious in their duties, it would hardly have been necessary for him to mention the fact that fitter men are preferable for army service.

Privy Seal writ from King Edward I to Walter de Langton, Bishop of Chester, Treasurer (or his lieutenant), John de Langeton, Chancellor and John de Drokenesford, Keeper of the Wardrobe
The King's affairs in Scotland are much set back for default of good footsoldiers. They are to have chosen from the counties nearest the march of Scotland, in addition to the number already serving with the King, ten thousand foot-soldiers, the strongest and best who can be chosen, and cause these men to be brought to Carlisle without delay, by sheriffs and others who can best and soonest bring them. They are to have this matter especially at heart, and assign to it will give all their attention to this business, and who should be assigned to pay the wages of these men in coming to the King.

27 July 1300

The wage differential between the knight and the esquires is a social distinction; both were men-at-arms but the knight enjoyed greater prestige and perhaps was expected to have higher costs. There seems to be no clear rationale to explain the expression of sums of money in medieval accounts. Robert le Graunt received £4 5s but Sir Alexander Comyn was paid 104s 8d: just as usefully expressed as £5 4s 8d. An account like this would have been compiled from several different documents and therefore may represent the preferred formats of different secretaries, but it does seem curious that a fiscal administrative system as sophisticated as that of Edward I should not have developed a standard practice for all of the king's departments.

Note relating to the accounts of Nicholas Fermbaud, Keeper of Bristol Castle, for Edward I, detailing payments made by him to Scottish prisoners of war from the campaign of 1296 (some from the battle; some from the castle garrison)
£57 15s 10d, paid by him to Richard Siward junior, knight, John de la More, John de Clogham and John fil Alexander de Moreva, esquires, and to their 2 guards, for their expenses from 30 Sept. 1296 to 30 Sept. 1298,

at the daily rate of 4d for the knight, 3d for each esquire, and 3d for each
guard. Also 104s 8d paid to Alexander Comyn, knight, for his wages from
30 Sept. 1296 until 10 Aug. 1297, on which day he was released. £4 5s,
paid to Robert le Graunt, esquire, for his expenses from 30 Sept. 1296
until 5 Sept. 1297, on which day he was released. £27 7s 6d, paid to John
de la More and John de Clogham, esquires, and to one guarding them,
for their expenses from 30 Sept. 1298 until 30 Sept. 1300. £4 7s 3d paid
to John de Moreve for his expenses from 30 Sept. 1298 to 14 Sept. 1299,
when he died in the same prison. 69s 4d paid to Richard Siward junior,
knight, for his expenses for 208 days from 30 Sept. 1298 till 26 Apr. 1299,
on which day he was freed at Benstede. 27s, paid for a horse taking Richard
from Bristol to Benstede, and for 2 valets accompanying him for 11 days,
going and returning. 50s 3d paid to a guard for [Richard] from 30 Sept.
1298 until 19 Apr. 1299, when he was relieved of this duty because of the
freeing of the prisoner.

Autumn 1300

The expense of maintaining an extensive network of garrisons across
Scotland was enormous. This document relates to the expenditure on wages
for the troops committed to the security of one sheriffdom, Roxburgh.
The operational premise of the garrison is revealed by its composition. The
chief function of the archers and the crossbowmen would have been maintaining the security of the establishments from which the men-at-arms
could operate. It is important to bear in mind that the garrison strength
was not simply that of the wages roll. Men of the local community of
Roxburgh – landholders, the burgesses of the town – would have had to
discharge their customary military service obligations (the duties they had
owed to John I and his predecessors) to the government of the day if they
wanted to retain their properties and their position in the community. In
Roxburgh in 1300 the government of the day was that of the occupation.
In addition to the men serving for wages and those serving for established
land tenure, there may have been men serving for land granted by Edward
I to men who had served in the invasion of 1296. Any such grants made
from the property of forfeited men would carry the existing burden of
responsibility; the amount of service at the disposal of the sheriff would
have been unchanged since King John's reign. However, grants made
from properties belonging to the Scottish Crown may have increased the

availability of men-at-arms without affecting the pay accounts, since these men would not be eligible for wages nor for the other important record of army service *restauro* (a scheme whereby men serving for wages were entitled to have one of their horses valued by Crown officers so that the owner could be recompensed should the animal be lost on active service). The last entry in this account is for £13 6s 8d paid for the 'restoration of a horse' for an esquire in Sir Robert's retinue. The apparent precision of the sum is misleading: it is in fact a 'round sum' expressed in a different format of account. The same sum could be expressed as twenty merks, much more suggestive of a 'broad brush' approach to valuation than of a precise assessment of the value of the beast The sums were not intended to reflect the immediate market value of the horse or its current condition, but to indicate the general value of a beast of that quality in reasonable condition in most marketplaces – very similar to the concept of a 'book value' in the motor trade. No mention is made here of the income of the sheriffdom: that would appear elsewhere in the 'compotus' (the financial report of the sheriff to the Crown; a précis of the income and expenditure of the king's officers in the county).

Account of Sir Robert Hastang, Sheriff of Roxburgh

Receipts – He received £686 13s 11d from Mr John de Weston, clerk, at divers times in this period, as much in money as in victuals. [He received three payments, each of £40: from the sheriff of York at the exchequer in May; from Robert de Woodhouse, clerk, in October; and from Sir Ralph de Manton in part payment for a horse. He also received £1 10s from Ralph at Holmcoltram on 2 October.] He received £13 6s 8d from the sale of goods remaining after the last accounting and £74 17s 2d from further such sales. Sum total of receipts, £896 7s 9d. [Expenses] Of this, his own wages from 14 Jan to 5 July 1300 were £34 16s, being 174 days at 4s daily. Wages for 1 knight for the same time at 2s daily, £17 8s. For 62 esquires for the same time, each at is daily, £539 8s. For 40 crossbowmen for the same time, each at 4d daily, £116. For 160 archers for the same time, each at 2d daily, £232. Total, £938 12s. [Hastang's wages for 128 days from 6 July to 10 November 1300 were £25 12s; those of one knight and twenty-three esquires for the same time were £12 16s and £147 4s respectively. The wages of thirty crossbowmen for 137 days, until 19 December, were £68 10s and those of 100 archers for the same time were £114 3s 4d; all rates of pay as above. Total for this period: £368 5s 4d.] Sum total of his expenses, £1307 17s 4d. Subtracting the receipts and £2 for the wages of certain esquires who left his contingent, the balance owed him on this account is £408 18s 6d.

He is also owed £13 6s 8d for restoration of a horse of one of his esquires, making £422 5s 2d in all.

14 January–10 November 1300

The treasurer and the keeper of the wardrobe were the chief financial officers of Edward I's government but, after the manner of medieval admin- istrators, rather more than office work was expected of them. Hugh de Cressingham had been killed at the battle of Stirling Bridge, serving his king as a knight and commander rather than as a bureaucrat. His may have been an extreme example, but all of Edward I's subordinates were expected to take on whatever tasks he allotted to them and to be involved in all the aspects of the king's business. The associate of Wallace referred to below is Sir William de Vipont (Vieuxpont). Sir William was a Lothian landholder who was captured in the campaign of 1296. He was kept at Winchester Castle in Hampshire where he received an allowance of 3d per day (see *CDS* vol. ii, 1283, 1294). He presumably entered the peace of Edward I through the terms of the Strathord agreement of February 1304, but was certainly in the Plantagenet camp in the summer of 1307 when he was serving as a man-at-arms at Ayr. His Plantagenet service was relatively brief; he had defected to the Bruce camp at some point before October 1309, when he was granted (or possibly had confirmed) baronial status for his property at Bolton in the constabulary of Haddington (East Lothian) by Robert I. Since Lothian was still very firmly in the control of Edward II's government in 1309, the grant of Bolton was rather dependent on the eventual success of the Bruce party. William may have fallen foul of the Plantagenet administration in some manner that drove him into the Bruce camp as his best prospect for advancement but, assuming that the man was not an idiot, he presumably chose the options in life that he felt offered the most to him and to his dependants. In short, at some point he made the political decision to oppose the occupation and join the Bruce party. At the time of the grant, 20 October 1309, the Bruce cause was prosper- ing, but had yet to make serious progress in the south-east of Scotland. If William Vipont was not in trouble with the occupation, he must have been very confident that the Bruce cause would eventually triumph. He was not dependent on Bruce leadership and patronage; he had continued to serve John I long after Robert Bruce had defected to the English, and it would seem that he had opposed Robert I's kingship for at least the first year of the Bruce campaign for the throne. It would seem reasonable to assume that, at some point between summer 1307 and autumn 1309, William came to a reasoned conclusion that the Bruce party would win and that becoming an adherent of the Bruces would be better done sooner rather than later. The reluctance of Edward I and Edward II to permanently alienate members of the political community by forfeiting their properties is demonstrated by the fact that although William was very definitely in the Bruce party after 1309, his property was not declared forfeit until the spring of 1312, when his lands were granted to Sir Alexander Moubray, a Scottish knight who had served Edward I and Edward II with rather more consistency.

Privy Seal writ from Edward I to Walter Langton, Bishop of Chester, Treasurer, and to John de Drokenesford, Keeper of the Wardrobe
He has heard that a knight of Scotland who was of the company of William Wallace [visited? was apprehended at?] Bleyues [Blaye, Department Gironde], behaving suspiciously, spying out the strength of the place, for which he was arrested. The addressees are to instruct the constable of Blaye, Guillaume Reymon de Gensalz, to have the knight put aboard the first ship for England and sent to Porchester castle under safe guard, to be handed over to the constable there until the King sends orders. A letter to the constable of Porchester under the great seal is to be carried by the knight's escort; meanwhile the King will warn the constable to expect the prisoner, whom he is to guard until the King's further orders are known.

CDS vol. iv no. 236, 30 December 1301

As well as the perennial problems of finding recruits and the stores and money required for their upkeep, Edward was plagued by the problems of delivering supplies to the point of consumption from the point of collection. The practice of demanding ship for the king's service was a long-established one and was never limited to the Cinque Ports. There was no standing fleet of warships; other than perhaps one or two vessels that reflected his royal state, the king depended on the conscription of both ships and sailors for his naval operations. The modern practice of STUFT (Ships Taken Up From Trade) vessels lent to the navy is not dissimilar in a sense, but such shipping is not enlisted for battle, only to serve the logistical requirement of the operation. The ships may be armed, but they are not deployed to fight. In the medieval world a warship was any vessel that could be filled with armed men, and perhaps fitted with two fighting towers fore and aft to provide a platform for archers. The total of fifty-six ships sounds impressive, but merchant vessels were not very large, generally between 100 and 300 tuns' burden. When Edward Balliol (the son of John I) and Henry Beaumont made their landing at Kinghorn, Fife in August 1332 and opened the second War of Independence, their army of about 2,000 men was carried in a fleet of eighty-eight ships. The Balliol/Beaumont army apparently included about 500 men-at-arms and therefore a minimum of 500 horses, and very possibly as much as double that number had to be accommodated.

> The barons of the Cinque Ports notify the King that the towns of these ports with their members can aid in his Scottish war with 12 good, large ships. [There follows a list of thirty other ports, including two in Wales and six in Ireland, with the number of ships they are to supply.] The total of these ships is 56, which the King can have for Scotland at his request without great grievance, as they understand. All should be at Dublin on the quindene of Pentecost [4 June] to go in the King's service at his wages.
>
> *6 February 1301*

Compensation for chargers lost on royal service was limited to men serving for wages (see above), which may have included most, but probably not all, of the men-at-arms (referred to here just as 'horsemen') and knights available to Prince Edward. A *socius* was a man serving in the company of another. What precisely was the difference between a *socius* and any other member of the retinue is not clear, though it may have been acceptable for men serving without pay, but in the retinue of a favoured leader, to have their horses 'insured' at the king's expense as an incentive to provide service.

> [*Extract*]: *Roll of horses valued in A.R. 29 Edward I, which were in the company of Edward, Prince of Wales in the Scottish War. 3 manuscripts. only the main retinues are given here*
> 6 July – Sir Guy Ferre junior, with 1 knight and 6 horsemen. 8 July – Sir Robert de Scales with 1 companion (socius), 2 knights and 11 horsemen. 9 July – Sir Robert de Tony with 3 knights and 11 horsemen. 10 July – Sir Hamo de Mascy with 1 knight and 10 horsemen. 13 July – Sir John de Engaine with 7 horsemen. 18 July – Sir William de Grandison with 2 knights and 8 horsemen. 19 July – Gilbert de Clare with 1 companion and 11 horsemen; Sir Robert de

Monthalt with 3 knights and 13 horsemen. 20 July – Sir Thomas de la Roche with 1 knight and 8 horsemen; Sir Roger de Mortimer with 3 knights and 13 horsemen. 22 July – Sir Reginald de Grey, John de Grey his banneret, 3 knights and 23 horsemen; Sir Ralph de Gorges, 1 knight and 6 horsemen, being part of the retinue of John de St John; Sir William de Leyburne with 3 knights and 12 horsemen; Sir Edmund de Hastings with 1 knight and 5 horsemen. 30 July – Sir Maurice de Berkeley with 2 knights and 9 horsemen.

July 1301

Sir Alexander Balliol was a consistent supporter of the Plantagenet cause for the better part of twenty years but was able to enter the peace of Robert I after the battle of Bannockburn in June 1314. Intelligence was just as important in the wars of the fourteenth century as in any other; here Sir Alexander acknowledges the receipt of intelligence from the king, and adds his own contribution to the intelligence picture. His agents have been able to inform him that the Scots intend to hold an 'inspection' of their forces at an appointed place on the march. It would seem a curious action – gathering one's forces in the vicinity of the enemy in order to have an examination of equipment – but the significance of the event is perhaps more of a political nature. The Scots and English governments were competing for civil, judicial and military authority within communities as well as the physical possession of the landscape. Weapon showings – 'wappinschaws' – would have been (at least in theory) regular events in Scotland before the war; their administration was one of the responsibilities of sheriffs, earls and other great lords. Both parties laid claim to the allegiance of communities and appointed sheriffs, constables, bailies and other officials to impose government in the name of King John or King Edward. By holding a weapons day, the Scots were putting pressure on the local political community, demanding that they declare their allegiance publicly by effectively recognising the right of the Balliol government to collect the army service of the sheriffdom and thereby rejecting the authority of the occupation government.

Letter from Alexander de Bailiol of Cavers to Edward I
He has heard from the King's letters that Sir John de Soulis has gone towards Galloway with a great company of Scots. The writer had and still has his spies among them, and will inform the keepers of the march as soon as he hears

the Scots are coming. The King has told him that if he provided spies they should remain under his control, and he will do his best for the King. The King must not take it amiss that the writer has not given him news more quickly, for he would hate to send the King anything other than certain news. As to what the King has told him concerning Sir Walter de Borudoun, who is staying at Chastel Terres [Carstairs], the writer will be ready whenever Sir Walter commands him. The writer and his fellow keepers of the march are threatened by a possible Scottish raid to destroy the writer's lands and to seize and defend the forest, so that they have arranged to gather next Sunday [24 September] at a place on the march to inspect their forces. Asks for the King's orders, as to one who is ready to obey.

September 1301

Once again Edward was bedevilled by a shortage of hard cash. Desertion, as we have already seen, was a huge issue for medieval armies generally, but was naturally more of a problem if the troops could not be paid. The logistical effort applied by the officials of Edward I to the problems of maintaining armies and garrisons in Scotland was immense, but it was not designed to carry the entire supply requirement; regular pay was vital because the men were expected to purchase their food rather than have rations issued, hence the regular request of English kings for merchants to bring their wares to the army.

Privy Seal writ from Edward I to the treasurer or his lieutenant and the barons and chamberlains of the Exchequer
He is greatly surprised that they have sent him so little money; each time some has come, the amount has been far too small. For this reason he has been unable to pay his troops; most of them have now left, and he cannot stop daily desertions from those still with him. The addressees are strongly charged to send all the money they can, as soon as possible. If shortage of money does not prevent him, the King hopes to end the campaign satisfactorily; thus they should ensure that their inefficiency does not force him to withdraw. In fact, the King thinks that he should now be sufficiently supplied from the revenues of last Michaelmas, the fifteenth, the tenth granted by the pope, and from other sources. Because his son is joining him, money for the prince and his company is to be sent direct to the King, and not to Carlisle; however, the garrisons of Dumfries and Lochmaben are to be supplied according to previous arrangements. They are ordered to send victuals to the King. So that they may be

better advised of the exact amount of money needed, he sends a roll under his seal, giving estimates of his weekly requirements, without including his son's company, of which he does not yet know the number. They are charged on their faith, as they love the King's honour and profit and do not desire his perpetual dishonour, to do their best to ensure that his Scottish business goes well.

11 October 1301

Edward blamed his lack of money for his failure to pursue operations against the Scots: in particular for preventing the completion of a bridge across the Firth of Forth, a major piece of military engineering. Why exactly money should have been so effective a barrier to completing a bridge is open to question and may be an attempt to motivate his financial departments to greater efforts. His exploits against the Scots had not been especially impressive in 1301, and though it may be true that only the absence of a bridge prevented King Edward from striking a mighty blow – in fact several mighty blows – against the Scots, it is not immediately apparent why that should be the case. True, the Scots held Stirling Castle, but if Edward's force was fit for an offensive into Fife, it would surely have been powerful enough to provide a force to isolate the castle at Stirling while the balance of the army crossed by the bridge and the fords in the area.

Privy Seal writ from Edward I to the treasurer or his lieutenant and the barons and chamberlains of Exchequer
The King complains that he is still seriously short of money, so that none of his promises to pay his troops have been kept and many men have deserted. This situation grows worse daily. But for lack of money, he would have completed the bridge across the Firth of Forth; he is sure that if he had crossed 'this season' he would have done such exploit against his enemies that his business would have quickly reached a satisfactory and honourable conclusion. The addressees are ordered, as they wish to protect the King's person from harm and his campaign from failure, to send as much money as possible, since the King intends to spend the winter in Scotland. Money sent into Scotland is to be sent to the King only, with the following exceptions: to Galloway for the garrisons of Dumfries and Lochmaben and to others guarding that march, and to Earl Patrick, who is at Noef Chastel sur Are [Ayr]. When the queen and the prince of Wales join the King, money is to be sent straight to the King, except as above. Alexander le Convers, clerk, the bearer of this letter, will give further information about the state of the army and the campaign.

16 October 1301

Edward was nothing if not assiduous; his officials may not have been able to find the money he needed, but not for the sake of Edward neglecting to ask for it. His losses through desertion do seem to have been particularly heavy, but service in Scotland was not especially popular in the summer, so the approach of winter was no doubt a factor that accelerated the diminution of the army through absenteeism as well as through illness.

> Writ from King Edward to the treasurer or his lieutenant and the barons and chamberlains of exchequer, complaining of the continuing shortage of money; so many of his troops, both horse and foot, have deserted that he has not enough left to complete his campaign, and is in danger of losing what he had previously won. He is now going to Linliscu to spend the winter, hoping not to lose any more ground. The addressees are to send him as much money as possible in the future, otherwise, by their default, he will be dishonoured for all time. He will not accept the excuse that it is dangerous to transport large quantities of [cash?]. Also, provisions are very scarce, and must be sent to him. Further information will be given by the bearer of this letter, Walter de Bedwynde, who is to take a reply back telling what steps are being taken to raise the money.
>
> *22 October 1301*

Moneys paid for military service were not recorded in a terribly consistent manner. The way in which an account was compiled and recorded probably has more to do with the practices of whichever department had been given the responsibility for paying the bill than the nature or application of the goods or services. The heavy cost of maintaining garrisons is shown by the arrangements for the transport of £2,000 from Berwick to Roxburgh. In an age when the real unit of currency was the silver penny, £2,000 is perhaps better thought of as 480,000 pennies. These would have to be counted and the total audited by men accustomed to handling money in large physical quantities: in this instance a little over three-quarters of a ton of coins – a wagon load, in fact. Economic historians have suggested that by the standards of the close of the twentieth century the penny took the place of the £20 note, though that interpretation may be based on a limited understanding of the actual current cost of unskilled and semi-skilled day labour, as opposed to what one might imagine that cost to be. It might be more appropriate to think of the penny as the equivalent of the modern £50 note – not strictly in terms of purchasing power, since there is no relationship at all between medieval and modern produce prices, but as a reflection of the order of purchasing power that people expect to receive in return for their time and effort. The account includes a rare reference to medical services, a payment of 40s (£2) to a Mr Causcy for his efforts on behalf of men from the garrison of Stirling (though the castle had fallen to the Scots in 1299, some two years previously) and on behalf of men wounded recently in a fight near Beverly.

To Robert de Barton, clerk of the chancery, assigned with Hugh Gobyon and William de Felton to choose footmen in Northumberland and take them to the King's army at Berwick, for his wages from 29 May-19 July at 18d daily, by his own hands [at Berwick], 78s. To Robert de Farnham, the King's naperer, for a horse bought to carry the King's napery in the war, by his own hands at Kelso, 13s 4d. To William de Felton, for 5 lances bought by him to carry 5 of the King's banners in the war, at Kelso, 10s. To Mr John de Arderne, for the carriage and escort of money from Berwick to Roxburgh at the end of July, by his own hands at Roxburgh, 3s. To John de Okham, clerk, for the carriage of 2000 marks from Berwick to Edinburgh for 3 days, and from there to the King at Peebles for one day, both for the hackneys carrying the money and their guards, by his own hands at Glasgow, 12s 2d. [On 8 September at Bothwell, Reginald Ingeniator was paid 2s for a sling bought for the engine of Jedburgh, for which ropes costing 8s were also bought on 12 September.] To Nicholas, cokinus, for a horse bought by him and delivered to the wardrobe for carrying a tent, by his own hands at Glasgow, 20s. To William Trenchefoill, for 2 great ropes bought for the engine of Edinburgh, by his own hands at Edinburgh, 16s 2d. To William de Gretham, monk of Durham, following the King in the war with St Cuthbert's banner, for expenses from 29 June when he left Durham to 8 Oct., by an account with him at Dunipace on 9 Oct., 102s. Sum of the page, £25 10s 7d. To Mr Roger Causcy, surgeon, for his labours in healing [?] footmen of the garrison of Stirling following the King and recently wounded near Beverley, by his own hands at Dunipace, 40s. To Benedict de Cantebrig', for 3 large and 2 small ropes bought from him for 2 of the King's engines, by his own hands at Berwick, 5 marks. Sum of the page, £9 11s 5½d.

May-October 1301

The wages alone of the garrisons amounted to a serious drain on Edward's already-stretched treasury, but were only a portion of the total cost involved. It may have been normal practice for men to buy their own provisions from their wages, but if the local economy could not or would not provide the merchandise, the garrison men would not be able to buy it. Vast quantities of grain, meat and wine were purchased or seized for delivery to garrisons in Scotland. Payment for materials could be deferred by the Crown, often very successfully, but was difficult to evade entirely; further, the more the Crown postponed or defaulted on debts, the worse for the credibility of the king, resulting in merchants becoming more effective at hiding their activities from his officers.

Roll of garrison wages

To William le Latimer junior, for his own wages at 4s daily, and those of 1 knight at 2s daily and 6 esquires, each at is daily, from 20 July, when the horses were valued, until 22 Sept., by an account made with him at Bothwell on that date, £39. (Marginal) He received victuals in part payment from Richard de Bremesgrave at Berwick, to the value of £3 2s. To Hugh Bardolf, for wages of himself, 4 knights and 14 esquires, from 17 July, when the horses were valued, until 11 Oct., when he left the King's army with 3 knights and 11 esquires, £111 16s. To the same for wages of John Carbonel, knight, and 3 esquires, staying in the army after the others left, from 11-31 October, by an account made with Carbonel at Linlithgow on 31 October., £5 5s. To Robert de Scales for himself, 1 knight and 6 esquires, from 11 July, when the horses were valued, until 13 July, £1 16s. To the same for himself, 1 knight and 7 esquires, from 13 July, when the additional horse was valued, until 26 July, £8 9s. To the same for himself, 1 knight and 8 esquires, from 27 July, when the additional horse was valued, until 8 Aug., £9 2s. To the same for himself, 2 knights and 10 esquires, from 9 Aug., when the additional horses were valued, until 29 Aug., when 1 esquire left the King's service, £18. To the same for himself, 2 knights and 9 esquires, from 28 August to 22 Sept., when 2 esquires left the King's army at Bothwell, £20 8s. To the same, for himself, 2 knights and 7 esquires, from 22 September to 3 Oct., when a knight and an esquire left the army, £8 5s. To the same, for himself, 1 knight and 6 esquires, from 3-31 Oct., by an account made with him on 2 Nov., £17 8s.

1301

Berwick had been the wealthiest of the Scottish burghs before 1296, and its possession continued to be something of a bone of contention between the English and the Scots until the Union of the Crowns in 1603, though the Scots had last held the town – and only briefly – over 100 years previously. The function of the Berwick garrison extended beyond the maintenance of law and order and excluding the Scots from the county to providing a strong mobile force that could respond to threats and incursions throughout south-east Scotland. The cost of the wages alone was greatly in excess of the income that could normally be derived from the sheriffdom of Berwick, though given its reserve function the cost of the garrison of Berwick would be offset by a reduced man-at-arms elements in a number of other establishments: the same principle held true for most, almost certainly all, Scottish sheriffdoms throughout both of the Plantagenet occupations.

An accounting of wages for the garrison at Berwick

For the Berwick garrison from 20 November to 21 May, £385 16s 6d. For the Roxburgh garrison, £189 2s. For Robert de Hastang, constable of Roxburgh castle, 40 marks. For the Jedburgh garrison, £67 2s. For Richard de Hastang, constable of Jedburgh, 40 marks. [All for the same period.] For the Edinburgh garrison from 27 Nov to 21 May, £127 4s 8d. To William le Latimer, 200 marks. For 56 men at arms at Berwick, from 21 May to 17 July, £173 17s. For crossbowmen at Berwick, £97 7s 6d, for archers there, £202 5s 8d, and for Mr Reginald, machinator there, £1 8s 6d. [All for the same period.] [Total wages for the various elements at Berwick from 18 July to 19 November were £565 2s 1d, and for the constable and garrison at Berwick in the same period were £58 17s 1d.] For Robert de Hastang and his troop at Roxburgh, from 24 July to 19 Nov., £208 5s. For archers, crossbowmen and workmen [etc.] there, £79 18 10d. For Richard de Hastang and his troop at Jedburgh, £65 9s. For archers, crossbowmen and workmen there, £43 12s 8d. [All for the same period.] For Hugh de Audleigh, staying in Selkirk forest in the King's service, from 25 August to 30 Oct., £31 5s; for Thomas de Grey serving with him, £3. For Robert de Farnham, from 12 October to 19 Nov., 19s 6d. Expenses of various couriers, £4 4s. To William le Latimer for the keeping of the town and castle of Berwick from 12 June, £22. [Payments were made to workmen for repairs to an unnamed castle: total £19 13s 4d. Weston's own wages from 20 November 1300 to 19 November 1301 were £21 2s 6d. A total of £46 was paid for restoration of lost horses.] Receipts – [A total of £892 7s 5d was received at various times from the exchequer. £46 was received from William le Latimer on 25 May, and another £50 on 4 June. A total of £647 8s 10d was received from the wardrobe at various times from 18 July to 20 October, including £158 received on 20 July to pay the wages of the Berwick garrison from 21 May to 17 August.] Further receipts – From the sheriff of Northumberland on 4 Oct., for payment of the Berwick garrison, £58. From Richard de Hastang, constable of Jedburgh, on 18 Oct., £26 19s. From Robert de Hastang, sheriff of Roxburgh, on 19 Oct., from sale of victuals, £45 10s 9d. From Richard de Bremesgrave, regarding

victuals in Berwick, Roxburgh, Jedburgh and Edinburgh, for the arrears of
a.r. 28 until 25 Nov. 1300, and from then until 2 Mar. 1302 [sic], £710 5s 6d.
[Six payments were received from the wardrobe between 8 February and 19
July, totalling £13 10s 11d. A number of small payments were also made by
the wardrobe as arrears of February 1300, for payment of various arrears of
wages, totalling £26 17s 9d.] Sum total of receipts, £2467 0s 2d. [List of 18
horses valued at Melrose on 13 Oct. 1301, including those of Sir Thomas de
Grey and Sir Hugh de Audleigh. List of 14 dead horses; a total of £136 6s 8d
was paid for restoration. Prests – [Four prests to Patrick, Earl of Dunbar, for
provisions; one undated, others on 18 June and 8 October 1299 and on 16
January 1300, totalling £7 4s 8d.] To Robert de Tony, for expenses in going
from Carlisle to the King at Linlithgow, on 30 Oct. 1301, £2. [Various small
payments to messengers, etc., but incorporating a payment of £43 14s 3d to
Richard de Winton. Total: £58 7s 3d.] Total payments in a.r. 29, £2804 5s
7d. Balance owed to Weston on this account, £337 5s 5d.

1300–01

Although Linlithgow had been an administrative centre under Scottish
kings there was, so far as is known, no fortified establishment. Edward I
selected it as a suitable location for a 'peel', a camp fortified with a ditch
and palisade rather than a stone castle with a myriad of social functions. The
peel was a considerable burden to Edward and his administrators. Initially
he planned to build a great stone castle of the same stature as those he
had built in Wales, and for the same reasons: to provide a secure military
centre and a strong visible presence in the community to overawe the
opposition. He may even have planned to make it the headquarters of his
Scottish domain, a good choice given its relatively central location. King
Edward even employed the same man to supervise the construction, but
could not find the necessary funds. Even the relatively cheap expedient of
a ditch posed a problem. King Edward's officers could enlist labour from
the community, but could not retain it if the wages were not forthcoming.
The term 'covered' means horses with armour, chain mail, leather, cloth or
a mixture of the three. Historians have suggested that only the wealthiest
knights, bannerets and magnates would have acquired such equipment;
however, it is perfectly clear from record material and the painstaking work
of Dr Aytoun (*Knights and Warhorses*, Boydell) that in order to draw the full
man-at-arms wage of one shilling a day (or a knight's wage of two shillings

a day) the soldier had to show that he had the full range of arms, armour and horses necessary for the work, including barding for their horses.

There was a second peel not far from Linlithgow, at Livingstone, where there is still an area called Peel. Although it has generally been assumed that the Livingstone peel was a Plantagenet installation, there does not seem to be any evidence of orders for its construction, but equally there are no references to a peel there in earlier Scottish documents. Sir Archibald de Livingstone served Edward I faithfully, providing a retinue of ten men-at-arms and twenty archers (see *CDS* vol. ii, various). His name obviously links Sir Archibald with the barony of Livingstone in a more direct fashion than might be expected to happen to a man who was merely the appointed constable or keeper of a peel. One possibility is that Sir Archibald had 'upgraded' the security of an existing hall-house compound of his own and made it available to the administration, presumably in the hopes of advancing his career prospects by making a very positive gesture of commitment to the new administration. Sir Archibald certainly had the peel in his keeping throughout most, if not all, of the period from its first appearance in record until the fall of Lothian to the Bruces in 1314. A satellite establishment like Livingstone was not likely to survive for long without its principal in war time, and there seems to be no record of the Livingstone peel after the battle of Bannockburn; it may therefore have been one of the castles or 'strengths' slighted or reduced by Robert I when he gained control of Lothian. It was not garrisoned by the administration that Edward III endeavoured to impose in Lothian after Halidon Hill in 1333 and which was finally ejected in 1341.

Retinues in the Linlithgow garrison

In the castle of Linlithgow. Sir William de Felton has 15 covered horse, of which 1 is for [his] service. Sir Archebald de Levyngeston, 10. Sir Adam de Swynebourne, 4, of which 1 is for [his] service. Sir Edmund Foliot, 3. Sir John de Fulbourne, 3. Sir Laurence de la Ryvere, 3. Sir John de Luda, 3. [Sir Nicholas de Scotevill, 3, Sir Robert de Cantilupo, 2, and 3 from the knights of William de Rythre: all noted as having not yet come.] Each knight takes 2s and each valet 12d daily, excepting Levyngeston's men, for whom he takes a lump sum at a fixed rate. [Names of 5 more men with 1 each, at 8d daily, and of 16 sergeants at arms, including Peter de Lybaud, each at 12d daily.] For service for lands held in Scotland – From the earl of Warwick, 3 men at arms. [Marginal – they have not come.] John la Ware, 1; Thomas de Umframvill, 1 (not come); Henry Touk, Robinet le Taillor and John Heiward, 1. Total, 6, who will stay at their own costs. Total of men at arms, 85; lacking 12. Also 100 footmen who are workmen completing the castle. In the garrison of Edinburgh. Sir John de Kingestone, 1 knight and 9 other men at arms, for whom he takes a fixed sum. [12 named soldarii at 10d each daily, 2 named sergeants at arms at 12d.] Service for lands in Scotland – Robert fitz Walter, 2; Kyngestone, 3; Sir Robert de Tony, 2; Sir Peter de Malo Lacu, 3; Sir William de Cantilupo, 2 (not come); Sir Robert de Scales, Sir Walter de Mouncy and Sir John de Merk, 1 each. Total 17 [sic], at their own costs, also 2 from Sir Adam de Welle, who stay in the castle of Yestre and will ride in Kyngeston's company at his command. Total of 41 men at arms [sic]; lacking 2. Footmen – An attillator, a carpenter, a smith and garcon, a watchman, 20 balisters and 20 footmen taking daily wages as before at the time of truce. Castle of Terres [Carstairs]. Sir Walter de Burghdon, 10 men at arms. [20 named soldarii, including Peter de Lybertone, and 40 footmen, all at rates of pay as in vol. ii no. 1321(6).] For lands in Scotland – Sir Walter de Teye, 3; Sir John fil' Marmeduc, 2 (not come); Sir Fulc fil' Warin, 2 (not come); John Spring, Robert le Conestable and John de Geytone, 1 each. Total of men at arms, 40. Kirkintilloch. Sir William Fraunceys, 3 covered horse; Sir John de Gymmynges, 2; Sir Henry de Pynkeny, 3. [19 men-at-arms, including Thomas de Rameseye and Gilbert de Meneteth. Total: 27. 2 smiths, a watchman, an attillator, 19 balisters and 19 archers, all named.] 20 archers chosen by Sir William Fraunceys at Linlithgow, whose names he has. Total of footmen and officers, 64. Town of Berwick. Sir Edmund de Hasting', 6, for whom he takes a fixed sum. Sir John de Newengham, 2; Mr John de Weston, 4; Seitann Mar, socius, Robert de Evencle and Richard Walraunt, 1 each; John de Pencatlan, 1. Sir John Burdoun has 5 men at arms for keeping the sheriffdom. Berwick castle, 4 men of John de Segrave, at full wages. Total 25, of whom 20 suffice for the garrisons, and 5 to ride with Segrave. [8 balisters and 8 footmen in the castle, 40 balisters and 140 footmen in the town, balisters at 3d and archers at 2d daily.] Total of 53 men at arms assigned to stay and ride with Segrave. Roxburgh castle. Sir Robert de Hastang, 10, for whom he takes a fixed sum. Latimer – [Details of men in his company, as in vol. ii no. 1321(11). Total: 38. Footmen, as Edinburgh.] Jedburgh castle. Sir Richard de Hastang, 5 men at arms, for whom he takes a fixed sum, and 1 for his lands in Scotland. [Footmen as Edinburgh, but with only 10 balisters and 10 footmen.] Castle and forest of Selkirk. Sir Alexander de Balliolo, 30 men at arms. [Footmen as Jedburgh.] Dumfries and Lochmaben. Sir John de St John has 20 men at arms in these garrisons, at 12d daily. [Footmen: each garrison as Edinburgh but with 20 balisters and 30 footmen.] Men at arms assigned to stay at Lochmaben and ride in St John's company.

From his own retinue, 52; from that of Sir Robert de Clifford, 10 (not yet come); a sergeant, [named], 1; all at the King's wages. For lands in Scotland – St John, 10; Henry de Lacy, earl of Lincoln, 10; [Robert de Clifford, 3, Henry de Percy, 3, John de Botetourte, 4, William de Ferariis, 3, Alan la Zouche, 3: all not yet come]. Total of men at arms assigned to St John, 98; lacking 25. Bothwell castle. From Sir Aymer de Valence, for lands in Scotland, 12. From Sir fil' Pagan [sic], for the same, 2; from Sir Walter de Bello Campo for the same, 2. [Castles and sheriffdoms of Peebles and Ayr, as vol. ii no. 1324(6, 11).] Total of men at arms assigned to stay in these Scottish garrisons, 507; lacking 50.

Winter 1302

Unusually, this account has references to men serving for land in Scotland. Sir Robert Clifford, Sir John de St John and the Earl of Lincoln had all been granted extensive lands in Scotland from the forfeited supporters of John I. Naturally they owed military service for these lands and had no doubt granted portions of them to other men to provide that service; however, finding men who would make their lordship a reality in these properties was undoubtedly something of a challenge, even in areas, if there were any, that were beyond the range of the Scots. As the war dragged on it must have become increasingly difficult to persuade the recipients of grants in Scotland that the effort was worthwhile. The syntax in this document may be slightly misleading, but at least forty-seven men-at-arms, most of them due service for land, had 'not come' to discharge their obligations. There were probably rather more Scots serving in these garrisons than the document would suggest. Later evidence shows that the ten men-at-arms in the retinue of Sir Archibald Livingstone were mostly, if not entirely, Scots. Some Scottish names are obvious – Gilbert de Menteith and Thomas de Ramsay, for example – but the high incidence of surnames of French or English derivation makes the identification of nationality by name impossible in many instances.

A letter from the bishop of Lichfield and Coventry relating the defeat of the Scots under William Wallace at Falkirk

On Saturday the Feast of St Peter in chains there came a messenger from Sir Walter de Langestone, bishop of Coventry and Lychfield and treasures to our lord the King of England, bringing a letter from the said bishop to the mayor, aldermen and barons of London in these words;

To his dear friends, the mayor and the barons of London, Walter, by the grace of God, bishop of Chester, greeting and true friendship. Because we well know that you willingly will hear good tidings of our lord the King and of his affairs in Scotland, we give you to understand that on the Monday next before the feast of St James, there came tidings unto the lord the King where he was staying, six leagues beyond Edinburgh, that the Scots were approaching directly towards him. As soon as he heard this, he moved with his host to those parts where the Scots were; and on the morrow the King arrived in good time, and found his enemies prepared to give battle. And so they engaged, and, by the grace of God, his enemies were soon discomfited, and fled; but nevertheless, there were slain of the enemy in the day's fight two hundred men-at-arms and twenty thousand of their foot soldiers; wherefore we hope that affairs yonder will go well from henceforth, by the aid of our Lord.

Unto God [we commend you]. Written at Acun, on Sunday after the feast of St James, in the twenty-sixth year of our lord, the King Edward.

And so the said messenger was given by hand of the chamberlain the sum of twenty-six shillings by order of the mayor, John le Blunt, and of the aldermen; John de Canterbury, Thomas Romeyn, Nicholas Fardone, Nicholas Pyckot, Wiliam de Betoigne and John Donestaple [Dunstable], the chamberlain at that time.

Reports of medieval battles tend to be brief and rather uninformative: this letter is no exception to that tradition. In wartime people are inclined to be more interested in the outcome of combat than in its progress. The only information, beyond the news of the victory, relate to the claimed scale of the action. The bishop's figure of 200 men-at-arms killed in action on the Scottish side may be a fair estimate and if so would have implications for the traditional belief that Wallace's army was recruited from the labouring classes. English and Scottish observers would have been perfectly clear about what exactly constituted a 'man-at-arms', and though it was not inevitable that a man-at-arms would be of noble status, it was much, much more likely than not. The distinction between men-at-arms and foot soldier might seem like a curious one; however, that too would have been clear to medieval observers. A man-at-arms might fight on foot; noble cavalry had been dismounting for battle for 200 years at least by the time of Falkirk. The distinction lies in there being a choice: the men-at-arms could be deployed with or without their horses while the common soldiers, naturally enough, could only fight on foot. Two hundred men-at-arms killed would be a heavy price even for a severe defeat. These would be the best-armoured men on the battlefield, and they were worth a good deal more alive than dead: even the modest ransom of a minor Scottish noble or burgess was better than nothing at all. Casualty incidence and rates are a thorny question in any era and it would be unsafe to make any assumptions about the lethality of medieval battle. Even the military records of England, and they are far more complete than those of any other medieval nation, do not give enough information about numbers of combatants and casualties to give even the most vague rule of thumb. However, it is safe to make certain observations about the definition of 'casualty'. Battlefield casualties are seldom the determinant factor in the decision-making aspect of battle, but it is very rare indeed for even a professional force to withstand 20 per cent casualties. That does not imply anything remotely approaching 20 per cent fatalities, though given the nature of medieval medical science there would obviously been a closer relationship between casualties and fatalities than would be the case in the wars of the twentieth century. If the bishop's figure of 200 Scottish men-at-arms killed is to be taken at face value, we might reasonably expect that they represented a substantial portion of the men-at-arms present, but almost certainly not a majority. If they constituted as many as one out of five of the men-at-arms in the Scottish army – which would be an immensely heavy rate – it would indicate that there was something in the region of 1,000 men-at-arms in Wallace's army. If this was the case, the traditional view of Wallace as a man deserted by the nobility – the very people who enjoyed privileged rank in return for their military responsibility to king and country – must be questioned. A complement of 1,000 men-at-arms would be quite respectable for a Scottish king with possession of his entire realm, let alone for a Guardian with limited control of Scotland south of the Forth and some degree of opposition north of it, not to mention the fact that several leaders in Scottish political society were actively aligned against him.

The figure of 20,000 dead among the Scottish infantry cannot be seriously entertained, of course. In the seventeenth century, with a popular cause and the administrative machinery of a state that was surprisingly sophisticated by the standards of the time, the Scottish government found it hard work to maintain an army strength of rather less than 20,000 for service in England during the wars of the Three Kingdoms. If Wallace's army mustered 20,000 in total at Falkirk it was probably the largest Scottish army to be committed to battle throughout the whole medieval period.

EDWARD I'S PROGRESS THROUGH EASTERN SCOTLAND, MARCH–AUGUST 1296

This remarkable document traces the movements of Edward I and his armies from his passage of the Tweed at the end of March until his return to England in August. The speed of his army is not particularly noteworthy. Although it has often been described as a 'lightning' campaign, the mean march distances were not unusually great. Although Edward had penetrated as far north as Elgin, his movements do not seem to have been aimed at making any inroads into the west any further north than the Clyde. This was not Edward's first visit to Scotland; he had travelled at least as far as Perth in 1291, receiving homages and fealties from the nobility and the burgesses. Geography was not an advanced discipline in the Middle Ages, and nor was cartography: it is conceivable that Edward did not fully appreciate the sheer size of the northern and western lordships, nor the degree to which the eastern counties would be vulnerable to incursions from regions outside the control of the occupation government. The scope of the operation was not simply military: in fact by the end of May 1296 it must have already been abundantly clear to Edward and his staff that there was no imminent threat of a military action from the Scots. By leading his army through the most densely populated areas, the ones most vulnerable to military action, King Edward could impress the people with the might of his kingship and, hopefully at any rate, discourage resistance.

In the twenty-fourth year of the reign of King Edward of England, Easter day fell on the day of the Annunciation of our Lady. On the Wednesday in Easter week, being the twenty-eighth day of March, the said King Edward passed the river Tweed with 5000 armed horse, and 30,000 footmen, and lay that night in Scotland at the priory of Coldstream, and the Thursday at Hutton, and on the Friday he took the town of Berwick-upon-Tweed by force of arms without tarrying. On the same day, sir William Douglas, who was within the castle, surrendered it, and the King lay that night in the castle, and his people in the town, each person in his house which he had taken; and the King remained there nearly a month.

On the day of St George, 24th April, news came to the King that they of Scotland had besieged the castle of Dunbar, which belonged to the earl Patrick, who held strongly with the King of England. It was upon a Monday that the King sent his troops to raise the siege. Before they came there the castle had surrendered, and they of Scotland were within. When the troops of the King of England came there, they besieged the castle with three hosts

on the Tuesday that they arrived before it. On the Wednesday, they who
were within sent out privately, and on Thursday and Friday came the host
of Scotland all the afternoon to have raised the siege of the Englishmen.
And when the Englishmen saw the Scotchmen, they fell upon them and
discomfited the Scotchmen, and the chase continued more than five leagues
of way, and until the hour of vespers. And there died Sir Patrick de Graham,
a great lord, and 10,055 by right reckoning.

Historians have tended to take this document at face value; however, there
is a very clear Plantagenet propaganda agenda. As a great and mighty prince,
Edward must needs be accompanied by a great and mighty army, and
the writer is more than happy to give him one. However, it is extremely
unlikely that King Edward's army amounted to 35,000 people in total, let
alone that many combatants. The strength of medieval armies is, in general, a thorny topic. Chronicle writers tended to use large numbers as an
indication of power rather than as literal statements. Three and multiples of
three are often used in a literary, not literal, sense. Heroic figures – Wallace
or Bruce – are from time to time attacked by three assailants, who they
repulse through their personal prowess; a band of 'thirty' implies a small but
generally rather dedicated body of men, often found in threatening situations from which they escape with great panache. A party of 300 indicates a
strong force, almost invariably of gallant men-at-arms, but not an army. An
army of 3,000 would be one of modest stature and one of 30,000 would
be a very great host. Any greater number – more often than not 100,000
– just implies an absolutely immense force. The modern colloquial use of
the terms 'hundreds', 'thousands' and 'millions' is not dissimilar.

Making realistic assessments of the size of medieval armies by extrapola-
tion from the figures offered by chroniclers is therefore less than reliable. It
is, for example, less than likely that any late medieval English king was able
to raise as many as 5,000 men-at-arms from their own resources, though
there were in excess of 5,000 knight service tenancies and obligations.
The writer's use of the term 'armed' is a normal medieval application; an
'armed' man (or horse) bore armour, not arms. Several other terms were
used to denote armoured horses: 'covered', 'barbed' or 'barded' being the
most common. In order to qualify for the full man-at-arms pay of one
shilling a day, a soldier would have to have suitable armour for his charger
as well as for himself.

It is possible that the English army of 1296 did include 5,000 horsemen,
but not all horsemen were cavalry soldiers at all, let alone men-at-arms.
The mounted archer – that is, an archer who travelled on horseback but

dismounted to fight – had yet to become a major feature of English armies, but mounted infantry *per se* were hardly an innovation and the army would almost certainly have included a number of light cavalry for reconnaissance and security duties.

The same issues apply to casualty counts. Although the writer claims some 10,055 Scots dead 'by right reckoning', he is describing an action that did not take place. The action at Dunbar involved formations of the man-at-arms element of either army. It is possible, though unlikely, that the entire Scottish noble cavalry force was present, but certain that only one English formation out of three or four took part. There was only one Scottish fatality significant enough to be mentioned by name, Sir Patrick Graham, which suggests that Scottish casualties were not in fact very heavy at all and certainly not extensive in comparison to the number of Scots who spent time as prisoners of war in 1296–97 – virtually all of whom were taken at or in the aftermath of the action at Dunbar or when Dunbar Castle surrendered. The greater part of the Scottish army, like that of any other northern European nation, consisted of the infantry, but there is no evidence that the Scottish infantry were engaged at all at any point in the Dunbar campaign; thus it is not at all likely that any great number of them were killed, and definitely not 10,000.

On that same Friday [27 April], by night, the King came from Berwick to go to Dunbar, and lay that night at Coldingham, and on the Saturday at Dunbar, and on the same day they of the castle surrendered themselves to the King's pleasure. And there were the earl of Atholl, the earl of Ross, the earl of Menteith, sir John Comyn of Badenoch the son, sir Richard Suart, sir William de Saintclair, and as many as fourscore men-at-arms and seven-score footmen. There tarried the King three days.

On Wednesday [1 May], the eve of the Ascension, the King went to Haddington; on the Sunday after to Lauder; on Monday to Roxburgh, to the Friars Minors; on the Tuesday to the castle, and the King tarried there four-teen days. On the fifteenth day, being Wednesday, he went to Jedborough; on the Thursday to Wyel, on the Friday to Castleton, on the Sunday afterwards back to Wyel; on the Monday to Jedborough, on the Friday to afterwards to Roxburgh, the Monday afterwards to Lauder, the Tuesday to the abbey of Newbattle; the Wednesday to Edinburgh to the abbey, and caused to be got ready three engines casting into the castle day and night. On the fifth day they treated of peace. On the eighth day the King slept at Linlithgow, and left the engines under good guard throwing before the castle. On the Thursday he went to Stirling, and they who were within the castle fled, and none remained but the porter, who surrendered the castle; and there came the earl of Strathearn 'to the peace,' and there tarried the King five days.

On the Wednesday before the feast of St John [20 June], the King passed the Scottish sea, and lay at Auchterarder, his castle. On the Thursday at St John of Perth, a good town, and there abode Friday, Saturday, and Sunday; this same day was St John the Baptist's day. On the Monday he went to Kincleven castle, on the Tuesday to Cluny castle, and there abode five days; the Monday after to Inverqueich castle; on the Tuesday to Forfar, a castle and a good town; on the Friday after to Fernwell; the Saturday to Montrose, a castle and a good town, and there abode the Sunday, Monday, and Tuesday; and there came King John of Scotland to his mercy, and surrendered entirely the realm of Scotland to him, as one who had done amiss. Likewise there came to his mercy, the earl of Mar, the earl of Buchan, sir John Comyn of Badenagh, and many others.

On the Wednesday [11 July] he went to Kincardine in the Mearns, a manor. On Thursday he was in the mountains, to Glenbervy; on the Friday to Durres, a manor among the mountains; on the Saturday to the city of Aberdeen, a good castle and a good town upon the sea, and there he tarried for five days. And there was brought to him his enemy, sir Thomas Morham, whom sir Hugh de Saint John took, and eleven others in arms with him.

On the Friday [6 July] after he went to Kintore; on the Saturday to Fyvie castle; on the Sunday to Banff castle; on Monday to Cullen manor; on Tuesday he was in tents upon the moor, on the river of Spey, which he crossed on Wednesday, and lay on the opposite side of the same river at the manor of Rapenach, in the county of Moray; on Thursday he was at the city of Elgin, a good castle and a good town, and there he abode two days.

On Sunday [29 July] he was at the manor of Rothes; on the same day the King sent sir John de Cantelow, sir Hugh le Spencer, and sir John Hastings to search the district of Badenagh; and the bishop of Durham with his people he sent back over the mountains by another road from that which he himself took. On the Monday he went to Invercharrach, where there are no more than three houses in a row in a valley between two mountains; on Tuesday to Kildrummy, a castle of the earl of Mar, and there abode the Wednesday, the day of St Peter, in the beginning of August. On Thursday he was at the hospital of Kincardine in the Mearns; on Saturday at the city of Brechin; on Sunday to the abbey of Aberbrothock, and it is reported that the abbot told the Scots that there were only women in England. On Monday he was at Dundee; on Tuesday at Baligerny, the red castle; on Wednesday at Perth; on Thursday at the abbey of Lundores, and there he remained the Friday, St Laurence's day. On Saturday he was at the city of St Andrews, a castle and a good town; on Sunday at Markinch, where are only the Minster and three houses. On Monday he was at the abbey of Dunfermline, where nearly all the Kings of Scotland lie. On Tuesday to Stirling, and there he remained on Wednesday, the day of the Assumption of our Lady. On Thursday to Linlithgow; on Friday to Edinburgh, and there he remained the Saturday. On the Sunday to Haddington; Monday to Pinkerton, near Dunbar; Tuesday to Coldingham; Wednesday to Berwick. And he conquered the realm of Scotland, and searched it, as is above written, within twenty-one weeks, without any more.

At Berwick he held his Parliament; and there were all the bishops, earls, barons, abbots, and priors, and the sovereigns of all the common people; and there he received the homages of all, and their oaths that they would be good and loyal to him. To the well regulated people he forthwith gave up all their own goods and those of their tenants; the earls, barons, and bishops he permitted to enjoy their lands, provided they came at All Saints to the parliament at St Edmunds. Then he appointed the earl of Warren to be guardian of the land, and sir Hugh de Cressingham treasurer, sir Walter de Agmondesham chancellor. Then he tarried at Berwick three weeks and three days, arranging his affairs, and set out on his road to England on the Sunday after the feast of the Holy Cross. [16 September]

THE *SCALACRONICA* OF SIR THOMAS GREY

The *Scalacronica* of Sir Thomas Grey has a unique value among the chronicles that relate to the Scottish and English wars of the late thirteenth and early fourteenth century. Sir Thomas served in the armies and garrisons of the Plantagenet/Balliol administration of southern Scotland in the 1330s. He was a career soldier and spent most of that career fighting against Scots. Since he had extensive experience of the realities of war his accounts are of particular interest; he was not above writing very good reports of his own actions, but it is only fair to remember that men and women writing their memoirs do not do so 'on oath', and it is not as if it is hard to identify the passages that may have become more 'polished' in Sir Thomas's memory by the time he committed his words to paper. Sir Thomas came from a family with a strong military tradition; his father – also Sir Thomas – had served in the Scottish administrations of Edward I and Edward II. Father and son both had the misfortune to become prisoners of war: a fortunate occurrence for historians, in that Sir Thomas junior had the leisure time to write his chronicle and the opportunity, as he tells us, to consult various prose and verse chronicles in Stirling and Edinburgh.

> The said King Edward [the First] went to Scotland, invested the castle of Caerlaverock and took it, after which siege William Wallace was taken by John de Menteith near Glasgow and brought before the King of England, who caused him to be drawn and hanged in London.
>
> The said King caused the town of Berwick to be surrounded with a stone wall, and, returning to England, left John de Segrave Guardian of Scotland. The Scots began again to rebel against King Edward of England, and elected John de Comyn their Guardian and Chief of their cause. At which time ensued great passages of arms between the Marches, and notably in Teviotdale, before Roxburgh Castle, between Ingram de Umfraville, Robert de Keith, Scotsmen, and Robert de Hastings, warden of the said castle. John de Segrave, Guardian of Scotland for King Edward of England, marched in force into Scotland with several magnates of the English Marches, and with Patrick Earl of March, who was an adherent of the English King, came to Rosslyn, encamped about the village, with his column around him. His advanced guard was encamped a league distant in a hamlet. John Comyn with his adherents made a night attack upon the said John de Segrave and discomfited him in the darkness; and his advanced guard, which was encamped at a distant place, were not aware of his defeat, therefore they came in the morning in battle array to the same place where they had left their commander overnight, intending to do their devoir, where they were attacked and routed by the numbers of Scots, and Rafe the Cofferer was there slain.

The battle of Roslin is a curiosity in the military history of Scotland; some historians have seen it as a minor skirmish, others as a vast engagement of great significance. The action was certainly portrayed as a great victory by the Scottish diplomats in France, who did not hesitate to relay the reception of the news back to the Balliol party in Scotland, saying that success in battle had brought the Scottish cause prestige and honour. Once again, the numbers given by chroniclers have given rise to a completely unacceptable view of the battle. The chronicler Bower has a force of Scots march through a bleak February night from Biggar to Roslin. A very hardy individual might make such a march, but not an army intent on forcing battle on an enemy in the morning. The Scottish force was evidently a mounted one; a point confirmed by all the other evidence. So far so good, but Bower outs the Scottish force at 8,000 men, a very large army indeed for the time, had it comprised the different elements of the sort of army raised for general engagements: a combination of man-at-arms, spearmen and archers. However, this was very obviously not that sort of an army, but a striking force of heavy cavalry. No English king was ever able to raise a cavalry force of that magnitude and no Scottish king could ever hope to match the resources of their neighbours. The strength of Sir John Comyn's army at Roslin was almost certainly a matter of hundreds, not thousands.

Bower's use of numbers is well within the literary tradition of his day. To give as much prestige to the Scots as he possibly can, Bower puts 8,000 men at the command of Sir John Comyn, not because he expects the reader to take the sum at face value, but to ensure the reader that this was a major force undertaking an important operation; no doubt he thought 8,000 'sounded good'. Having given that level of force to the Scots, Bower was naturally obliged to accord a far greater strength to the English army – some 30,000. A number of Scottish writers have taken that figure literally, but it is safe to assume that had there been an English force of that stature involved it would have left a great deal more in the way of state records. Nonetheless, Roslin was an important engagement. By the standard of Scottish-English war it was a fight of some size. Numbers were not always of great significance in medieval conflicts; the nature of the fight was also an issue. One of the issues about Roslin from an English perspective was that the Scots had been successful in a conventional fight: a clash between men-at-arms of the kind that everyone in Europe understood. The Scottish nobility had demonstrated that they could take on the English nobility and give them a run for their money. This is not to say that either side were very proficient in their business; more than half a century later, when he was a very old man, the writer Petrarch saw the English knights as fine paladins, though in his youth they had been '…inferior, even to the wretched Scots', thus neatly damning the noble classes of both countries.

> Because of this news King Edward marched the following year into Scotland, and on his first entry encamped at Dryburgh. Hugh de Audley, with sixty men-at-arms, finding difficulty in encamping beside the King, went [forward] to Melrose and took up quarters in the abbey. John Comyn, at that time Guardian of Scotland, was in the forest of Ettrick with a great force of armed men, perceiving the presence of the said Hugh at Melrose in the village, attacked him by night and broke open the gates, and, while the English in the abbey were formed up and mounted on their horses in the court, they caused the gates to be thrown open; the Scots entered on horseback in great numbers, bore to the ground the English who were few in number, and captured or

slew them all. The chevalier, Thomas Gray, after being beaten down, seized the house outside the gate, and held it in hope of rescue until the house began to burn over his head, when he, with others, was taken prisoner.

The Thomas Grey referred to in this passage was the father of the author. Not content with being captured at Melrose in the service of Edward I, he went on to be captured at Bannockburn in the service of Edward II. Thomas Grey junior would follow his father's career path by serving against the Scots and also by being taken prisoner.

King Edward marched forward and kept the feast of Christmas [1303] at Linlithgow, then rode throughout the land of Scotland, and marched to Dunfermline, where John Comyn perceiving that he could not withstand the might of the King of England, rendered himself to the King's mercy, on condition that he and all his adherents should regain all their rightful possessions, and they became again his [Edward's] lieges; whereupon new instruments were publicly executed.

John de Soulis would not agree to the conditions; he left Scotland and went to France, where he died. William Oliphant, a young Scottish bachelor, caused Stirling Castle to be garrisoned, not deigning to consent to John Comyn's conditions, but claiming to hold from the Lion. The said King Edward, who had nearly all the people of Scotland in his power and possession of their fortresses, came before Stirling Castle, invested it and attacked it with many different engines, and took it by force and by a siege of nineteen weeks! During which siege, the chevalier Thomas Gray was struck through the head below the eyes by the bolt of a springald, and fell to the ground for dead under the barriers of the castle. [This happened] just as he had rescued his master, Henry de Beaumont, who had been caught at the said barriers by a hook thrown from a machine, and was only just outside the barriers when the said Thomas dragged him out of danger. The said Thomas was brought in and a party was paraded to bury him, when at that moment he began to move and look about him, and afterwards recovered.

The King sent the captain of the castle, William Oliphant, to prison in London, and caused the knights of his army to joust before their departure at the close of the siege. Having appointed his officers throughout Scotland, he marched to MS. England, and left Aymer de Valence, Earl of Pembroke, as Guardian of Scotland, to whom he gave the forests of Selkirk and Ettrick, where at Selkirk the said Aymer caused build a pele, and placed therein a strong garrison.

There is a sense in which Sir William Oliphaunt's garrison were the first Scots to commit themselves publicly to the political independence of their country, as opposed to upholding the rights of their king. There is obviously some difference between the two positions, a difference that was not easy to express in terms of medieval political theory. The form of state known as a kingdom needed a king to make its government 'complete'. Since King John had evidently declined to take any further interest in his realm it was not altogether unreasonable to take the view, as Edward did, that there was nothing left for the Scots to fight for by early 1304. The refusal of the garrison to accept the terms of the Strathord agreement must have been something of an embarrassment to the leadership of the Balliol party as well as an irritation to Edward I. What exactly the defenders of Stirling hoped to achieve by holding out is a mystery. A close siege pressed to its conclusion must inevitably be successful unless the siege force is driven off. Since there was no longer any kind of a Scottish army in the field other than a tiny band of men under William Wallace, there was no prospect whatsoever of a relief. Edward's refusal to accept the surrender of the Stirling garrison is usually attributed to his desire to see a new siege weapon in action, which may well have been the case, though in fact there would have been nothing to prevent him from having a demonstration of the 'war wolf' after the surrender of the garrison rather than before. More realistically, Edward may have considered it desirable to show that his patience had been exhausted. The Balliol party had been powerful enough and successful enough that they could not be denied a degree of 'official' status as combatants. Having eventually succeeded in neutralising the mainstream of support for King John, Edward may have been determined to show that any continuing resistance from 'splinter groups' would not be accorded the same generosity, but would be pursued relentlessly until they threw themselves on the mercy of the Crown – a message perhaps to William Wallace, but probably aimed at a rather wider audience of men and women who might otherwise be tempted to shelter and aid him.

Notes

CHAPTER ONE: WILLIAM WALLACE, KNIGHT OF SCOTLAND

1   John of Fordoun, Andrew of Wyntoun and Walter Bower all take pains to ensure the reader is aware that William Wallace was the son of a noble knight, a member of the aristocratic and political community of Scotland.

2   The term 'Scots' is used throughout this volume to indicate the form of northern Middle English spoken in southern and eastern Scotland in the thirteenth and fourteenth centuries.

3   The scarcity of Scottish state records from the thirteenth and fourteenth century is, obviously, a problem for Scottish medievalists; however, there are several sources which indicate the general practice of the king's chapel (chancery). See the introductions to *Regesta Regum Scottorum* vols v and vi, *Exchequer Rolls of Scotland* vol. i and *The Register of the Great Seal of Scotland* vol. i.

4   G. Donaldson, *Scottish Historical Documents* (Edinburgh 1970) pp.29-30.

CHAPTER TWO: OF NOBLE KIN: THE SOCIETY OF WILLIAM WALLACE

1   *The Wallace* was one of the first books to be printed in Scotland and one of the volumes most likely to be found in Scottish households in the eighteenth and nineteenth centuries. Robert Burns was particularly moved by Scotland's hero: 'Scots wha hae wi' Wallace bled…'.

2   See the *Register of the Great Seal of Scotland* (*RMS*) and the *Regesta Regum Scottorum* volumes for the reigns of William the Lion and Robert I for examples of the wide variety of burdens that could be attached to property tenure.

3   It has been widely assumed by historians that women did not play a significant part in medieval political communities. It is clear that women did not give military service – a political activity – in person and much more likely than not that they did not give jury service either, but they were responsible for ensuring that the duties attached to any property they owned were properly discharged. Several historians have asserted that women were not required to give homage to their superior lords or to the king; the latter can be disproved by a brief examination of the *Calendar of Documents relating to Scotland* (*CDS*) where, in addition to records of several individual acts of homage, a sizeable proportion of the names entered on the Ragman Roll are female. *CDS* vol. II, pp.194-211.

4   See the introduction to *RRS* vol. v.

5   Acts of the Parliaments of Scotland vol. i, p.404.

6   See Andrew Ayton, *Knights and their Warhorses*, for a detailed study of the English nobility at war in the fourteenth century.

7   R. Nicholson, *Scotland. The Later Middle Ages*, pp.48-54.

8   A.A.M. Duncan, *Barbour's Bruce*, pp.670-78.

9   A.A.M. Duncan, *Scotland. The making of the Kingdom*, pp.507-8.

10 There has not, as yet, been a scholarly monograph study of the battle of Bannockburn since McKenzie's volume published in 1913, which is now extremely dated.

11 M. Powicke, *The Thirteenth Century*.

12 G.W.S. Barrow, 'Lothian in the Wars of Independence' in *Scotland and its Neighbours in the Middle Ages*.

13 See the introduction to *RRS* vol. v, Robert I.

14 *CDS* vol. ii no. 857.

15 For an examination of military obligation in Scotland prior to the Wars of Independence, see G.W.S. Barrow's essay 'The Army of Alexander III in Scotland in the Reign of Alexander III', (ed.) N.Reid.

16 See Introduction to *RRS* vol. v, Robert I.

17 The armies raised by Scottish kings for the campaigns that resulted in the battles of Bannockburn, Myton, Halidon Hill and Neville's Cross were not the normal practice of war, but rare events engendered by unusual circumstances.

18 A.A.M. Duncan, *Scotland. The Making of the Kingdom*, p.381.

19 Harold Booton, 'Burgesses and Landed Men in North East Scotland'. Ph.D. thesis, Aberdeen University, 1987. Elizabeth Ewan, *Town Life in Fourteenth Century Scotland*.

20 See Mayhew and Gemmill, *The Changing Value of Money in Medieval Scotland* for a detailed examination of the Scottish economy and money supply in the late Middle Ages.

21 R. Nicholson, *Scotland. The Later Middle Ages*, chapter 1 and A.A.M. Duncan, *Scotland. The Making of the Kingdom*, chapters 12, 18 and 19.

22 P. McNeill and H. McQueen (eds), *Atlas of Scottish History to 1707*, pp.231-242.

23 I am indebted to Mr Alex Woolf of St Andrews University for his views on the relationship between feudal tenure and the deliberate fostering of markets in particular locations.

24 STS miscellany, vol. xi.

25 Several examples of these instructions can be found in *CDS* vols ii and iii and in *Rotuli Scotiae*.

26 *CDS* vol. iii, pp. 327-41.

27 *CDS* vol. iii, p.400.

CHAPTER THREE: THE ROOTS OF THE WAR

1   G. Donaldson, *Scottish Historical Documents*.

2   There were a number of kings in Europe who were the subjects of other kings; Savoy, Navarre and Sicily all fell into this category at different times.

3   *RRS* vol. v, Robert I.

4   Although Caddonlea was considered the traditional mustering point for Scottish armies heading south, it had been some considerable time since a Scottish army had been raised at all.

5   See the *Progress of Edward I* reprinted in this volume.

6   *CDS* vol. ii, pp.194-211.

7   Rev. Stevenson, *Documents Illustrative of the History of Scotland.*

8   C. Brown, 'We are Cummand of gentlemen'. Ph.D. Thesis, St Andrews University, 2004, also *Knights of Scotland* forthcoming.

9   *Camerar Scocie,* Accounts of the Chamberlain of Scotland.

10 CDS vol. ii no. 832 and many others.

11 G. Donaldson, *Scottish Historical Documents.*

CHAPTER FOUR: FROM GANGSTER TO GOVERNOR

1   James MacKay, *Brave Heart* (Edinburgh and London, 1995).

2   CDS vol.ii, p.194 etc.

3   A.A.M. Duncan, *Scotland. The Making of the Kingdom*, chapters 13, 14 and 15.

4   I am indebted to Mr Peter Armstrong for bringing this item to my attention and for sending me the relevant article from *The Herald* (formerly *The Glasgow Herald*).

5   Wallace had gathered an army of some thousands by the late summer of 1297; self-evidently, he was effective at recruiting.

6   See 'Wallace and Fordoun/Wyntoun/Bower/Blind Harry' extracts in this volume.

7   According to the charges brought against William, he 'in contempt of the King, had cut the said sheriff's body in pieces'.

8   Blind Harry, *The Wallace.*

9   Details of the locations of his imprisonment and of the allowances he and his com-patriots received as prisoners of war in castles throughout England and Wales can be found in great quantity in *CDS* vol.ii. Interestingly, prisoner of war allowances reflect social status in the same way as the pay structures of waged English soldiers of the time, though only a handful of Scottish men-at-arms received any form of pay and those who did were the recipients of salaries as knights of the king's household.

10 R. Nicholson, *Scotland. The Later Middle Ages* (Edinburgh, 1974), Chapter 1. For a detailed examination of the social, legal and financial structures of the later medieval town in Scotland, see Elizabeth Ewan, *Town Life in Fourteenth Century Scotland.*

11 The origins of this belief are obscure, being apparently quite well established by the middle of the twentieth century. It is still being perpetuated at the Bannockburn Visitors Centre.

12 *RRS* vol. v.

13 Barbour, *The Bruce.*

14 Maxwell's translation of *Scalacronica* was reprinted by Luath Publications in 2000, and a new scholarly edition by Dr A. King and Dr M. Prestwich is in preparation at the time of writing. As the observations of a professional career soldier, *Scalacronica* is a particularly significant account of the Scottish wars of the fourteenth century.

15 E.M. Barron, *The Scottish War of Independence.* Barron made a case that the study of the Wars of Independence had been almost completely focused on events and individuals in the south and east of the country. What he saw as 'Celtic' Scotland had borne the burden of the wars against the English, but their contribution had been ignored. Although he 'over-egged his pudding' – and was prone to distortions of fact about the geographic origin of specific lords – Barron did have something of a case.

16 For an introduction to the business of how armies and conflicts 'work' it would be difficult to suggest anything other than Michael Handel's *Masters of War, Classical Strategic Thought* (New York, 1992).

CHAPTER FIVE: THE BATTLE OF STIRLING BRIDGE

1   For Edward I to attend to the problem in person might give the Balliol party a certain degree of credibility.
2   The thousands who, according to English chroniclers, died on the battlefield do not seem to have been noticed by anyone else.
3   Even if there had been a shortage of arms after the spring of 1296, there had been ample time to acquire replacements before the late summer of 1297.
4   See 'Wallace and Fordoun' and 'Wallace and Bower' in this volume.
5   The provisions made for the support of Sir Edward Hastang under Edward II and Sir John de Strivelin of East Swinneburne (Swinburne, Northumberland) by Edward illustrate this sort of arrangement. See Chris Brown, *Knights of Scotland*, forthcoming, for a detailed examination of military service tenure conditions in Scotland in the later thirteenth to mid-fourteenth centuries.
6   The battle of Evesham.
7   This was the policy adopted successfully by Robert I against Edward I in the years after Bannockburn.
8   See 'The Resistable Rise of Edwardian Government' in Fiona Watson, *Under the Hammer* (East Lothian, 1998).
9   *CDS* vol. ii no. 1375.
10 Stevenson, *Documents Illustrative of Scottish History* no. ccccliii.
11 G. Cameron Stone, *Glossary of the Construction and Decoration of Armour*.
12 Maitland Club, *Documents Illustrative of William Wallace, His Life and Times*.
13 There was a '*galeator*' or 'helmet-maker' in Perth in the reign of William the Lion, but such specialists would be few and far between. Most of the armour worn by most of the troops was leather- and/or fabric-based and could be produced at home.
14 The website www.deremilitari.org carries a synopsis of arms and armour prices from England from the 1290s to the late 1330s. Scottish prices are likely to have been similar or very slightly higher.
15 'Munition' equipment: arms and armour issued to the soldiers as opposed to arms purchased privately by the soldier.
16 *Scalacronica* (Maxwell).
17 One of these castles was Dirleton, a major modern fortress in 1296; the other two may have been Yester and Hailes.

CHAPTER SIX: FROM VICTORY TO IGNOMINY

1   C. MacNamee, *William Wallace's Invasion of England* (1990).
2   G. Donaldson, *Scottish Historical Documents* (Edinburgh 1970) pp.45-46.
3   Maitland Club, *Documents Illustrative of William Wallace, His Life and Times*.
4   *CDS* vol, ii no. 1323.
5   Many of the military tenure obligations in north-eastern England and south-eastern Scotland had their origins in the earlier 'Thanage' and 'Drengage' tenures that pre-dated the 'feudal' arrangements introduced in the twelfth century. See A.A.M. Duncan, *Scotland. The Making of the Kingdom* (1975) pp.161 & 327 and chapter 15 of *Fief and Service* for an examination of the origins and development of different military land tenures in Scotland. Also Chris Brown, *Knights of Scotland* (forthcoming) for a discussion of the transition from Drengage to man-at-arms service in

south-east Scotland before the onset of the Wars of Independence.

6   There were something in the region of 200 Scots in English custody after the Dunbar campaign. Bain's *Calendar of Documents Relating to Scotland* vol.ii is inform-ative about the various arrangements made for their allowances, custody and accommodation, their ransoms and, increasingly after the summer of 1297, their exchange for men who had been taken prisoner by the Scots.

7   C. MacNamee, *William Wallace's Invasion of Scotland* (1990).

8   *Ibid.*

9   Stevenson, *Documents Illustrative of the History of Scotland* (London 1879) p.237.

10   G.W.S. Barrow, 'The Army of Alexander III' in N. Reid (ed.) *Scotland in the reign of Alexander III* (Edinburgh 1990).

11   R. Nicholson, *Scotland. The Later Middle Ages* (Edinburgh 1974) p.56.

12   C. MacNamee, *William Wallace's Invasion of Scotland* (1990).

13   For a detailed examination of the English army of the Falkirk campaign see H. Gough, *Scotland in 1298: Documents Relating to the Campaign of King Edward I in that Year* (London 1888).

14   M. Powicke, *The Thirteenth Century* (Oxford 1953) p.689.

15   R. Nicholson, *Scotland. The Later Middle Ages* (Edinburgh 1974).

16   *CDS* vol.ii no.1011.

17   G.W.S. Barrow, *Robert the Bruce and the Community of the Realm of Scotland* (London 1965).

18   A. Young, *Robert the Bruce's Rivals: The Comyns, 1212–1314* (East Linton 1997).

19   *Ibid.* chapter 4, 'A Responsible Aristocratic Governing Community, *c.*1260–86'.

CHAPTER SEVEN: EXILE AND DEFIANCE

1   R. Nicholson, *Scotland. The Later Middle Ages* (Edinburgh 1974) p.61.

2   Bruce and Comyn had assumed the Guardianship before the end of 1298. M. Penman, *The Scottish Civil War* (Stroud 2002).

3   All land was held from the king, not owned outright as we would understand it. 'Heritage' lands were properties whose tenure passed indefeasibly from father to son – so long as all of the stipulations of the original grant were fulfilled.

4   *CDS* vol.ii no.857.

5   King Phillip's letter of credence for William is printed in this volume, see 'Wallace in English State Records'.

6   Although Edward planned to build at least one modern stone castle – at Linlithgow – his financial situation meant that he had to settle for a timber 'peel' there and others at Selkirk and Lochmaben. Plans for a fourth peel at Dunfermline were apparently shelved when it became apparent that Edward could not find the money for labourers to dig the ditch that would provide the foundation for the rampart.

7   See Fiona Watson's *Under the Hammer* (East Linton 1998) for a detailed examination of Edward I's Scottish administration, in particular the chapter 'The Resistable Rise of Edwardian Government'.

8   *CDS* vol.iv no.477.

9   Stevenson, *Documents Illustrative of Scottish History* (Edinburgh 1879) nos cxxxi and cxxxii.

10   Stevenson, *Documents Illustrative of Scottish History* (Edinburgh 1879) no. dcxxxiii.

11   G.W.S. Barrow, *Robert the Bruce and the Community of the Realm of Scotland* (London

1965) p.184, quoting Palgrave, *Documents and Records Illustrating the History of Scotland* (London 1837). The instruction orders that 'Sir John Comyn, Sir Alexander Lindsay, Sir David Graham and Sir Simon Fraser shall exert themselves until twenty days after Christmas to capture Sir William Wallace and hand him over to the king, who will watch to see how each of them conducts himself so that he can do most favour to whoever shall capture Wallace, with regard to exile or legal claims or expiation of past misdeeds.'

CHAPTER EIGHT: BUT WHAT WAS IT ALL *FOR*?

1   Declarations of the clergy and, apparently, the nobility after the St Andrews Parliament of 1309 and of course the Declaration of Arbroath.

2   G.W.S. Barrow, *Robert the Bruce* (London 1965) pp. 252-4. A.A.M. Duncan, *Nation of the Scots and The Declaration of Arbroath* (London 1970).

3   For an account of the rule of the Guardians see N. Reid, '*Kingless Kingdom*', S.H.R. LXI ,1982.

4   G.W.S. Barrow, *Robert the Bruce and the Community of the Realm of Scotland*, xix-xxi, 23-24, 46-47 and also A. Young, *The Comyns – Robert the Bruce's Rivals* 1212–1314. (East Lothian 1998) pp. 93-95.

5   The Guardianship of 1295 was a committee of twelve, '...likened by contemporary English commentators to the Twelve Peers of France... in fact it was a return to the Guardianship of 1286'. Young, *The Comyns*, p.140.

6   For further discussion of the Community of the Realm as a political concept and in particular the medieval concept of national as opposed to personal liberty, see G.W.S. Barrow 'The Idea of Freedom in Late Medieval Scotland', *Innes Review* vol. xxx, 1980.

7   R. Nicholson, *Scotland in the Later Middle Ages* (Edinburgh 1974) p.26.

8   G.W.S. Barrow, *Robert the Bruce* p.xx.

9   The release of King John into papal custody was a major success for the Scots, but it did not procure his liberty.

10   Barrow, *Robert the Bruce* pp.134 & 168.

11   For further discussion see Barrow, *The Scottish Clergy and the War of Independence*, SHR xxxi (1962).

12   Fiona Watson, *Under the Hammer* (East Lothian 1998) p.45.

13   G.W.S. Barrow, *Robert the Bruce* p.117.

14   '...even though the lords themselves were present with the [English] King in body, at heart they were on the opposite side': *Chronicle* of Walter of Guisborough, quoted in Nicholson, *Scotland in the Later Middle Ages* p.54. Although the term 'good lordship' is one we associate more with the fifteenth century than the fourteenth or the thirteenth, that does not mean that it's absence or presence was not of crucial significance to the relationship between lord and tenant.

15   Duncan, *Nation of the Scots* and the Declaration of Arbroath.

16   This would have been a common experience among those landlords who sided with the Scottish administration but whose property lay in the occupied areas.

17   Watson, *Under the Hammer* p.30.

18   F. Watson, 'The Enigmatic Lion' in *Image and Identity* (Edinburgh 1998).

19   G.W.S. Barrow, *Robert the Bruce* p.147.

20   A. Young, *The Comyns* pp.21, 28, 69.

21 W.S. Barrow, *Robert the Bruce* p.179.

22 That the Scots could hold a parliament as far south as Rutherglen is a good indication of their confidence and of the effectiveness of the English occupation.

23 G.W.S Barrow, *Robert the Bruce* p.128.

24 *Ibid* p.149.

25 A.A.M. Duncan examines the income of Scottish kings before the war in *Scotland, the Making of the Kingdom* (Edinburgh 1975) pp.596-8.

26 F. Watson, *Under the Hammer* p.115.

27 *Ibid*, p.30.

28 *Ibid*, p.208.

29 C.J. Neville, 'Earls of Strathearn' SHR lxv 1986.

30 A.A.M. Duncan, *Nation of the Scots*.

31 N. Reid, *Kingless Kingdom*.

32 The innovation was limited to the deployment. For an examination of military service obligations see Barrow, 'The Army of Alexander III's Scotland' in *Scotland in the Reign of Alexander III*, (ed.) N. Reid (Edinburgh 1990).

33 It is difficult to see what more they could have hoped for.

34 Vague use of the words 'the right' in Robert Bruce's surrender pact suggest that Edward was prepared to consider using Bruce to keep John out of Scotland (F. Watson, *Under the Hammer*). Edward's confidence in Robert's dependability after the surrender of the Guardians has been questioned because of the requirement that he provide a keeper for Kildrummy Castle that 'he himself would be willing to answer for', but since Edward used the same phrase in an indenture with one of own lords – Clifford – perhaps we should not read too much into it.

35 Reid, *Kingless Kingdom*.

CHAPTER NINE: DEATH AND IMMORTALITY

1 See the Fordoun, Bower and Wyntoun chronicle extracts in this volume.

2 A larger property carried more of a burden (usually) than a smaller one, but not a different obligation.

3 Titles with the words 'holy', 'grail', 'Templar', 'mystery' and 'blood' often fall into this category.

4 Continental names abound in Scottish history: Fraser, Comyn, Lindsay, Sinclair and of course Bruce.

5 James McKay, *William Wallace: Braveheart* (Edinburgh 1995), p. 173.

6 G.W.S. Barrow, *Robert the Bruce* p.29.

7 A.A.M. Duncan, *Barbour's Bruce* (Edinburgh 1997), introduction.

8 A.A.M. Duncan, *Scotland. The Making of the Kingdom* (Edinburgh 1975) pp.378-391.

9 *Regesta Regum Scottorum*, introduction.

10 See Andrew Aytoun, *Knights and their Warhorses* (Surrey 1997).

11 G.W.S. Barrow, *Lothian in the Wars of Independence*.

12 C. Brown, Chapter 2, 'Lothian Families' in *Knights of Scotland* (Stroud), forthcoming.

13 Antony Bek, Bishop of Durham, was entrusted with the recovery of three castles, Dirleton and two others, in the summer of 1298 before the battle of Falkirk.

14 See the Fordoun, Wyntoun and Bower chronicle extracts in this volume.

Glossary

Advowson	right of appointment to a parish benefice
Aketon	a protective padded garment
Bailie	a sheriff's officer
Bondi	peasants
Carucate	a measure of land
Charger	a cavalry horse
Covered	armoured horses
Ferrand	a colour (of horses)
Haubergeon	protective padded garment
Hauberk	chainmail shirt
Hobelars	light cavalry or mounted infantry
Husbandmen	farm tenants
Jack	protective padded garment
Liard	a colour (of horses)
Librate	a measure of land
Magnates	the greater nobility
Marcate	a measure of land
Mark/merk	two-thirds of a pound; 13s 4d
Nativi	peasants
Oxgang	a measure of land
Restauro	compensation for warhorses lost on active service
Rustici	peasants
Servi	peasants
Sheriff	chief local officer of the Crown
Teinds	church taxation (tithes in England)
Verge	the household of the king of Scotland
Villeins	peasants
Wappinschaw	a day for military training and weapons inspection
Wardrobe	the cash department of the households of English kings

Select Bibliography

PRIMARY SOURCE MATERIAL

Acts of the Parliaments of Scotland. C. Innes, London (1844)

Anglo-Scottish Relations, 1174–1328, Some Selected Documents. E.L.G. Stones, London (1965)

Calendar of Close Rolls. HMSO, London (1892–1907)

Calendar of Documents Relating to Scotland vol. v. G. Simpson and J.Galbraith, Edinburgh (1988)

Calendar of Documents Relating to Scotland vols i–iv. J. Bain, Edinburgh (1881–88)

Calendar of Inquisitions (Miscellaneous). HMSO, London (1916)

Calendar of Inquisitions Post Mortem. HMSO, London (1908–10)

Carte Monialium de Northberwic. Bannatyne Club, Edinburgh (1847)

Chronicles of the Reigns of Edward I and Edward II. Ed. W. Stubbs, London (1882)

Chronicle of Holyrood. Ed. O. Anderson, SHS Edinburgh (1938)

Chronicles (of Jean Froissart). Tr.& ed. G. Brereton, London (1968)

Chronicon de Lanercost. Bannatyne Club, Edinburgh (1839)

Documents Illustrative of the History of Scotland. J. Stevenson, Edinburgh (1870)

Edward I and the Throne of Scotland, 1290–96. E.L.G. Stones and G.Simpson, Oxford (1978)

Exchequer Rolls of Scotland vol. i. Ed. J. Stuart and G. Burnett, Edinburgh (1876)

Liber Sancte Marie de Calchou. Bannatyne Club, Edinburgh (1846)

Liber Sancte Marie de Melros. Bannatyne Club, Edinburgh (1887)

Records of the Wardrobe and Household. Ed. F. and C. Byerley, HMSO (1985)

Regesta Regum Scottorum vol. v. Ed. A.A.M. Duncan, Edinburgh University Press (1988)

Regesta Regum Scottorum vol. vi. Ed. B.Webster, Edinburgh University Press (1982)

Registrum de Sancte Marie de Neubotle. Ed. C. Innes, Edinburgh (1849)

Registrum Honoris de Morton. Bannatyne Club, Edinburgh (1853)

Rotuli Scotiae. J. MacPherson, Record Commission, London (1814–19)

Scalacronica of Sir Thomas Grey. Maxwell (1913)

Scotichronicon of Walter Bower. Ed. D.Watt, Aberdeen (1991)

Source book of Scottish History. Ed. W. Croft Dickinson, G. Donaldson and I. Milne, Edinburgh (1952)

Scottish Historical Documents. G. Donaldson, Edinburgh (1974)

The Bruce. J. Barbour. Ed. A.A.M. Duncan, Edinburgh (1997)

The Chartulary of Coldstream. Ed. C. Rogers, London (1879)

The Chronicle of Lanercost. Tr. H. Maxwell, Glasgow (1913)

The Chronicle of Walter of Guisborough. Ed. H. Rothwell, Camden (1957)

The Exchequer Rolls of Scotland, J. Stuart and G. Burnett, Edinburgh (1978)

The Original Chronicle of Andrew of Wyntoun. Ed. J. Amours, Edinburgh (1907)

The Register of the Great Seal of Scotland. Ed. J. Thomson, Edinburgh (1912)

The Scottish King's Household. Ed. M. Bateson, SHS Miscellany, Edinburgh (1904)

Vita Edwardi Secundi. Ed. N. Denholm-Young, London (1957)

SECONDARY SOURCES AND SPECIALIST MATERIAL

Allmand, C. *The Hundred Years War*. (Cambridge 1998)

Armstrong, O. *Edward Bruce's Invasion of Ireland*. (London 1923)

Aytoun, A. *Knights and Warhorses*. (Woodbridge 1994)

Bain, J. *The Edwards in Scotland 1296–1377*. (Edinburgh 1901)

Balfour Paul, Sir James. *The Scots Peerage*. (Edinburgh 1904–14)

Barker, J. *The Tournament in England, 1100–1400*. Sutton (Stroud 1986)

Barrie, J. *War in Medieval Society*. (London 1974)

Barron, E.M. *The Scottish War of Independence*. (Inverness 1934)

Barrow, G.W.S. *The Kingdom of the Scots*. (London 1973)

– *Robert the Bruce and the Community of the Realm of Scotland*. (London 1965)

– *Kingship and Unity*. (London 1981)

– *Scotland and its Neighbours in the Middle Ages*. (London 1992)

– *The Anglo-Norman Era in Scottish History*. (Oxford 1980)

Beresford, M. *The New Towns of the Middle Ages*. (London 1957)

Black, G. *The Surnames of Scotland*. (Edinburgh 1999)

Blair, C. *European Armour 1066–1700*. (New York 1972)

Boardman, S. & Ross, A. (eds). *The Exercise of Power in Medieval Scotland*.
   (Chippenham 2003)

Braudel, F. *Civilisation and Capitalism*. (London 1981)

Brotherstone, T, & Ditchburn, D. (eds). *Freedom and Authority*. (East Lothian, 2000)

Broun, Finlay and Lynch (eds). *Image and Identity*. (Edinburgh 1998)

Brown, C. *The Second Scottish War of Independence*. (Stroud 2002)

– *Robert the Bruce. A Life Chronicled*. (Stroud 2004)

Brown, M. *The Black Douglases*. (East Linton 1998)

Burns, W. *The Scottish War of Independence*. (1874)

Contamine, P. *War in the Middle Ages*. (Oxford 1986)

Coss, P. *The Knight in Medieval England*. (Stroud 1993)

Croft Dickinson, W. *Scotland from the Earliest Times to 1603*. (Oxford 1977)

Cruden, S. *The Scottish Castle*. (Edinburgh 1981)

Davis, R. *The Medieval Warhorse*. (London 1989)

– *Conquest, Co-existence and Change: Wales 1063–1415*. (Oxford 1987)

Ditchburn, D. *Scotland and Europe*. (East Lothian 2001)

Dodgson, R.A. *Land and Society in Early Scotland*. (Oxford 1981)

Dowden, J. *The Medieval Church in Scotland*. (Glasgow 1910)

Duffy, S. *Robert the Bruce's Irish Wars*. (Stroud 2002)

Duncan, A.A.M. *Scotland, The Making of the Kingdom*. (Edinburgh 1975)

Dupuy, R.& T. *Numbers, Prediction and War*. (New York 1985)

Dupuy, T. *Understanding Defeat*. (New York 1990)

Easson, E. *Medieval Religious Houses in Scotland*. (London 1957)

Ewan, E. *Town life in Fourteenth Century Scotland*. (Edinburgh 1990)

Ferguson, W. *Scotland's Relations with England. A Survey to 1701*. (Edinburgh 1977)

Fisher, A. *William Wallace*. (Edinburgh 1986)

Fryde, N. *The Tyranny and Fall of Edward II, 1321–26*. (Cambridge 1979)

Gilbert, J.M. *Hunting and Hunting Reserves in Medieval Scotland*. (Edinburgh 1979)

Gillingham, J. & Holt, J. (ed.) *War and Government in the Middle Ages*.
   (Woodbridge 1984)

Grant, A. *Independence and Nationhood*. (London 1984)

Grant, I.F. *The Social and Economic Development of Scotland before 1603*. (Edinburgh 1930)

Hale, J. (ed.) *Europe in the Late Middle Ages*. (London 1965)

Hanawalt, B. *The Ties that Bound: Peasant Families in Medieval England*. (Oxford 1986)

Hardy, R. *The longbow, a Social History*. (London 1992)

Herbert, T. and Jones, G.E. *Edward I and Wales*. (Cardiff 1988)

Hewitt, H. *The Black Prince's Expedition 1355–57*. (Manchester 1958)

Hume Brown, P. *Early Travellers in Scotland*. (Edinburgh 1891)

– *History of Scotland*. (Cambridge 1911)

James, L. *Warrior Race*. (London 2001)

Jillings, K. *Scotland's Black Death*. (Stroud 2004)

Jones, A. *The Art of War in Western Civilization*. (Chicago 1987)

Keen, M. *Chivalry*. (London 1984)

Kosminsky, E. *Studies in the Agrarian History of England in the Thirteenth Century*.
   (Oxford 1956)

Lloyd, T. *The English Wool Trade in the Middle Ages*. (Cambridge 1977)

Lomas, R. *North-East England in the Middle Ages*. (Edinburgh 1992)

Lucas, H. *The Low Countries and the Hundred Years War*. (Michigan 1929)

Lynch, M. *Scotland: a New History*. (London 1991)

Macdougall, N. (ed.). *Scotland and War*. (Edinburgh 1991)

– *An Antidote to the English*. (East Lothian 2001)

MacFarlane, K.B. *The Nobility of Later Medieval England*. (Oxford 1973)

MacKenzie, W. *The Battle of Bannockburn*. (Glasgow 1913)

MacNamee, C. *The Wars of the Bruces*. (East Linton 1997)

MacQuarrie, A. *Scotland and the Crusades*. (Edinburgh 1997)

Mapstone, S. & Wood, J. (eds). *The Rose and the Thistle*. (East Lothian 1998)

Mason, R. (ed). *Scotland and England, 1286–1817*. (Edinburgh 1987)

Maxtone, A. *The Maxtones of Cultoqhuey*. (Perth 1936).

Mayhew, N. and Gemmill, E. *The Changing Value of Money in Medieval Scotland*.
   (Cambridge 1996)

McKenzie, W.M. *The Battle of Bannockburn*. (Glasgow 1913)

McKisack, M. *The Fourteenth Century*. (Oxford 1959)

McNeill, P. & Nicholson, R. *An Atlas of Scottish History to 1707*. (Edinburgh 1996)

Moor, C. *The Knights of Edward I*. (Harleian Society 1930)

Morris, J. *The Welsh Wars of Edward I*. (London 1901)

– *Bannockburn*. (Cambridge 1914)

Nicholson R. *Scotland. The Later Middle Ages*. (Edinburgh 1974)

– *Edward III and the Scots. The Formative Years of a Military career*. (Oxford 1965)

Oman, Sir Charles. *A History of England.* (London 1910)
– *A History of the Art of War.* (London 1898)
Penman, M. *David II.* (East Lothian 2002)
– *The Scottish Civil War.* (Stroud 2003)
Phillips, J.R.S. *Aymer de Valence.* (Oxford 1972)
Powicke, F. *The Thirteenth Century.* (Oxford 1953)
Powicke, M. *Military Obligation in England.* (Connecticut 1975)
Prestwich, M. *Armies and Warfare in the Middle Ages.* (New Haven 1996)
– *Edward I.* (London 1988)
– *The Three Edwards; War and State in England, 1272–1377.* (London 1980)
Rait, R. *The Parliaments of Scotland.* (Glasgow 1924)
RCAHMS Inventory of East Lothian. (HMSO 1926)
RCAHMS Inventory of the City of Edinburgh. (HMSO 1951)
RCAHMS, Midlothian and West Lothian. (HMSO 1929)
Reid, N. (ed). *Scotland in the Reign of Alexander III.* (Edinburgh 1990)
Ridpath, P. *Border History of England and Scotland.* (Berwick 1848)
Ritchie, R. *The Normans in Scotland.* (Edinburgh 1954)
Rollason, D. & Prestwich, M (eds). *The Battle of Neville's Cross.* (Stamford 1998)
Simpson, G. (ed.). *Scotland and the Low Countries.* (East Linton 1996)
– *Scottish Handwriting.* (Aberdeen 1977)
Smith, J. (ed.) *New Light on Aberdeen.* (Aberdeen 1985)
Smout, T.C. *A History of the Scottish People.* (Glasgow 1969)
Stevenson, J & Wood, M. *Scottish Heraldic Seals.* (Glasgow 1940)
Stone, G. Cameron. *Glossary of the Construction of Arms and Armour.* (London 1978)
Stringer, K. (ed.). *Essays on the Scottish Nobility.* (Edinburgh 1985)
Sumption, J. *The Hundred Years War.* (London 1990)
Tuchman, B. *A Distant Mirror.* (London 1979)
Tytler, P.F. *A History of Scotland.* (Edinburgh 1828–43)
Vale, J. *Edward III and Chivalry.* (Woodbridge 1982)
Watson, F. *Under the Hammer.* (East Linton 1998)
Whittington, G & Whyte, I.G. (eds). *A Historical geography of Scotland.* (London 1983)
Young, A. *Robert the Bruce's Rivals: The Comyns.* (East Linton 1997)

UNPUBLISHED THESES AND PAPERS

The Kingship of David II. Michael Penman, St Andrews University (1998)
Burgesses and Landed Men in North-east Scotland in the Later Middle Ages. Harold Booton, Aberdeen University (1987)
Military Service of Northumbrian Knights. A. King, Durham University Medieval Conference (2001)
Technology and Military Technology in Medieval England. Randall Storey, University of Reading (2003)
A Lyon in the Field, Continuity and Change in Scottish Warfare 1057–1460. C.A. Brown, BCLA, Galashiels (1985)

ARTICLES

'The Development of Scottish Border Lordship, 1332–58.' M. Brown, *Historical Research* vol. lxxv no.171 (February 1997)

'A Late Fourteenth-Century Coin Hoard from Tranent.' J. Bateson & P. Stott, *Proc. Soc. Antiq. Scot.* 120 (1990)

'Archaeological Excavations at Cockpen Medieval Parish Church, Midlothian, 1993.' J. O'Sullivan, *Proc. Soc. Antiq. Scot.* 125 (1995)

'Chronicle Propaganda in Fourteenth Century Scotland.' S.Boardman, *Scottish Historical Review* 76 (1977)

'Edinburgh Castle, Iron Age fort to Garrison Fortress.' P.Yeoman, *Fortress Magazine* 4 (1990)

'Excavations at Springwood Park, Kelso.' P.Dixon, *Procs. Soc. Antiq. Scot.*

'Excavations South of Bernard Street., Leith, 1980.' N. Holmes, *Proc. Soc. Antiq. Scot.* 115 *f.* (1985)

'In the Territory of Auchencrow: Long Continuity or Late Development in early Scottish Field Systems.' J.Donelly, *Proc. Soc. Antiq. Scot.* 130 (2000)

'Lothian in the First War of Independence.' G.W.S. Barrow, *Scottish Historical Review* 55 (1976)

'New Light on Old Coin Hoards from the Aberdeen Area.' D.Evans & S.Thain, *Proc. Soc. Antiq. Scot.* 119 (1989)

'North Berwick, East Lothian; its Archaeology Revisited.' D. Hall & D. Bowler, *Proc. Soc. Antiq. Scot* 127 (1997)

'Scottish Arms in the Bellenville Roll.' C. Campbell, *Scot. Geneal*, XXV

'Sprouston, Roxburghshire.' I. Smith, *Proc. Soc. Antiq. Scot.* 121 (1991)

'The Aftermath of War.' G.W.S. Barrow, *Transactions of the Royal Historical Society*, Fifth Series, 28 (1978)

'The Lunan Valley Project: Medieval Rural Settlement in Angus.' D. Pollock, *Pros. Soc. Antiq. Scot.* 115 (1985)

'The Sigillography of the Ragman Roll.' B. McAndrew, *Proc. Soc. Antiq. Scot.* 129 (1999)

'The Use of Money in Scotland, 1124–1230.' W. Scott, *SHR* LVIII (1979)

'The War of the Scots, 1306–23', Prothero Lecture, *TRHS* (1992)

'Thomas of Coldingham.' J. Donelly, SHR LIX (1980)

'War, Allegiance and Community in the Anglo-Scottish Marches: Teviotdale in the Fourteenth Century.' Dr M. Brown, *Northern History*, XLI (2004)

List of Illustrations

Index

TEMPUS REVEALING HISTORY

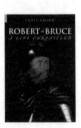

Scotland From Prehistory to the Present
FIONA WATSON
***The Scotsman* Bestseller**
£9.99
0 7524 2591 9

Flodden
NIALL BARR
'Tells the story brilliantly' ***The Sunday Post***
£9.99
0 7524 2593 5

1314 Bannockburn
ARYEH NUSBACHER
'Written with good-humoured verve as befits a rattling "yarn of sex, violence and terror"'
History Scotland
£9.99
0 7524 2982 5

Scotland's Black Death
The Foul Death of the English
KAREN JILLINGS
'So incongruously enjoyable a read, and so attractively presented by the publishers'
The Scotsman
£14.99
0 7524 2314 2

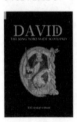

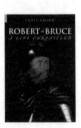

David I The King Who Made Scotland
RICHARD ORAM
'Enthralling... sets just the right tone as the launch-volume of an important new series of royal biographies' ***Magnus Magnusson***
£17.99
0 7524 2825 X

The Second Scottish War of Independence 1332–1363
CHRIS BROWN
'Explodes the myth of the invincible Bruces... lucid and highly readable' ***History Scotland***
£16.99
0 7524 2312 6

The Kings & Queens of Scotland
RICHARD ORAM
'A serious, readable work that sweeps across a vast historical landscape' ***The Daily Mail***
£20
0 7524 2971 X

Robert the Bruce: A Life Chronicled
CHRIS BROWN
'A masterpiece of research'
The Scots Magazine
£30
0 7524 2575 7

If you are interested in purchasing other books published by Tempus, or in case you have difficulty finding any Tempus books in your local bookshop, you can also place orders directly through our website www.tempus-publishing.com